TOGETHER WITH JESUS
Daily Devotions for a Year

Richard E. Lauersdorf

Northwestern Publishing House
Milwaukee, Wisconsin

To Beth, Mark, Jim, and Anne,
the children God gave us
and with whom we've spent
time together with Jesus

Fourth printing, 2005
Third printing, 2004
Second printing, 2004

Cover illustration: Steve Johnson and Lou Fancher

Scripture is taken from the HOLY BIBLE, NEW INTERNATIONAL VERSION®. NIV®. Copyright © 1973, 1978, 1984 by International Bible Society. Used by permission of Zondervan Publishing House. All rights reserved.

The "NIV" and "New International Version" trademarks are registered in the United States Patent and Trademark Office by International Bible Society. Use of either trademark requires the permission of International Bible Society.

Library of Congress Control Number 2003105345
Northwestern Publishing House
1250 N. 113th St., Milwaukee, WI 53226-3284
©2003 by Northwestern Publishing House
www.nph.net
Published 2003
Printed in the United States of America
ISBN-13:978-0-8100-1583-8
ISBN-10:0-8100-1583-8

From Jesus we can learn many things. Not only has he told us to search his Word, but he has also given us an example of the same. The gospels record a number of times when the Savior looked for a quiet spot away from the pressures of daily life to spend time in prayer and meditation, either alone or with his followers.

Those who spend time with the Savior, as we find him in his Word, and follow his example will discover benefit for their souls.

May God bless all who use this book of daily devotions.

MORE OF THE SAME

Jesus Christ is the same yesterday and today and forever. Hebrews 13:8

Last night in New York City's Times Square, the clock struck midnight, the crowd cheered, the confetti flew, and a new year began. Today city workers are busy cleaning up the celebration's debris. Tomorrow people, hurrying to their places of employment, will throng the sidewalks. And everything will be the same.

More of the same—that's what life seems to be for many of us. Though some may have new experiences and excitement this new year, life for many of us will be one day strung behind the other with the same tasks hovering before our eyes and the same troubles settling on our shoulders. It doesn't make much difference what number we write for the year.

Thank God one thing never changes. Would we want a Lord who changes his mind and issues a recall for promises he made yesterday? A Lord who forgets his full payment for all our sins and now demands that we cover sin's debt? A Lord who capriciously closes the door to heaven he once opened with his resurrection?

More of the same! That's what we need and that's what we have in the Savior Jesus, who is the same yesterday and today and forever.

Lord Jesus, fill our lives each day of this new year with more of your unchanging love. Amen.

A NEW YEAR BUT THE SAME PARDON

I will forgive their wickedness and will remember their sins no more. Jeremiah 31:34

What can you do with that water stain on the kitchen ceiling? Try covering it with ordinary paint, but it still bleeds through. Buy the special paint made to cover such stains, but you still see its faint outline each time you look at the ceiling.

Sometimes we act as if God deals the same way with our sins. As if Jesus merely covered them over and yet they're still there. Notice what the gracious Lord said. He does more than cover our sins—he removes them. He doesn't even remember our sins. Our sins are gone as if they never existed. All because he sent his Son to pay for them on Calvary's cross.

Thank God we didn't have to enter the new year with the stains of last year's sins upon us. They're totally gone—blotted out completely by the precious blood of the Savior. And the sins of this new year? There will be plenty of them. Old familiar ones that we fight against and yet fall back into. New ones that we stumble into because they sneak up on us. What shall we do, what can we do, with all their wretched stains?

The same thing we did last year. Bring them with tears of repentance to God, and thank him each day of this new year for forgiving our sins and remembering them no more.

Thank you, Lord, for your forgiveness that remains new for us each day. Amen.

A NEW YEAR BUT THE SAME PEACE

The Lord blesses his people with peace.
Psalm 29:11

Pixie, our toy fox terrier, was so high strung that she seldom relaxed. Perhaps it was her size that made everything seem like a threat to her. Only when she was in front of the fireplace would her ears finally go down and her legs stretch out.

We also know something about threats and stress. We've carried burdens from the old year into the new. And those burdens seem to pick up more weight day by day. And who knows what new problems will drop down on our shoulders tomorrow? It's enough to make us keep our ears up and never relax, to run around and "bark" in anxiety. We are so small compared to what we have to live with and what looms before us.

What's the solution? Where can we find release from our fears and relaxation under our burdens? There's only one place—one person—the Lord. He who prepared in Jesus the perfect peace we need for our souls will also provide what we need for our daily lives. With eyes on such a loving Lord, we can go forward even though the steps are painful. We can smile even in the midst of tears. When hearts of faith lie down before God's promises, the result is always peace.

Lord, fasten our hearts on your gracious
promises and fill our lives with peace. Amen.

A NEW YEAR BUT THE SAME POWER

Be strong in the Lord and in his mighty power.
Ephesians 6:10

Those nails just wouldn't budge. Finally, I reached for the pinch bar, that three-foot-long metal rod with a claw on the end, and wrenched the nails one by one out of the board. Power when I needed it, that's what that pinch bar gave me.

None of us is a stranger to temptation. Each of us has his own areas of weakness that the sly devil explores and the sinful world exploits. And the evil hearts within us never sleep or give up the struggle. Know what I'm talking about? How long would the list be if we were to catalog the soft spots where temptations sink in so readily? How many times have we been pinned to the mat of sin by the old evil foe instead of winning the match?

Will it get any better this new year? Will our struggle against sin be more successful? Not if we use only the puny hammer of our own efforts. More power is needed. And the Lord Jesus offers us just that. "[He] appeared . . . to destroy the devil's work," Scripture tells us (1 John 3:8). Not only has God's Son paid for our sins, but he has also broken Satan's stranglehold on us. When Satan is successful in our lives, it's not because Christ's power has failed. Rather it's because our hold on his pinch bar isn't as firm as it should be.

> Lord, tighten our grip on your Word
> through which you give our faith your
> mighty power. Amen.

A NEW YEAR BUT THE SAME PROMISE

[I will] take you to be with me that you also may be where I am. John 14:3

"Are we there yet?" "How much longer?" Five minutes down the road and the kids in the backseat start asking these questions.

So do we. In fact, as one year runs into another, these questions come up with increasing frequency. How many new years do we have left? How many days in this new year will there be for us? We leave the answers to those questions in the Lord's hands. He knows much better than we what the measure of our days should be.

We do know, though, where we are going. The Lord himself has told us. Jesus said it was to be where he would be. We call the place heaven, but we don't know its location. We know something about that place, though we, who are so used to this vale of tears, have a hard time imagining an existence totally free from temptation, tears, and troubles. Best of all, heaven will mean being with Jesus.

And we know how to get there. Jesus has answered that question so clearly for us. The only way is through his blood that has cleansed us from all sin and his righteousness that clothes us for heaven. That's his promise, and it holds true into a new year and into all eternity.

Lord Jesus, keep us ready for heaven
by covering us with your blood and
righteousness. Amen.

A NEW YEAR BUT THE SAME STAR

We saw his star in the east and have come to worship him. Matthew 2:2

We don't know much about the Magi. Scripture doesn't reveal from what country they came, how many they were, what occupations or names they had. What we need to know about them, though, the biblical account has recorded. They were led by some mysterious star—"his" star—right to Jesus' side. And when the Magi saw their infant Savior, they knew what to do. They knelt down and worshiped him.

The Magi were the first in a long line of Gentiles brought to the Savior, a line that by God's grace includes us also. They were led by a star. Our star is even better. "Your word is a lamp to my feet and a light for my path," the psalmist wrote (119:105), and we heartily agree. Wherever we open that Word, we see the Savior. All of its teachings revolve around its central message of God's Son coming into the world to pay for sin and prepare peace again with our Maker. Guided by that star, we have knelt at Jesus' baby bed and cruel cross. We have rejoiced in his resurrection and received the promise of his return. "We have seen his star," we say with the Magi, not in the east but, better still, in his Word.

Now the Lord has given us a new year in which to be guided by his Word to our Savior. Modern Magi know where their eyes belong—on God's wondrous star.

Help us to live in your Holy Word, Lord, and to see our Savior there. Amen.

THANK GOD FOR THIS SNOW

Though your sins are like scarlet, they shall be as white as snow. Isaiah 1:18

Some people like snow, at least the first snow of the winter. The glistening flakes cover the earth's dead vegetation and all looks pristine and pure. But when the snow keeps coming or shows up in spring, grumbling begins.

In the land of Palestine, situated at the same latitude on the globe as the state of Arizona, snow was not too common. Only one verse mentions snow falling there (2 Samuel 23:20), though, at times in winter it coated the mountain peaks, just as it does outside Tucson. All who read Isaiah's words, however, knew what he meant. He was using snow's purity as a contrast to the starkness of sin. As scarlet as our sin may be, it's wiped out by the snow-white forgiveness God offers in Christ.

Thank God for this snow. How could we get up and start another day without the promise of his forgiveness? How could we go to bed each night without the assurance, "Were as scarlet my transgression, It shall be as white as snow By your blood and bitter passion" (*Christian Worship* [CW] 304:6)? Even more, how could we ever face eternity, where we need to be snow white in the judge's sight?

Regardless of where we live or how many snowflakes we see each winter, we can never get too much of this snow.

Cover us, Lord, with your Son's forgiveness that we may be pure in your sight. Amen.

THE DIVINE WEATHERMAN

He spreads the snow like wool. Psalm 147:16

The TV weatherman had just finished his presentation to the grade school class. When he asked for questions, up went a hand and out came the question, "Do you make it snow?"

"No," he chuckled, "I only tell you about the snow."

The psalmist knew who made the snow. So do we. When the road home from work is snow covered and slippery, the driveway plugged by the passing snowplow, the sidewalk almost buried under the drifting snow, who of us stops to think of the One who sent it? More likely, if we're students or perhaps teachers, we're happy that school is canceled. Or, if we have to start the snow blower and do the shoveling, we're not too tickled.

Next time it snows, stop for a moment and consider the hand behind it. It's that of our almighty God. He alone fills the clouds with moisture, forms the lacy snowflakes, and sends them fluttering to earth. It's our all-knowing God who waters the fields, fills the reservoirs, and provides for his creatures. His divine hand sends not only the snow but everything else good for his children.

From this divine weatherman we look for weather that is always "fair."

Gracious Lord, help us see your hand at work in the changing seasons of our lives. Amen.

MAKE IT SNOW

As the rain and the snow come down from heaven, and do not return to it without watering the earth and making it bud and flourish . . . so is my word that goes out from my mouth: It will not return to me empty, but will accomplish what I desire and achieve the purpose for which I sent it. Isaiah 55:10,11

The pastor had given up. For months he had shared God's Word with the lady, only to be rebuffed by her. Then weeks after giving up, his phone rang. It was the woman asking how to join the church. What he couldn't do, the Lord had done. The young pastor had learned a valuable lesson. His job was to share the Word; the Lord's job was to make it work in the human heart.

God, who gave the Word, said he would make it work just as he does with the snow. But just as he decides where and when the snow will fall, so he determines where and when his Word will bring dead hearts to faith. If only we could see the Holy Spirit at work through that powerful Word, we would be more encouraged in our attempts to share it. Since we cannot, we need to remember this important truth: Our job is to share the snow, not to make it grow.

So let it snow! On our relatives, neighbors, friends, coworkers, fellow students—whomever. They need the life-giving message of their only Savior from sin and only Deliverer from death. Into our hands God has placed his Word. In his hands rest the results he has promised.

Lord, bless our sharing of your powerful Word. Use it to bring dead hearts to life. Amen.

ORDERS REMAIN UNCHANGED

Go into all the world and preach the good news to all creation. Mark 16:15

Every hour on the hour, 365 days a year, a soldier reports for duty at the Tomb of the Unknown Soldier in Arlington National Cemetery. The precision of the changing of the guard is impressive. Even more impressive are the orders handed on. Always the command is the same, "Orders remain unchanged."

Can't we say the same about the command the risen Jesus has given his soldiers of all times? "Go," he charged, "into all the world." "Preach the good news," he commanded, "to all creation." "And when you have done it," he continued, "pass the order on to those who follow you." The orders of the day for believers are always the same. Not to guard a tomb in which an unknown body rests but to tell all creation of their living, loving Savior, their only Savior.

Soldiers of the cross, how goes it? Whom have we told? "I can't reach very far," you say. Well then, how about your family, your neighborhood, your small corner of the world? "I can't do very much," you excuse. Well then, how about your prayers and dollars for missions? Few of us will ever personally cross the oceans and convey the saving message of his cross to distant worlds. But we can help build the boats that carry those who go. And we can fish in the lakes right in our own backyards.

Lord, here I am. Move me, use me, and bless my efforts to tell others about you. Amen.

SAFE IN OUR FATHER'S ARMS

God is our refuge. Psalm 46:1

How secure a father's arms can feel. When our eldest was a little girl, she was afraid of dogs. When visiting at a member's home, she'd walk along with us to the door. But let a dog bark, and it was "Carry me." Only when my arms were around her did she feel safe.

Know the feeling? Those who have walked a ways in life know how many dogs are behind the doors and how loudly they can bark. They know also how ill equipped they are to walk on unafraid. Best of all, they know where to turn, to the refuge of their Father's waiting arms.

Is it physical pain? Some part of the body that refuses to function, some clump of cells that is growing wildly? Of course, we fear these things, but then we know where to turn. Is it some sorrow that saps our spirit? A loved one that we have lost, a family member that has disappointed us? Certainly the tears flow, but then we know where to turn. Is it some temptation that we face? Some sin that has its hooks deep in our daily life? Indeed our steps may stumble, but then we know where to turn. Is it the future that troubles us? Uncertainty about our own ends and the graves that await us? Surely, we swallow in apprehension, but then we know where to turn.

When God's children cry out in the stress of life, "Carry me," they find a Father's waiting arms.

Lord, we are weak, but you are strong. Carry us each day and into the eternal day. Amen.

ALWAYS IN FASHION

He has clothed me with garments of salvation.
Isaiah 61:10

Sunday's newspaper contained a special section detailing the latest in clothing. What about men's suits? Should they be double breasted or have three buttons? Are the lapels broad or narrow? What about women's wear? Are the hems up or down? What colors are in vogue? What about accessories? Here were "must read" articles for those who would be fashionably dressed.

Christians know something about proper dress. In fact, only Christians know about the right clothing for heaven. The garments of salvation are not union made but divinely tailored. They carry no dry-cleaning labels but are always pressed and spotless. They are not made for hanging in the closet but for everyday wear. And they are the only dress that gets us into heaven's party.

Already at our baptisms God clothed us with the garments of his salvation. By his grace, Christ's forgiveness covered us and his holiness counted for us. Through his Word, as we hear and read it, he wraps that beautiful robe more tightly around us and fastens its buttons more securely. When my final day comes, it will be his doing that I can step "clothed in his righteousness alone, Faultless to stand before his throne" (CW 382:4).

Those whom God dresses with the garments of salvation are always in fashion.

Jesus, please let your blood and righteousness
be my beauty and my glorious dress. Amen.

HE NEVER EVEN LEAVES HIS CHAIR

The One enthroned in heaven laughs; the Lord scoffs at them. Psalm 2:4

What's a person to do? The world in which we have to swim is becoming increasingly polluted. All around us—in movies and on television, in ads and commercials, and even within some churches—beats the appealing chant that man can have it all, do it all, ignore it all. So what are we supposed to do? Shrug our shoulders and ask what else is new? Throw in the towel and surrender? Thank God we have gray hair and won't see what our grandchildren will have to face?

Or should we join David in today's verse? He raised his eyes to heaven, and what he saw comforted him. The sinful efforts of the world aren't enough to make the One who sits on heaven's throne even leave his seat. Their feeble attempts to war against him and his own are only enough to make him laugh. The almighty Ruler of all has never heard anything so humorous as man's empty boasting. He's never seen anything so funny as mankind's incompetent attempts to get along without him.

Of course, the times are evil. But we're not going to give up. Why should we? We're going to win. He who sits in the heavens is laughing, and we with him. His Word will still stand. His ways will still endure. And when the dust settles in the future as in the past, it will be victory that we shall see.

Almighty Lord, fix our faith on you so
that we have comfort in the midst of life's
turmoil. Amen.

JUST ANOTHER DAY?

Whatever you do, whether in word or deed, do it all in the name of the Lord Jesus, giving thanks to God the Father through him.
Colossians 3:17

How ordinary life can seem. Day after day we get up, clean up, and hurry up, off to the duties of another day. Then we return home, have some supper, clean up the kitchen, watch some television, and head back to bed. But don't forget to set the alarm, because tomorrow it starts all over again. Often, even though there are moments of excitement, life seems rather ordinary. We run in the same old ruts and do the same old things. We are born, we live, we sweat, and we die.

But for Christians it's never just another day. Each day the Lord gives us golden opportunities to serve him—to show our appreciation for the eternal life that he has already given us. Whether it's bringing home the bacon or balancing the checkbook, changing the diapers or cleaning the kitchen floor, digging into our homework or doing sports, we try our best. We picture God looking down from heaven and smiling at our attempts to show our gratitude for what he has given us in Jesus our Savior.

Just as a hot dog without mustard doesn't taste right, so life without Christ has no zip. But add the Savior and life takes on new meaning. Then "just another day" becomes another day to serve him in grateful love.

Lord, take our moments and our days, let them flow in ceaseless praise. Amen.

THE ONLY BREAD

I am the bread of life. He who comes to me
will never go hungry. John 6:35

Where can you find good bread these days? The packaged
variety on the shelf is little more than cardboard out of the
toaster. The sumptuous looking French loaf in the supermarket bakery is little more than thick crust and flimsy pockets
when cut. Where do you find good bread?

Like the body, the soul needs bread or it will die. But unlike
with our bodies, stuff that just looks like bread will not do
the job. Some set before the hungry soul the loaves of man's
own works. But such bread is less than cardboard with no
vitamins of forgiveness. Others serve up the packaged loaves
of man's own theology. But such bread is full of holes, holding no sure promise of an eternal home. Where do you find
good bread? The hungry soul needs to know.

In Jesus! When he described himself as the bread of life, he
had more than flour, shortening, and water in mind. He
meant his perfect life that would fulfill all of God's commands
and his precious blood that would be spilt in full payment for
all sins. The soul, famished because of sin, can feast on Jesus'
payment and be filled. The soul, hungry for a perfect life to
present to God in the judgment, can reach for Jesus' righteousness and be satisfied. For the hungry sinner, Jesus is not
just good bread. He's the only bread.

Lord Jesus, help us feast on you through our
use of your Word. Amen.

A DIVINE SEAL
OF APPROVAL

And a voice came from heaven: "You are my
Son, whom I love; with you I am well pleased."
Mark 1:11

Before I purchased those strings of outdoor Christmas lights,
I looked for the little tag on them. "Underwriters Laboratory
Seal of Approval," it said. Even then, several of them lasted
only one season. Man's approval, after supposedly rigorous
testing, doesn't mean all that much.

When Jesus began his public ministry with his baptism, a seal
of approval was placed on him. "My Son," the Father called
him, "true God with me and the Spirit from all eternity."
"Whom I love," the Father added. Human love pales into
insignificance in face of the love the heavenly Father has for
his Son. "With [him] I am well pleased," the Father asserted.
"That's my mission my Son is embarking on," he was saying.
Already in eternity the plan to save sinners had been set in
place, etched firmly by the awesome love of God. Now Jesus
had come to carry out that plan. Three years later, he would
finish the work with his death.

Those who see only a man on the cross miss the point completely. That's God's own Son who died for sinners. On him
and him only does the Father put his stamp of approval. To
him and him only can sinners look for sure salvation.

> Lord, when I doubt, remind me that you sent
> your Son to die for me. Assure me that his
> divine blood has covered all my sins. Amen.

HIS LOVE DETECTOR

The next day Jesus decided to leave for Galilee.
Finding Philip, he said to him, "Follow me."
John 1:43

Her hobby was sweeping the sandy lake shores and grassy park areas with a portable metal detector. In her "junk room" were jars of coins and boxes of rings, lost by people on the paths of life. With joy she told stories about class rings and wedding bands returned to their owners.

Jesus swept the land of Galilee with a different type of detector. With redeeming love he came to seek and save the lost. And Philip was one of them. Like some ring lost in the sand, Philip could do nothing to find the Savior. All the sinner can do is burrow deeper into the dust of sin and be lost forever in the darkness of hell. With unfailing love, Jesus looked for and reclaimed Philip as his very own. When sinners are found, the Savior rejoices. So do the angels in heaven. So do the sinners who once were lost but now are found. In the Savior they have pardon for their sins. In the Savior they have peace with God. In the Savior they have promises of heaven.

What detector does Jesus use to find lost sinners today? Just as with Philip, it's the message of his love. The Savior uses us to sweep the shores of this world with the gospel in Word and sacrament. When the lost are found, we rejoice. So does Jesus who sends us. Sinners are back where they belong, with him.

Lord, thank you for finding me in your love.
Use me to help find others who are lost. Amen.

FATHER AND SON
IN BUSINESS TOGETHER

"Why were you searching for me?" he asked. "Didn't you know I had to be in my Father's house?" Luke 2:49

It used to be that sons walked in the footsteps of their fathers. Proudly the company letterhead or the sign on the truck door stated, "Plumbing by Jones and Son." In our day of widening opportunities, we don't find as many fathers and sons in business together.

With Jesus it was and is "Father and Son in business together." Between his presentation as a 40-day-old baby in the temple and the beginning of his public ministry as a 30-year-old man, we have only one account of Jesus. It tells of a 12-year-old staying behind in the temple. When his anxious parents found him, he asked, "Didn't you know I had to be in my Father's house?" Didn't they understand that he was there in the temple, engaged in his Father's business?

It was big business. Into it Jesus sank all the energy he had and even shed his blood. And I'm one of the beneficiaries of their joint work. For me Jesus became a baby in a mother's womb, a 12-year-old in the temple, a 33-year-old on the cross. For me he shouldered the load of sin, shuddered under its punishment in the fires of hell, shouted of its payment, "It is finished."

Now he wants me involved. The world still stands so that more may be saved. I'm still alive so that more may be told.

Lord, let it be Father, Son, and me in business together. Amen.

NOT JUST ANY NAME WILL DO

Everyone who calls on the name of the Lord
will be saved. Romans 10:13

Our four kids used to laugh at us. In the heat of the moment,
we'd call them by the wrong names. But we'd tell them, "It's
okay; any name will do unless we call you Pixie"—the name
of our dog.

In the serious matter of salvation, not just any name will do.
In spite of the current trend to let every god be god and
everyone's religious opinions be as valid as another's, the
Bible still insists on one name only for salvation. Salvation is
found only in Jesus. Only he is "the way and the truth and
the life" and "no one comes to the Father except through
[him]" (John 14:6). Only the precious blood of Jesus, God's
own Son, "purifies us from all sin" (1 John 1:7).

When it comes to us, then any name will do. "Everyone," Paul
said. It matters not what my name is. How often I have
sinned or how far I have strayed. What language I speak or
what color my skin. He who is the world's only Savior came
for everyone. He came for me. For me he said of sin's penalty,
"It is finished" (John 19:30). For me heaven's door is open.
For me he will say at life's end, "Come, . . . take your inheritance, the kingdom prepared for you" (Matthew 25:34).

Jesus' name is the only name of salvation. I thank God I know
that blessed truth. And I thank God that in his grace he knows
my name among all the names of those who call upon him.

> Lord, all my life let it be, "Jesus, Jesus, only
> Jesus Can my heartfelt longing still" Amen.
> (CW 348:1)

THE GREATEST DISTANCE IN THE WORLD

If you confess with your mouth, "Jesus is Lord," and believe in your heart that God raised him from the dead, you will be saved. Romans 10:9

What's the greatest distance in the world? Not the miles across the Atlantic or down to Antarctica, but the distance between the human head and heart. Those 18 inches are the most difficult in the world. Why? Because only God the Holy Spirit can travel them. Millions hear about Jesus Christ as their only Savior, but only some believe. The rest shake their heads in rejection or nod in seeming approval, only to go their own ways. Their ears have heard but not their hearts.

What about me? Can I say with my heart, "Jesus is my Savior whom God raised from the dead"? Can I say with conviction: "His death counted for me. His resurrection assures my resurrection. Because he lives, I also will live, body and soul in heaven some day"? Then thank God the Holy Spirit. Through the gospel he carried the message from my head to my heart. My faith is his gift. Through that gospel he still works when faith wavers to bridge the distance between head and heart.

The Spirit helps me travel another distance, the one between my heart and mouth. When Jesus has moved from my head to my heart, then he'll also move from my heart to my mouth. I'll proclaim gladly what I believe and thank him for it. I'll tell others what I believe and ask them to join me. By God's grace it'll be head to heart to mouth, with the name of Jesus, my precious Savior.

For faith's gift I thank you, Lord. For faith's continuance I trust you, Lord. Amen.

HE KNOWS ME

"How do you know me?" Nathanael asked. Jesus answered, "I saw you while you were still under the fig tree before Philip called you." Then Nathanael declared, "Rabbi, you are the Son of God; you are the King of Israel." John 1:48,49

The two had never met before that day. Yet the One knew the other perfectly. Jesus knew Nathanael's name and character, what he had been doing, and what he needed. Sound familiar?

Jesus knows me too. He knows the sudden sins that sweep down on me like some hurricane hitting the Mississippi coast. He knows the wreckage they leave on my conscience. And he knows the daily sins that are as close to me as my skin—that I don't always recognize as wrong. Like Nathanael, who was looking for the Savior to come, I need Jesus. And he knows this. So he speaks to me through his Word. He tells me that he forgives me because he's already paid for my sins.

Jesus has greater things waiting for me too. He promised Nathanael that he would see the heavens open. And so he did. With his work of redemption, Jesus opened heaven. Can the Savior offer me anything greater? What surpasses knowing heaven is my home? What offers more peace than to know Jesus, my Way, is complete and never changes?

With Nathanael, it's time for me to say joyfully, thankfully, "Jesus, you are the Son of God, my eternal King, my beloved Savior."

Thank you, Jesus, for being my Savior and for the heaven you have waiting for me. Amen.

WHAT DOES JESUS HAVE TO SAY?

"The time has come," he said. "The kingdom of God is near. Repent and believe the good news!" Mark 1:15

"What will he have to say?" the patient worries as she enters the doctor's office. "What will she have to say?" the young man wonders as he rehearses his marriage proposal. Sometimes words can be so important. But none more so than those of our Savior. To us too, in this first month of another year, the Savior says, "Repent and believe the good news."

What Jesus has to say can be summed up with four *Rs*. He tells us to *realize* that we have sinned—more times than we can count, more ways than we can remember. He tells us to *regret* that we have sinned. Not just to mouth the words "I'm sorry" but to hang our heads in shame before our Holy Father. Then he tells us to *rely* on his full forgiveness to cover those sins. To find in him the pardon we need and the peace to stand before our loving Father again. Last of all, he tells us to *resolve* to fight against our sins. Not just to take his pardon and run but to promise with his power to amend our sinful lives.

There is no shelf life on Jesus' message of repentance. What he has to say never goes out of date regardless of how many new years come. Sinners like you and me need to hear again and again his important words, "Repent and believe the good news."

Lord, open my ears to hear and my heart to receive your good news. Amen.

ON THE PHOTO?

Whoever does the will of my Father in
heaven is my brother and sister and mother.
Matthew 12:50

At her family's Christmas gathering, my wife always takes a picture. Each year more are on the photo as new babies are born
and new spouses are brought in. This makes me wonder what a
photo of Jesus' family would look like. Even more important,
who would be on such a photo if one could be taken?

Jesus tells us. "Whoever does the will of my Father in
heaven," he says, "is my brother and sister and mother."
What does he mean with "does the will of my Father in
heaven"? He tells us that too. In John 6:40 he explains, "My
Father's will is that everyone who looks to the Son and
believes in him shall have eternal life." The heavenly Father's
dearest wish is that everyone recognize Jesus as his own Son
sent from heaven to pay for sinners so that they can live with
him forever. To put it another way, he wants us to believe
that only Jesus can turn us from enemies into beloved family members.

In earthly families, blood bonds us together. In Christ's family, it is faith, the gift of the Spirit. When God brings me to
faith in his Son as my only Savior, I'm Jesus' brother or sister or mother. I'm a dear family member, closer to him than
to anyone else, sure of sharing his home in heaven.

Am I on Jesus' family photo? I pray so. God make it so by
his grace.

Lord, bond me into your eternal family by giving
me faith in you as my only Savior. Amen.

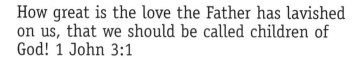

IN MY HANDS?

How great is the love the Father has lavished on us, that we should be called children of God! 1 John 3:1

What's the greatest blessing we enjoy in our earthly families? It's love, isn't it? If love is absent, we can have the best of food and clothing, you name it, and yet have nothing.

In Christ's family, love is also the greatest blessing. And Christ's love is by far the greatest. Just think of it—a love that brought him to earth to shoulder the world's sins, sweat drops of blood under their load, and hang silhouetted between heaven and hell for their payment. A love that laid him in a tomb and raised him again to show that sin was paid for. Was there ever another love like this?

There's more! A love that makes him chase after sinners, catch them with his Word, and keep them at his side so they can be his forever. Still more—a love that does this for me. That found me at the baptismal font, speaks to me through Sunday's sermon, assures me at his table, "Here are my body and my blood, given for you." A love that accompanies me on life's walk, carries me when the road is too difficult, and finally cradles me in his arms for the eternal journey. Oh, the height of Jesus' love!

That's what my Father placed into my hands when he made me his child. What more could I ask for? Just one thing—that his marvelous love keep me safe till in heaven I can thank him personally.

Love me, Lord, love me now and forever. Amen.

ON THE JOB?

Repentance and forgiveness of sins will
be preached in his name to all nations,
beginning at Jerusalem. You are witnesses
of these things. Luke 24:47,48

What's our job? To mow the lawn, take out the garbage? Bring
home the "bacon" so the bills are paid? Clean our rooms, do the
dishes, prepare the meals? A functioning family is one where
each member knows his responsibilities and carries them out.

As members of Christ's family, we have responsibilities too. Or
perhaps we should call them privileges. They are efforts we put
forward in willing, grateful response to what the Savior has
done for our salvation. Of course, such actions cover our whole
lives. We want everything in word and deed to be done to his
glory. But one privilege stands out above all others. That's the
work the risen Savior has given us—to be his witnesses. We
who have seen his cross and empty tomb tell others. We share
with the needy the good news of the forgiveness of sins.

On the job? Perhaps I can't become a pastor or a teacher. Perhaps I can't fly to distant continents or move to expanding
areas of our country. But I can still witness. I can tell the
child on my lap, the neighbor down the street, the coworker
on the job about the Jesus who loves them. I can speak my
prayers and bring my offerings for the gospel-spreading
efforts of my congregation and synod.

On the job? That's right, Lord, with the good news you've
brought me and with the desire you've given me to share it.

Lord move me, use me, bless me. Amen.

MY FRIEND
SANCTIFIES MY JOYS

On the third day a wedding took place at Cana in Galilee. Jesus' mother was there, and Jesus and his disciples had also been invited to the wedding. John 2:1,2

What does a Christian look like? Doesn't it bother you to see how the world portrays the believer? Like a person who has just sucked a lemon or has a constant frown on his face.

Did you know that Jesus' first recorded miracle was at a wedding celebration? He had just begun his ministry, just been baptized in the Jordan, just been tempted in the wilderness, just called his first disciples, when we find him at a wedding reception. He was busy, as we can well imagine, but not too busy to accept the invitation of this bride and groom. As a friend he was there rejoicing with them and even increasing their joy with his miracle of changing water into wine.

Does this tell us something about the Christian? The world has it all wrong. Believers are not the gloomiest; they are the happiest people on earth. Who but the Christian can have real joy in this sin-muddied world? Only a life that is faith filled, love filled, and hope filled can be a joyous one. And such a joyous life is found only in Christ, our heavenly Friend. When his forgiveness fills our lives and his love colors our days, smiles, not frowns, are in place. When our heavenly Friend stands beside us at our celebrations and in our daily lives, our smiles are heightened and our joys brightened.

Lord Jesus, fill my heart with joy and my life with smiles through your presence. Amen.

MY FRIEND SATISFIES MY NEEDS

Jesus said to the servants, "Fill the jars with water"; so they filled them to the brim. Then he told them, "Now draw some out and take it to the master of the banquet." They did so, and the master of the banquet tasted the water that had been turned into wine. John 2:7-9

In that Cana home it wasn't long before needs arose. To us the lack of wine may not seem serious, but to the bridegroom it spelled embarrassment. But their heavenly guest took care of their need. When the servants carried the cupful from the water-filled pots to the caterer of the feast, it was obvious what Jesus had done. Miraculously that cup now contained wine, far better wine than what the bridegroom had originally provided. And Jesus was not stingy with his gift. The heavenly Friend provided at least 120 gallons of this wine, more than enough for the occasion.

Want to talk about needs? How can we help it? Daily life is filled with them. What can we do about those huge ones, like the stain caused by our sins, the pressures of those special sins, the weaknesses when it comes to daily temptations? Where can we turn with those lesser and yet weighty cares, like a loved one in the hospital, a wayward child in our home, a job on shaky ground? Where can we find solutions to new problems, patience to put up with old ones, courage just to keep on living?

Let that miracle at Cana remind us! Jesus' first miracle was not to stop a pain or heal a disease but to make wine at a wedding, as a reminder that our needs, big and little, are seen and satisfied by him.

Lord Jesus, remind me your hands are strong enough to handle all my needs. Amen.

MY FRIEND STRENGTHENS MY FAITH

This, the first of his miraculous signs, Jesus performed in Cana of Galilee. He thus revealed his glory, and his disciples put their faith in him. John 2:11

Far greater than the miracle of water turned into wine was the invisible miracle that day at the wedding. As always Jesus' miracles were not to make a grand display of himself or dazzle those around him. They were intended as signs to point sinners to him for the greater needs of their souls. The miracles were powerful displays of his ability to rescue the people from sin, death, and the devil. Though many missed the point, his disciples at Cana that day didn't. Of them we read, "His disciples put their faith in him." See what this heavenly friend did for them. He strengthened their faith. He became closer and dearer to them, more precious and glorious than ever before.

Do we want faith and friendship with Jesus strengthened? There is a way, one that the world despises and that even some lukewarm friends of Jesus at times disregard. As we hear his Holy Word in our churches and read it at home, he sends the Spirit to renew our faith. As we receive the Lord's Supper at his altar, he refreshes our hearts. And through the miracle of Holy Baptism, he makes and then reminds us of his promise that we are his and he is ours forever.

Jesus comes not as a guest who wants to visit but as a friend who wants to stay. And when he does, great are the blessings that he brings for our faith.

Come, Lord Jesus, as the guest in my heart and home with your strengthening for my faith. Amen.

THE REAL
THIRST QUENCHER

Whoever drinks the water I give him will never thirst. John 4:14

Ask the person who has come out of surgery or the athlete who has given his all what the liquid lifted to his lips does for him. What a problem thirst can be and how necessary to quench it.

Though man may not fully feel or freely acknowledge it, his soul begs for relief from the burning anguish of sin. In his ignorance and stubbornness, he turns to the world's wells. But like the alcoholic, the more he drinks the less his thirst is quenched. Instead of labeling these wells as "unsafe for human consumption," Satan gilds the spouts to deceive the thirsty traveler. But soon comes the time when the wells of power, possession, pleasure, and philosophy, where people have let down their buckets in mad profusion, will be shown to have offered only poison for the soul.

Only one well can quench the soul's thirst. Jesus said it clearly, "Whoever drinks the water I give him will never thirst." With his atoning death on Calvary's holy mountain, he opened the pure and healing fountain that flows to you, to me, to all. Now he channels his thirst-quenching forgiveness to us through the riverbeds of the Word and sacraments. If all who lived on earth were to come and drink, never could they drain his forgiveness dry.

Lord, draw me to your Word and lead me to drink deeply of the water of life you offer. Amen.

THE BIBLE TELLS ME SO

The centurion replied, "Lord, I do not deserve to have you come under my roof. But just say the word, and my servant will be healed."
Matthew 8:8

What's faith? "A mask for hypocrites," some reply. "A wheelchair for weaklings," others ridicule. "Useless foolishness," still others remark. Like blind people talking about color, they prattle on.

More important is the question, On what does faith rest? The centurion could answer that question. He wasn't looking for a sign. He didn't even ask that Jesus come to his house. All he wanted was Christ's promise. "Just say the word," he said full of trust, "and my servant will be healed."

On what does faith plant its feet? On what do I base my trust for forgiveness from God and a future home in his heaven? Is it, "I feel I'm forgiven"? Perhaps I feel that way today, but what about tomorrow? Basing faith on my emotions is like walking on a frozen lake where one day the ice is thick enough, the next day it is too thin. Or is it, "I hope so"? Hope is only wishful thinking if it doesn't have a concrete basis. Like quicksand such hope turns spongy beneath faith's feet.

God's Word is the only solid foundation for faith. "Jesus loves me, this I know, for the Bible tells me so," is the only sure song for faith. Because the Bible says so, I believe that Jesus paid for my sins with his precious blood and innocent death. Because Jesus promised, I believe that all who the Spirit brings to faith in him will not perish but have eternal life.

Lord, help me to say with the centurion, "Just say the word," and I will be saved. Amen.

SLEEPING IN THE STORMS OF LIFE

[They] woke him, saying, "Lord, save us! We're going to drown!" Matthew 8:25

"How can you go to sleep so quickly?" asked his roommate. John had heart trouble that severely limited his activities and children who seldom came to visit him in the nursing home. Yet each night on his bed he would say his prayers out loud, then roll over and go to sleep. John's answer? "I say my prayers to Jesus. Then I go to sleep. No use in both of us staying awake."

He had caught the secret of sleeping through the storms of life. So did the disciples that night out on the lake. They weren't sleeping, but Jesus was. The fierce storm had them all wide awake. Pulling on the oars, bailing out the water, using their considerable seaman skills did no good. They were even beginning to think that Jesus was no good as he slept on, seemingly unconcerned.

How wrong they were! He had come from heaven to rescue them from the hurricane of sin. He would go to the cross so that with nail-pierced hands he could invite sin-tossed souls, "Come to me, . . . and I will give you rest" (Matthew 11:28). When such loving, almighty hands are wrapped around the storms of life, those who sail with God are safe. Perhaps the disciples didn't roll over and fall asleep the next time they ran into a storm out on the lake. But they trusted that their Jesus wasn't sleeping either. It's not that I stop rowing, but that I start trusting Jesus in the storms of life.

Jesus, in your wounds is pardon for all my sins. In your hands is relief for all life's storms. Amen.

"SHINE, JESUS, SHINE"

> He [Jesus] said, "I am the light of the world. Whoever follows me will never walk in darkness, but will have the light of life." John 8:12

Batteries are getting better all the time. They stay fresher and last longer. But sooner or later they fail. Like the time we were tenting in the wilderness and one of the children had to use the bathroom. Sure enough, the lantern that worked when we slipped into our sleeping bags was dead. So in the dark night we had to feel our way to the primitive bathroom.

Not so with Jesus. Like some all-powerful searchlight, he penetrates the dense midnight of sin, pushes aside the dark pall of death, and points the way through earth's gloom to heaven. Not only does he light the way. He is the way. With his death and resurrection, he paid for sin and now stands like some well-lit ladder to heaven. With his redemptive work, he's the laser that beams us up to eternity. Jesus stands revealed in Scripture as the lasting light of salvation for all times.

If some people don't have this light, it's not because he's not shining. If the light is dim, it's not because Jesus is losing his juice. Rather, it's because no one has told the sinner. Or the sinner prefers stumbling around in the darkness. Or has cloaked Jesus' pure light with the rags of his own works.

> "Shine, Jesus, shine! Jesus, Light of the world, shine upon us; Set us free by the truth you now bring us." Amen. *(Let All the People Praise You,* 270:1)

THE DIVINE DELETE KEY

> The blood of Jesus, his Son, purifies us from
> all sin. 1 John 1:7

Used to be we'd reach for the bottle of "white out," brush it on our mistakes, and then type over them. Next came the erasing ribbon that lifted the type from the page so we could make our corrections. Now we have the computer with its delete key. How far we've come!

Sin is not just some "typo" on the page of life that we can correct. Each thought, word, and deed that goes astray offends God and earns us death. Whiting sin out in our memories won't work. Regardless what we try, the print remains to trouble us. Typing over sin with our own works won't do it either. Those efforts only smudge our sins, leaving them clearly visible to the divine judge. Even if we had some delete key for our sins, they'd still be in the computer trash file, damning us before our God.

There's only one way for sin to be erased. In fact, it's already been done. At Calvary when his Son said, "It is finished," God hit the delete key on his heavenly computer. His Son's precious blood paid for every sin of every sinner. The sins were totally erased, not just typed over or transmitted to some trash file. When God looks at me, he sees a clean page because of his Son's blood. Unbelievers will go to hell, not because Jesus' blood didn't cover them, but because they rejected its payment. Something to think about the next time I use the delete key on the computer. Better still, something for me to treasure all my days.

> Please, God, help me to appreciate Jesus'
> precious blood. Amen.

BUILT BY GOD

For we are God's fellow workers; *you are . . . God's building.* 1 Corinthians 3:9

"I helped build that church," stated the elderly gentleman with joy. He had noticed the visitors admiring the beautiful structure and just had to tell them that he had been involved.

God's church is not brick or block; it is all believers in Christ. Its construction started in the Garden of Eden when God proclaimed the promise of the Savior. The Holy Spirit has been its general contractor throughout the years. His construction equipment is the gospel in Word and sacrament. Through the good news of forgiveness, he works in the hearts of people. He brings them to faith and mortars them as living stones into God's eternal church.

Wherever the gospel is used, God's church is built. Though we cannot program him or predict in whose heart he will work, the Holy Spirit builds through the Word. When the gospel is spoken from the pulpit or beside the workbench, when people pick up the Bible or read a tract, when the good news is presented on videotape or a child's cassette, the Spirit is at work. Across our land and around our globe, wherever the gospel is proclaimed, God is building his church.

"Built by God" is not just some abstract theological truth. It's my comfort. Thank God for his work in my heart. What a gift of his grace that I am part of his church!

May the Spirit keep me mortared in his church through the gospel. Amen.

BUILDING WITH GOD

For we are God's fellow workers; you are . . .
God's building. 1 Corinthians 3:9

"This church is being built by God," said the sign on the construction site. Under those words someone had scrawled, "Plumbing by Johnson and Son." There's more truth than fiction to such thinking when it comes to building God's invisible church of believers in Christ.

The Master Builder is hiring. Those whom the Spirit brings into God's church become members of his construction team—no ifs, ands, or buts about it. Their work is not to create faith in people—that's the Spirit's work alone. But they do handle the Spirit's construction equipment, the gospel in Word and sacrament, through which the Spirit mortars people into God's church.

How calloused are my hands? How much have I sweated while building with the Lord? Is my partnership with him drudgery or privilege? Some hobby in which to dabble at my leisure or some work that demands my best? Paul, a fellow builder with God, gives me an answer. He told the Corinthians, "I will very gladly spend for you everything I have and expend myself as well" (2 Corinthians 12:15). I won't go wrong when I follow his example.

Can I even imagine my joy when I finally stand in heaven at Jesus' side, brought there by his grace? And what added joy when looking around, I can say in my heart, "I helped build that church."

Lord, thank you for cementing me into your
church. Use me now to work on others. Amen.

BE WISE—
BUILD ON ROCK

Everyone who hears these words of mine and puts them into practice is like a wise man who built his house on the rock. Matthew 7:24

Jesus has more in mind than a course in architectural design or intelligent house building. He's talking about lives and souls, about using our lives to be built on him and read-ied for heaven.

What's the rock foundation for wise builders? "No one can lay any foundation other than the one already laid, which is Christ Jesus," Paul wrote (1 Corinthians 3:11). "Faith comes from hearing the message, and the message is heard through the word of Christ," the same apostle said in Romans 10:17. Such words take the guesswork out of what the rock founda-tion is. It's Christ Jesus, God's own Son, and his Holy Word in which he tells us all we need to know for life and salvation.

Those who build on this sure foundation will be ready for life's storms. When sin's downpour hits the roof, the eaves troughs of God's grace will be there to funnel the guilt away to Jesus who has already paid for all sin. When trouble's lightning bolts strike, faith's lightning rods will deflect the charge to the ground called Christ, who cares for us so lov-ingly. When the hail stones of loss and sorrow hit, life's roof, though dented, will remain intact because the almighty God is our refuge and strength. And when death's final storm comes, life's house, though shaken, will stand in eternity.

"On Christ, the solid rock, I stand; All other ground is sinking sand." Lord, help me so to pray and to build. Amen. (CW 382)

GOD IS NO CROOK

There is now no condemnation for those who are in Christ Jesus. Romans 8:1

Every pastor's been asked and had to answer it. Many a Christian on a sickbed or in trouble has thought or said it. "God must be punishing me for my sin," is the comment or, should we say, the question. Many times the believer even has a specific sin in mind. Always the troubled Christian needs an answer. Perhaps I've even been in their shoes.

How I need to listen to Paul's words! "There is now no condemnation," he asserts strongly. Write in the word *punishment* for *condemnation,* and you can see what he has in mind. There is no more punishment for me, no more sin that the righteous judge is singling out for which to hit me. Can that be so? "Yes," Paul says, "for those who are in Christ Jesus." Because Jesus has paid for all my sins, they are totally and completely gone. Because the Spirit has brought me to faith in Jesus, I am wholly holy in God's eyes, cleansed from sin's every stain and clothed with Jesus' robe of righteousness.

"What do you call someone who tries to collect twice for some debt?" the pastor asked a Christian, troubled by some sin on that hospital bed.

"A crook," the believer answered. "Only a cheat would try to collect double."

"God's no crook," the pastor replied. "He has already charged Jesus for your sin and accepted the payment rendered. So how could he be charging you again for it?"

> Lord, fill my heart with the peace that
> comes from knowing Jesus has paid for all
> my sins. Amen.

CAN'T YOU SEE IT?

"No eye has seen, no ear has heard, no mind has conceived what God has prepared for those who love him"—but God has revealed it to us by his Spirit. 1 Corinthians 2:9,10

As we were driving through Yellowstone Park, off in the distance, barely discernible, was a bull elk. "Can't you see it?" my wife asked.

"No," I had to answer, until I pulled off onto the shoulder and closely followed the pointing of her finger.

Better than this is what the Spirit does for us. By nature our eyes are more than clouded by cataracts, our eardrums more than punctured, our minds more than impaired when it comes to knowing Jesus. Not only can't we know him, we can't even want him if we do learn about him. People can try to tell us about the Savior. Preachers can try to point us to him. But when they ask, "Can't you see him?" our answer can only be "No." Such is our horrible legacy from our first parent's sin in the Garden of Eden. In our natural spiritual condition, God's wisdom of salvation in Christ is only foolishness.

Until God reveals this blessed truth to us by his Spirit. The Holy Spirit brings the Savior up close to us through the gospel. With the Word he not only points out Jesus but works to power faith within our unbelieving hearts. Not only does he ask, "Can't you see him?" He also creates faith in us to know and trust Jesus as our only Savior. When the Holy Spirit does his work, I can see Jesus. And that's the most precious sight in the world.

Holy Spirit, thank you for opening my eyes to see and my heart to trust Jesus as Savior. Amen.

WE CAN TAKE HIS WORD FOR IT

For no matter how many promises God
has made, they are "Yes" in Christ.
2 Corinthians 1:20

"I guarantee it," says the clothing chain president in his TV
commercial, meaning we can take his word for it. He wants
us to believe that his company's suits are the best quality and
the best price. At least, so he claims.

When God makes his claims, we can take his word for it. Isn't
that what Christian faith is all about? It's the confidence that
whatever God says he means. Note what Paul said. All God's
promises are "yes" in Christ. Everything he has promised for
our salvation in Christ he has done. Everything else he promises for our lives, he will also surely do. Christ is God's "YES,"
in big letters and bold print, for all his claims.

At the baptismal font, when God promises, "Whoever believes
and is baptized will be saved" (Mark 16:16). I can trust his
words are true for me and for my children. In the church service, when he promises, "Take heart, . . . your sins are forgiven" (Matthew 9:2), I can bank on his words. At the
Communion Table, when he assures me, "This is my body . . .
this is my blood . . . for the forgiveness of sins" (Matthew
26:26,28), I can go home in peace. Not only does my God
promise, but in Christ he has put his powerful love behind all
his claims. And that is not all. What he has done for my salvation in Christ is the guarantee of what he will do for me in
all the changing scenes of life.

Lord, in Jesus show me that I can take you at
your word whenever you speak. Amen.

LET ME SEE
HIS SHINING FACE

There he was transfigured before them. His
face shone like the sun, and his clothes
became as white as the light. Matthew 17:2

Who took his photo or painted his portrait? Since that time, artists have only imagined what Jesus looked like. We really don't know. From the account of his transfiguration come some ideas.

How do we describe the glory shining in Jesus' face and through his clothing that day? Not some outside glory beaming down on him, but arising from within him. A glory that far outshone the sun's brightest rays in the sky. The radiant glory of God himself, for that's who Jesus is!

From such a shining face, we can only fall back in fear. When God and man stand face-to-face, man must step aside. God wanted a face-to-face relationship with us. But Adam's sin spoiled it all. Now when God comes, sin's curse can only turn us away from his glorious face.

"Move over Peter, James, and John," we have to say. "Make room for our sinful faces down in the dust of that mountain top." Like them, we can't look at Jesus' holy face. But we dare not stay there with sinful faces in the dust of despair. We need to look from Jesus' holy face to his loving face. We need to learn what he has done with our sins so we can have that face-to-face relationship with him already here on earth and forever in heaven.

Lord Jesus, remind me how you made me
holy by your blood so I could see your holy
face. Amen.

LET ME SEE
HIS LOVING FACE

Two men, Moses and Elijah, appeared in glorious splendor, talking with Jesus. They spoke about his departure, which he was about to bring to fulfillment at Jerusalem. Luke 9:30,31

On the Mount of Transfiguration, we see another side of Jesus' face. Kneeling there, we hear voices. There's Moses, buried by God in an unknown grave. Next to him stands Elijah, taken alive by God in a fiery chariot to heaven. These two Old Testament believers are returned to speak with Jesus.

About what? Those three went right to the heart of the matter—Jesus' death that was coming up in Jerusalem. The King James Version puts it in a strange way—Jesus would accomplish death. We suffer death; there's nothing we can do about it. But Jesus accomplished death. That was a part of his work of salvation. The cup of suffering with every bitter drop, the cross of nails with every bitter pain, the opened tomb with every blessed comfort, the salvation of the world—this he was going to bring to fulfillment. And this is what they talked about on that mountaintop.

"Move over Peter, James, and John," we feel like saying, "make room for us. We'd like to stay forever on that mountaintop and bask in the sunshine of such love." But like them we have to walk back down into the sin- and tear-filled plains of life. And it's down there that Jesus' love becomes very real for us. In daily life, where joy and sorrow, laughter and tears run together, we need to know that Jesus loves us. In the midst of sin and problems, I need to see his loving face.

Lord, let the sight of your loving face assure me of your salvation and strength for my life. Amen.

LET ME SEE
HIS ETERNAL FACE

Two men, Moses and Elijah, appeared in glorious splendor, talking with Jesus. Luke 9:30,31

One more time we look at Jesus on that Mount of Transfiguration and note that his is an eternal face. To appreciate this truth, we need to look at our own faces. What do we see when we do? Faces marked by the hands of change. Faces where disease and pain have left their marks. Faces finally that will be cold in a coffin.

Oh, how we need to look at Jesus' face on that mountain! There we gain a preview of what we can expect someday with him. Moses and Elijah at his side on that mountain reinforce our expectation and conviction. Dead at the age of 120, Moses stands there alive some 1,500 years later. Carried to heaven in a fiery chariot almost 900 years earlier, Elijah lives too. They are real. They listen, think, talk, and are recognized by the disciples.

In those two we see what a bright future awaits us through our eternal Savior. Some of my loved ones have disappeared from my sight. I'll see their faces no more on this earth. But in heaven I shall, just as surely as I've seen Moses and Elijah standing there with Jesus. Someday, who knows when, my face will disappear. But that won't be the end for me any more than it was for Moses and Elijah. Instead, all believers and I will join those Old Testament Christians to stand at Jesus' side forever.

Yes, let me see my Savior's face, first here on earth and finally in heaven. Amen.

GRACE SAYS IT ALL

The kingdom of heaven is like a landowner who went out early in the morning to hire men to work in his vineyard. Matthew 20:1

In Palestine, when the grapes were ripe in September, it was pick them before the rains came or lose them. So Jesus' listeners could understand when in his parable he talked about the owner hiring workers. They also understood the union scale for such work and how one's check was figured. What they couldn't understand is why all the workers received the same pay.

They missed the point because they were looking at the wrong person. Jesus' picture story with a meaning was not about the labor of the workers but the generosity of the owner. What about me? Do I understand that people are carried to heaven not because of what they do or don't do but because of God's generosity? Do I appreciate that people enter God's heaven purely through his grace? *Grace* is the rich word for some gift completely undeserved, something I in no way have coming.

Why should God send his own Son to rescue me from the eternity in hell that I so richly deserve? Why should he single me out in the surging sea of humanity to hear the news of his salvation? Why should he struggle with my rebellious heart and bring me to faith in Jesus as my only Savior? Why, why, why? Grace is the only answer that fits. It really is. As Paul says in Ephesians 2:8,9, "By grace you have been saved, through faith . . . it is the gift of God—not by works, so that no one can boast."

Thank you, loving Lord, for the amazing grace that saved a wretch like me. Amen.

GRACE COVERS US ALL

> When they received it, they began to grumble against the landowner. "These men who were hired last worked only one hour," they said, "and you have made them equal to us who have borne the burden of the work and the heat of the day." Matthew 20:11,12

"Unfair," the workers in Jesus' parable thought when all received the same wage. Those who had worked just one hour before the whistle blew received as much as those who had broken their backs under the blaze of the noonday sun. Yes, unfair according to the ways of the world but not according to God's grace.

Get the point! Forgiveness of sin and eternal life in heaven are pure grace. They are undeserved favors from the hand of a loving God. Every believer shares in them equally. Those who are brought to faith in the morning hour of life, and those who come later in the evening hour. Those who are baptized as a baby, as well as the deathbed convert. The murderer who repents the night before his execution along with the faithful grandmother. Words like *first* and *last* simply have no meaning when it comes to the kingdom of heaven. The word to use is *grace*. God's grace that covers us all.

Grace is a comfort word. When my sins give me alarm, when my last breath is drawing near, when I need the assurance that heaven is my home, nothing does it like God's grace. Nothing comforts better than the truth, "Plenteous grace with thee is found, grace to cover all my sin" (CW 357:4).

Lord, please make my concern not that your grace comes to others but that it covers me. Amen.

EVERY DAY
A VALENTINE'S DAY

This is how we know what love is: Jesus Christ
laid down his life for us. 1 John 3:16

"Will you be my valentine?" Remember cards like that?
Remember when we used to send them? Perhaps we still do
to show our love for someone special.

Ever stop to think that every day is Valentine's Day with God?
He doesn't limit his show of love to one day a year. He loves
every day and has been doing so since the world began.
Notice too that his love is active. He doesn't merely say, "I
love you," or simply send a card. He shows his love in actions.

How did he show his love to me just this past week? In the
form of family members who laughed with me when I was
happy and cried with me when I was sad? In the form of
strength against temptation, healing for a hurting body,
success in some venture, and guidance for some decision?
God's love flows down on me constantly. Every day his love
sends me valentines.

Best of all, God has shown his love in sending his Son to lay
down his life for me. Jesus loved me so much that he was
willing to take my place on the cross so sin's punishment
might be paid and sin's debt erased. Because of this gift, the
devil can't harm me, the grave can't hold me, and eternity
can't harbor any fear for me. Behind this divine gift of salvation stands a love that is undeserved and indescribable.
And that love is real every day. What a blessed valentine
from my God every day!

Lord, I need your love in Jesus. Please be my
valentine today and always. Amen.

HEAVEN IS MY HOME

Our citizenship is in heaven. And we eagerly await a Savior from there, the Lord Jesus Christ. Philippians 3:20

Away from home for a month, I welcomed the sight of the American flag fluttering over the embassy in Lagos, Nigeria. It reminded me of my blessed country and made me long for home.

Every Christian knows that feeling. Except, the home for which believers long is a heavenly one. "I'm but a stranger here. Heaven is my home," we love to sing. At funerals the words bring tears to our eyes. Even more so should those words color our lives. I still have to live in this world and use the things of this world. But God help me live as one who is just passing through, not one who is trying to put down permanent roots. God help me rejoice that my name is recorded in his book of life in heaven. God help me treasure the blessings I have as a citizen of heaven—forgiveness for every sin, help for every trouble, comfort for every sorrow, and heaven in the end.

Yes, heaven in the end. "We eagerly await a Savior from there," Paul wrote, using a word that describes how children wait for Christmas. As a citizen of heaven, I don't walk around with my eyes fixed on this ball of mud. My eyes and heart know only one direction, upward, eagerly waiting for the Savior to return. When he does, on the last day of this world or my last day in this world, I'll fully enjoy my heavenly citizenship and revel in all its blessings. When that day comes, I'll see heaven's flag waving and be truly at home with the Lord.

Lord, keep me safe as a pilgrim in this world till you take me to my heavenly home. Amen.

DON'T TRUST GOD SO MUCH

The tempter came to him and said, "If you are the Son of God, tell these stones to become bread." Jesus answered, "It is written: Man does not live on bread alone, but on every word that comes from the mouth of God." Matthew 4:3,4

You wake up in the middle of the night in a cold sweat, only to discover the monster about to grab you wasn't real. Too bad the same can't be said of the devil and his attacks on believers.

"Don't trust God so much," Satan was telling Christ with his first temptation. More than bread for an empty stomach was involved. At stake was Christ's trust in the heavenly Father. Did that Father really care for him? Could Jesus really trust him? If so, then why this lonely hunger in the desert?

Sound familiar? "If," the devil starts in on me, always with that insidious little "if." "If you are God's child, how come you have trouble? How come you're sick? How come your loved one has cancer or your teenager is rebellious? He says that he loves you, but can you call that love?"

What to do? Look to Jesus. "The reason the Son of God appeared was to destroy the devil's work," Scripture tells us (1 John 3:8). In the desert we see this truth in action. On Calvary's cross, I see this truth complete as Christ forever routed Satan for me. Now when Satan knocks on my heart's door, I can say, "Away from me." Satan can't win when Christ fights alongside me.

Lord Jesus, strengthen me when the devil attacks so that you and I together gain the victory. Amen.

TRY GOD OUT

> Then the devil took him to the holy city and had him stand on the highest point of the temple. "If you are the Son of God," he said, "throw yourself down . . ." Jesus answered him, "It is also written: 'Do not put the Lord your God to the test.'" Matthew 4:5-7

"Try God out," Satan urged Christ with his second temptation. Swaying together on that high peak of the temple, the devil breathed again that little "if." "If you are the Son of God, throw yourself down." And then he even quoted from Psalm 91 about how God has promised to protect his own. But watch out when the prince of darkness masquerades as an angel of light. God is to be trusted, not tested. His promises are to be humbly believed, not insolently stretched.

Sound familiar? Has that "roaring lion" sought to devour me with similar temptations? "If you don't help me, Lord, I'll never trust you again. If you don't answer my prayer, right now and just the way I want it, I'm going to leave." So cleverly can Satan wedge such thoughts into our hearts. "That's right," he says, "put God on the spot. Treat him like your own personal genie, who jumps out of the magical lamp when you rub it. And if he doesn't, forget about him."

What to do? Look to Jesus. "It is written," he answered, sending Satan flying with the cutting edge of God's almighty Word. When I swing the sword of the Spirit at Satan, he has to duck. When I train and fight with God's almighty Word, Satan has to slink away in defeat.

Lord, train me in your Word so that I am armed for battle. Amen.

TAKE THE EASY WAY

"All this I will give you," he [Satan] said, "if you will bow down and worship me." Jesus said to him, "Away from me, Satan! For it is written: 'Worship the Lord your God, and serve him only.'" Matthew 4:9,10

Take all the pages of history, past, present, and future; all the realms and riches of the world as it was, is, and will be; and we get an idea of what Satan showed Jesus on that mountaintop. Again comes that little "if," but what a liar Satan is! He offers what he doesn't have and demands what he doesn't deserve. "Take the easy way," he was telling Christ in this third temptation. "Here's a kingdom without a crown of thorns and without a cross of nails to be had just for bowing down before me."

Sound familiar? "Why work so hard? Look at what others get away with," the clever serpent tells the laborer. "Why not over-figure expenses and under-figure income? The government will just spend it anyway," he tells the taxpayer. "Why not give in and enjoy?" he asks the teenager. "Others are doing it." "Why not let down the standards and loosen the doctrine?" he hints to the church member. "Take the easy way," he tells us as he conjures up before our eyes the things of this world.

What to do? Look to Jesus. He fears, loves, and trusts in his Father alone. Through Jesus, I will one day stand in heaven, not only cleansed from my sins against the First Commandment but with its perfect keeping in my hand. On it will be printed, "Made by Jesus Christ."

Jesus, thank you for keeping God's commandments and making it count for me. Amen.

LOVE LISTENS TO JESUS

> One thing is needed. Mary has chosen what is
> better, and it will not be taken away from her.
> Luke 10:42

How can you tell when you're in love? No, we aren't asking about some checklist for prospective partners or quizzes for those already married. Here's a practical question for practical Christians. How can we tell that we're in love with Jesus?

Let's look at Mary. Remember the account. Jesus came visiting once again to that home in Bethany. Martha immediately started cooking up a storm in the kitchen. But Mary, instead of helping her sister, sat listening at Jesus' feet. All else was forgotten as she hung on his every word. Need we guess what Jesus talked about? He who did the talking that day described it as the "one thing needed" and that which is "better." From such hints we can safely surmise that the conversation was about his love. How he had come to earth to pay for sinners and lift them as ransomed souls to heaven. How he had to do this because divine love compelled him. No wonder Mary sat there listening.

I cannot love Jesus without him first loving me. Because of his saving love, I have something to listen to, something that never grows old. When he tells me through his Word how he left his glorious throne on high and came down to earth to bleed and die, I want to catch his every word. That's where I belong this Lenten season, at his feet listening to the one thing needed.

> Lord, help me never lose my love for the
> message of how you loved and saved me. Amen.

LOVE LIVES FOR JESUS

"Martha, Martha," the Lord answered, "you are worried and upset about many things, but only one thing is needed." Luke 10:41,42

Poor Martha! So often people have misunderstood Jesus' rebuke of her. There was nothing wrong with her wanting to prepare a meal for Jesus. Nothing wrong with her wanting that dinner to be the best for her Savior. Jesus wants us to serve him. He wants us to work as hard as we can out of love for him. What he was scolding Martha for was her timing. "First things first," he was telling her. First she was to sit at his feet and let him serve her with his Word. Then she could properly serve him.

Love wants to serve. Love and selfishness cannot stand side by side. They are as opposite as fire and water, sugar and vinegar. And Jesus deserves my loving service. My reaction to his amazing love is to want to love him back. From his cross comes not only pardon for our sins, but power to serve him. "We love because he first loved us," John said correctly (1 John 4:19). Wherever he has placed me, with whatever talents he has given me, with whomever I interact, I want to serve him. My life is no longer something I use for myself but something I dedicate in love to his service. My divine Lover has work for me to do, none of which is more important than telling others of his love. But remember, first things first. Before I can respond, "Love so amazing, so divine, demands my life, my soul, my all," I need to sit at the foot of his cross, drinking in the message of his love.

Lord, fill me with your amazing love so that I can become an instrument of your love. Amen.

RED WITH HIS BLOOD

These are the Scriptures that testify about me.
John 5:39

"Cut the Bible anywhere, and it bleeds red," said the pastor in confirmation class. He was right! The more we search the Scriptures, the more we see Christ and his precious blood. From Genesis to Revelation, the theme of Scripture is the Savior sent by God's love.

The Seed promised to fallen Adam and Eve in the garden was a reference to the Savior. The rainbow placed in the sky after the universal flood was a guarantee that God keeps his promises, including the main one about the Savior. The promise that brought Abraham to a strange land was centered in the Savior who was to come. When David tuned his harp and sang his psalms, his beloved theme was wrapped around the Savior. When Isaiah took up his pen, it was especially to write about the Savior who would be born of a virgin and wounded for our transgressions. When Malachi closed the Old Testament, it was with cheering references to the Savior coming like the sun in the morning sky.

We who live in the New Testament can read even more clearly. Like some red thread, Jesus is woven throughout the books. He came, he suffered and died, and he rose again. He paid for sin and restored peace between man and God. God made him carry our sin and gave us his righteousness. Now we can look forward to life eternal through him and with him. Open the Scriptures where you will, and there stands Jesus, my only Savior.

"They testify about me," Jesus said. God help me always to see him. Amen.

SINLESS IN HIS PERSON

Can any of you prove me guilty of sin? If I am telling the truth, why don't you believe me?
John 8:46

Whom can we believe these days? We've learned to take the words of the salesman, the politician, and others with a "grain of salt." The more they urge, "Believe me," the more we back away. Thank God, there is one Person we can believe—totally. What he says, we can trust—completely.

The Pharisees didn't. Instead of trusting him, they tried to trap him. If they could discredit his person, they would automatically also discredit his teachings. So Jesus challenged them, not just to accuse him of sin but to make the accusation stick. How ironical! Not only was Jesus the only One who was ever without sin but his mission on earth was to make them sinless by paying for theirs.

Why do I need a sinless Jesus? Because a sinless Jesus is one who never speaks a lie or stretches the truth. When he says he will never leave me nor forsake me, I can take that as gospel truth. When he says my sins are plunged into the depths of the sea, that promise stands sure as the heavens above. When he says he will walk with me through the valley of the shadow, he's going to be there. When he says I will stand beside his throne in his heaven some day, I'm going to be there. Because my sinless Jesus says so! Jesus says, "Believe me." How foolish not to!

Yes, Lord, I believe—by your grace and the Spirit's working. Help me ever to do so. Amen.

LIFE-GIVING
IN HIS WORD

I tell you the truth, if anyone keeps my word,
he will never see death. John 8:51

The fear of death is universal. Death is not a familiar topic of conversation over morning coffee at the restaurant or on break at the plant. Nor do women at the beauty shop lace their discussions with it either. We'd just as soon forget about death. When we have to face it, we try to cover it up and get away from it as quickly as possible. Why? Because down deep inside ourselves, we know what comes after death. We know there's a God to face and a judgment to answer. And that makes death the king of terrors.

So when Jesus spoke about never seeing death, wouldn't we have expected those Pharisees to sit up and pay attention? When he promised that those who hear and believe his Word would never have to set foot in hell, shouldn't they have been listening with wide-opened ears?

I don't much like death either. It's not my favorite topic of conversation. Nor is there any greater grief than caused by the loss of a loved one. But I don't have to be afraid of death. Not since Jesus filled Calvary's cross and emptied Joseph's tomb. Yes, "the wages of sin is death," and that's what the sinless Son of God came to pay. He carried my sins on his sinless shoulders, suffered for them in the fires of hell, and satisfied my debt forever. In him I have the guarantee that I shall live forever. Jesus says, "Believe me." How foolish not to!

Yes, Lord, I believe—by your grace and the
Spirit's working. Help me ever to do so. Amen.

ETERNAL
IN HIS EXISTENCE

"I tell you the truth," Jesus answered, "before Abraham was born, I am!" John 8:58

For the people of Israel, there was no greater hero than Abraham. Yet he had been dead for 2,000 years. So when the 30-some-year-old Jesus said, "Before Abraham was born, I am," they laughed. They saw only the human and not the divine Jesus. They understood his contrast, "Abraham *was* born, I *am*." They heard what he was saying, that he always was and would be because he was eternal God. But to them, calling himself God was blasphemy, punishable by stoning to death. So they reached for their stones. How foolish! The eternal God had come to earth just as he had long promised for just one purpose, to save sinners like them. And they wanted to kill him.

What a Jesus he is! He is Jesus Christ, the same yesterday, today, and forever. What a comfort to know that he is the eternal, unchanging Son of God whose blood will surely cleanse me from all my sins! Change and decay I see all around me, but my eternal Jesus stays the same. Years ago when my forefathers put his cross upon the altar in my church, it was in honor of that Jesus. Today it still stands, and the Jesus whom it represents is still the same—my eternal, unchanging Savior. Should the world continue, who knows how many more years, so that my children and grandchildren see that cross on the altar, Jesus will still be the same.

That eternal Savior says, "Believe me." How foolish not to!

Yes, Lord, I believe—by your grace and the Spirit's working. Help me ever to do so. Amen.

SALVATION FOR THE SOUL

When Jesus landed and saw a large crowd, he
had compassion on them, because they were
like sheep without a shepherd. So he began
teaching them many things. Mark 6:34

It was past dinner time. They were hungry. What kept that
crowd spellbound so long that day in the wilderness? Perhaps not all had come for the right reason. Perhaps not all
would go home with the right answers. But Jesus had
offered rich food for their souls. His heart, seeing what the
crowd really needed, spoke to them about forgiveness and
peace, rest and heaven.

Even his miracle that day was designed for their souls. By
multiplying the loaves and fishes, he wanted to point them
to the greater miracle, how he as the Savior was the only
bread that could feed their souls. Some were fed and satisfied
that day. Others went home still hungry, though they had
dined on miracle loaves and fishes.

When I sit at the Savior's feet, as the crowd did that day, for
what am I hungry? Do I think of him the way the anonymous
poet did who wrote: "My Master was so very poor, a manger
was his cradling place. So very rich my Master was, kings
came from far to gain his grace. My Master was so very poor
and with the poor he broke the bread. So very rich my Master was that multitudes by him were fed. My Master was so
very poor they nailed him naked to a cross. So very rich my
Master was, he gave his all and knew no loss"? But oh, the
gain when my soul is fed by him!

Feed me, Bread of Heaven, and my soul will be
satisfied. Amen.

SANDWICHES
FOR THE STOMACH

Jesus then took the loaves, gave thanks, and distributed to those who were seated as much as they wanted. He did the same with the fish.
John 6:11

Where could they get something to eat? In the wilderness, there were no supermarkets with stocked shelves or convenience stores packed with snacks. In their treasury, there was hardly enough money to buy a bite to eat for every one of the five thousand. In the crowd was only a lad with five loaves and two fishes, hardly enough to make sandwiches for everyone. What were the disciples going to do?

Remember what happened when Jesus took over? In his powerful hands, the fish sandwiches grew into enough to feed the crowd. When all were satisfied, more was left over than what the boy had even started with. Don't you wonder if the disciples ever forgot the powerful lesson learned that day? How the Lord Jesus provides for the needs of the body.

Do we remember or do we forget? Christians get hungry too. Inflation affects their income, recession their savings. Tornadoes don't just hit the houses of unbelievers. Sickness doesn't just invade non-Christian bodies. The believer is no barometer with the needle of life always stuck on FAIR. The difference lies in my reaction. Someone once said, "There are three ways to react to trouble. You can take it on the chin. You can take to drink. You can take to religion." Where do I turn? He who served up fish sandwiches to the crowd that day will supply what I need.

Lord, help me to cast all my cares on you, trusting that you care for me. Amen.

WHAT WOULD I WRITE?

Jesus took the Twelve aside and told them, "We are going up to Jerusalem, and everything that is written by the prophets about the Son of Man will be fulfilled." Luke 18:31

Dear God, I'm writing to you about those special services my church holds during Lent. I don't know how to say this, but I don't think I'll be at many of them. When I finally get home from work and take my shoes off, I want to leave them off. It's easier to let the children sit in front of the TV. Also, I don't want to miss my favorite show. If I record it, the tape will just sit there with all the others. Besides, I know all about your Son's suffering and death. I hear about it every Sunday and won't be missing much. Please understand and excuse me. Signed—a church member.

Dear Church Member, I was sorry to receive your letter. Did you know that I'm not always happy about going to church either, especially when people don't come to worship me? But I go. I'm there to bless my children through my Word. Especially do I want to bless them through the news of my Son's suffering and death. During Lent I want people especially to hear what my Son has done for them. I have no greater gifts than his forgiveness, peace, and sure promise of heaven. When you find out what I offer, you'll have joy in coming. I'll be looking for you. Signed—God.

There's no mail delivery to heaven, and these are just fictional letters. But as Lent approaches, the question is, What would I write?

Lord Jesus, take me up to Jerusalem with you so that I may enjoy your gift of salvation. Amen.

HE TOOK A TOWEL

He poured water into a basin and began to wash his disciples' feet, drying them with the towel that was wrapped around him. John 13:5

What kind of towel was it? Made of wool, perhaps, from sheep of nearby Bethlehem? Stained with color, perhaps, from some nut or berry in a day before our modern dyes? We don't know. Far more important is it for me to note who took that towel and what he did with it.

What love that foot-washer exhibited that Maundy Thursday evening. He, into whose hands the Father had placed all things, now filled a basin and picked up a towel. That night the Savior washed feet with water in the upper room. The next morning he washed souls with his blood on Calvary's cross. That night his hands took a towel. The next morning they were pierced by nails. How can I miss the love behind it all? A love that took up a towel and handled dirty feet. A love that tasted hell's doom and a grave's darkness because he was handling the world's sins. From that love came such wonderful cleansing for sinners like Peter and John, Matthew and me.

Cleansed by Jesus' blood, I still have to walk the world's dusty roads. In the Lenten season, more than any other time of the year, I need to check my feet again, noting clearly what greed and envy, what love for the world's goods and lack of love for my neighbor have been layered there. Seeing the dirt, it's time again to kneel before his cross with the plea, "Wash me, Savior, or I die."

Lord, wash not just my feet but all of me with your cleansing blood. Amen.

TEARS FOR LENT

The Lord turned and looked straight at Peter.
Then Peter remembered the word the Lord had
spoken to him. . . . And he went outside and
wept bitterly. Luke 22:61,62

When's the last time I cried? Might it sound strange to suggest that Lent is a good time for Christians to have tears in their hearts, if not also in their eyes, just like Simon Peter?

If only I could see the hurt in Jesus' eyes each time I choose sin. You see, there is no such thing as cheap grace. Each one of my sins cost Jesus dearly. Each one made him shudder in the garden, struggle on the cross, sigh his last breath in death. And repentance is not a light matter. It's the sinner seeing the look on his Savior's face and gulping in shame, "I'm sorry, Lord, so sorry I have sinned against you." Am I ready to join Peter in those tears of repentance this Lenten season?

When the Savior looked at Peter that night, it wasn't, "I warned you about this. You got yourself into it, now get yourself out." Instead, there had to be love in that look. That look had to say, "Peter, I still love you, and I forgive you."

This holy season, can I leave the cross and its message of God's love for sinners without tears of gratitude? Jesus still loves me! He knows my daily defeats and denials. He's well aware of all my sins and shortcomings. And he forgives me! Can it be? Oh, thank God that it is!

Please, Lord, let it be tears in my heart, if not
in my eyes, this Lenten season. Amen.

WERE YOU THERE?

He was delivered over to death for our sins.
Romans 4:25

Were you there? "Yes," we answer gladly on some occasions. Not so gladly if it's an unpleasant situation. How about when asked, "Were you there when they crucified my Lord?"

Notice the little pronoun in our verse? "*Our* sins," Paul said. We're quick to pick up on the sins of others in Christ's death. Like the hatred of the Jewish leaders, the cowardice of Pilate, Judas' greed, and the disciples' faintheartedness. But what we so easily spot in others can remain unseen in ourselves. Paul sets the record straight with that pronoun *our*. My shortcomings, which no paint can gild regardless how thick I apply it, were part of that Calvary equation. Soldiers swung the hammer, but my sins pierced him. Hell chained him in its torments, but my sins forged some of the links.

Notice something else in Paul's words? God was there on Calvary. He "delivered" Jesus "over to death for our sins." Divine justice demanded that every sin be punished. Man could not cancel, chisel away at, or cover up the awful debt. Only one remedy would work, the one God's love alone could provide. He delivered his own Son over to death at Calvary to bear the punishment for our sins.

There when they crucified my Lord? Thank God, my happy answer can be "Yes," there seeing and believing what God's love did with all my sins.

Thank you, Lord, for being there at Calvary as the only one who could pay for my sins. Amen.

LENT AND LOVE

To him who loves us and has freed us from our sins by his blood . . . to him be glory and power for ever and ever! Amen. Revelation 1:5,6

For weeks Michelangelo, painting the ceiling of the Vatican's Sistine Chapel, had been on the scaffold. So accustomed had his eyes become to looking up that it hurt to turn them downward to the ground. Our problem is often the opposite. We fasten our eyes on the ground and don't raise them to heaven. This season it's time to look heavenward and marvel anew at God's love behind our salvation.

He "has freed us from our sins," John wrote. Lent is not only a time for the upward look at God's love but also for the inward look at myself. The more honestly I scrutinize myself, the more marvelous God's love appears. What do I see when I look at myself? Someone worthy of God's love or with sin's dirt imbedded beneath the fingernails of daily life? Someone whose walk is squeaky clean or whose mind, tongue, and actions look as though they've spent time in sin's mud holes? The inward look quickly reminds me how amazing God's love is to reach so low to sinners like me.

What did it cost God to free me from my sins? "Blood," John said. The cross was no decoration or ornament for Jesus. It was filled with pain and flecked with blood. Worse were the tortures of hell. All the pains of hell that were sin's wage were his to collect. Love that only God could display took him to that cross and kept him there. It's time to look up again and marvel at such love.

Lord, fill me with thankfulness and awe each time I hear the message of your salvation. Amen.

THOSE NAIL-PIERCED HANDS

They have pierced my hands and my feet.
Psalm 22:16

Scars on our hands—perhaps from some knife that slipped or disease that crippled. There's usually a story behind those scars. Jesus' hands have scars too and behind them is the greatest story the world has ever heard.

David foretold it, and the gospels record it, using simple words. But there was nothing simple about it. Splintery wood and sharp nails, torn flesh and screaming nerve endings, constant pain and slow death—such was involved in crucifixion. Far worse were the tortures of hell. All the pains of hell that were the wages for the world's sins crushed down on Jesus pierced on that cross. Only the devils and the damned in hell can begin to understand. We can only guess at what this involved for Jesus.

There's no guessing, though, as to who pierced his hands and his feet. Calvary's scene won't mean much until the *they* becomes *we*. Better still, it needs to be *"I* pierced his hands and his feet." I with my many sins did it! Nor dare I stop with the thoughts of my guilt. The gloom of guilt is dispelled by the glorious truth that Christ has paid for all my sins with his suffering and death. Clearly and plainly the Bible tells me, "By his wounds we are healed" (Isaiah 53:5).

So look at those nail-pierced hands! They have a story to tell. They speak of full payment for the world's sins. They speak— they shout—to me about my salvation!

Lord, help me to listen. Amen.

FOR ME
HE WAS CRUCIFIED

[He] loved me and gave himself for me.
Galatians 2:20

"For me?" exclaims the young wife opening the present she had hardly dared to hope for. Few are the times in life that we receive something unexpected and undeserved and can use those words. Yet as we gaze at the cross on Calvary, that expression belongs in our hearts and on our lips. "For me!" All this the Savior did for me, all unworthy though I be.

What held Jesus to that horrible tree? Not strands of hemp hurriedly put on his hands in Gethsemane's shadows nor the hatred of the mob howling for his blood. Not even Pilate's unjust command or the nails that skewered Christ's flesh. It was the power of his love. In eternity, divine love had decreed that God's Lamb be sacrificed on that rough altar. Now at Calvary it was done. Divine love, amazing love, unbelievable love bound Jesus to that cross, fashioned by our sins.

All this for me! His holy hands were pierced in payment for the sins I commit daily. His perfect feet were scarred because of the many times my feet have not walked in the way of God's commands. Thorns marred his sinless head in ransom for my wayward, selfish, and often senseless thoughts that blemish my days. "Was it for crimes that I had done he groaned upon the tree? Amazing pity, grace unknown, and love beyond degree!" (CW 129:2).

Yes, thank you, Lord, for the love that crucified Jesus for me. Amen.

FOR ME HE DIED

[He] loved me and gave himself for me.
Galatians 2:20

Though some of us in the 21st century will live longer than our grandparents, the statistic remains ultimately the same. One out of one dies. Death still waits to claim each one of us with cold arms.

Then what? Then comes the unthinkable, not just being erased from the land of the living but from the sight of the gracious God in a never-ending hell. That's not what God wanted for me. He wanted me to live forever in perfect peace and harmony with him. But sin brought its wage of death.

So why did Jesus have to die? "The soul who sins is the one who will die," a just God had warned (Ezekiel 18:20). Jesus had no sin. Yet he died—with a death so frightful it caused him to cry out, "My God, my God, why have you forsaken me?" (Matthew 27:46). The full fury of God's righteous anger and the full force of hell's pain washed over him on that cross. When God looked at his sinless Son, he saw on him the full load of the world's sins. With Jesus' death came the world's redemption. "It is finished," Jesus could say of sin's payment, even as he laid his sinless soul into the hands of his heavenly Father.

All this for me! Though death still buzzes like some bee around me all my days, it cannot harm me. Jesus has removed its sting. His death is my death; his payment for sin covers also me. He means us too when he asserts, "Whoever lives and believes in me will never die" (John 11:26).

Lord, thank you for offering yourself for my sins that I might live with you in heaven. Amen.

FOR ME
HE WAS BURIED

[He] loved me and gave himself for me.
Galatians 2:20

What more desolate spot can there be than a cemetery? What more heart-rending scene than a funeral? Those of us who have left loved ones beneath a mound of dirt in the cemetery know the feeling. So did that small group of Jesus' followers that first Good Friday. Heartbroken and hope-shattered they took his dead body down from the cross, wrapped it in strips of linen cloth, and laid it to rest in the garden tomb. For them it looked like the end. It seemed as if they had based their hopes for salvation and heaven on the wrong one. How slowly they must have trudged home after that hurried funeral.

Little did they know! On the third day Joseph's tomb would be empty again. Their Savior would be gloriously alive again. Their future would be stretching into an endless eternity. That tomb in which they had buried Jesus was the setting for his and their glorious Easter victory.

All this for me! Someday I'll fill a rectangular spot in some cemetery, but I need not be afraid. "I know that my Redeemer lives" is my triumphant shout ever since Joseph's borrowed tomb was emptied that first Easter day. By God's grace I can say, "When from the dust of death I rise To claim my mansion in the skies, E'en then this shall be all my plea: Jesus has lived and died *for me*" (CW 376:5).

Jesus, thank you for loving me and giving yourself for me. Amen.

PRAISE FOR
HIS NAME—IMMANUEL

"The virgin will be with child and will give birth to a son, and they will call him Immanuel"—which means, "God with us."
Matthew 1:23

What a beautiful name for my Savior, Immanuel—*God with us*. In it are wrapped two comforting truths. The first is that Jesus is God. Eliminate that truth and what would that baby mean to me? He'd be just another baby, cute, no doubt, like all of them. And what would that figure on the cross 33 years later mean to me? He'd be just another innocent victim nailed there by some miscarriage of justice. No, he must be God, or else he can't be my Savior. If he's not God, then his blood could hardly purify me from all sin.

The second truth in his name Immanuel? He's "God *with us*." What a comforting thought. God's not far off, distant in the heavens, glancing at us from across the miles. He's with us in our flesh, on our globe, under our sin. He's with me in my sin, not to cause them or share in them but to save me from them. He's already paid for every one of them. He's with me in my sorrows and trials. He knows what they are like. He suffered many of them also and knows just how to help me with them. He's with me in my service to him. Though I often get weary and seem to take three steps forward then five steps backward in my efforts, he's there to keep me trying.

What a name, *Immanuel,* my Savior-God has, one that deserves my praise all my days!

Lord, thank you for coming to the manger and the cross to be my only Savior. Amen.

PRAISE FOR HIS NAME—JESUS

You are to give him the name Jesus, because he will save his people from their sins.
Matthew 1:21

"What are we going to name the baby?" expectant parents ask. Sometimes the name picked fits; sometimes not. But with the One lying in the manger, riding into Jerusalem, hanging on the cross, the name picked fit superbly. Why?

First of all, because it was a name given from heaven. It was given nine months before his birth to his mother and also sometime later to his foster father. "Give him the name Jesus," the angel said. He was God himself come down from heaven, and so his name was given from heaven. He came to do the work that only heaven could do—save sinners. And he's going to take people to heaven to be there where he is. The name Jesus just rings with thoughts of heaven.

Second, the name Jesus fits because he is my helper. Does anyone reading this not know that Jesus means "Savior"? The penitent thief, hanging next to Jesus on Calvary, knew. He begged, "Jesus, remember me when you come into your kingdom" (Luke 23:42). From Jesus comes forgiveness for my sins, ability to stand before God with confidence, a heart filled with all-surpassing peace. He's my Savior!

What a name, *Jesus,* my Savior-God has, one that deserves my praise all my days!

Lord, thank you for teaching me your name Jesus and what it means for me. Amen.

PRAISE FOR HIS NAME—THE LAMB

Look, the Lamb of God, who takes away the
sin of the world! John 1:29

Other than in a children's petting zoo, we seldom see lambs.
To the Jews, lambs were commonplace, raised in the fields for
food and for sacrifice. Over the years thousands must have
been slain in the temple, at least two every day, not count-
ing the ones brought as special sacrifices.

Notice Jesus is not just called *a* lamb. He is *the* Lamb because
he is God's Lamb. He was sent by God. He was God's choice. He
was God's perfect Lamb, as Peter put it "a lamb without blemish or defect" (1 Peter 1:19). This heaven-sent Lamb had no
spots on the outside or defects on the inside. God's Lamb was
perfect and holy, as he had to be for his important mission.

Notice also why God sent his Lamb—to take away sin. Animal blood could not pay for a single sin of a single human
being. Only the blood of the God-man could. All those sacri-
ficial lambs pointed to the great Lamb that a loving Father
would send to take sin away—he sent his own Son. And
notice whose sins this divine Lamb paid for. Not just Israel's
sins, not just my sins, not just your sins, but the sins of the
world were laid on and paid for by this Lamb of God. What a
Lamb he is, one I just have to have—one of whom the world
needs to hear and of whom I need to speak.

What a name, *the Lamb,* my Savior-God has, one that deserves
my praise all my days!

Lord, thank you for becoming the Lamb and
shedding your blood for me. Amen.

PRAISE FOR
HIS NAME—KING

Now to the King eternal, immortal, invisible, the only God, be honor and glory for ever and ever. Amen. 1 Timothy 1:17

In our country the word *king* doesn't resonate. Perhaps there's a flicker when we read about England's queen or watch reports about despotic kings in the Middle East, but otherwise, who cares? Yet when Scripture calls Jesus the King, we listen with interest.

Look what my King brings. Earthly kings tax and take from their subjects. Jesus only gives, even offering up himself for me. Earthly potentates demand with heavy hand. Jesus offers with winsome love. Earthly rulers fill their coffers with the coins of their people. Jesus, through his death, has prepared treasures in heaven for me. What a King he is! Just look at what he brings.

Look also where he takes me. He's the eternal, immortal King who takes me to immortality and an eternal kingdom. Jerusalem above awaits with no more death to slay me or sin to stain me. Just perfect care for all his subjects and me, and perfect peace for our hearts. Already here on earth I am a citizen of his kingdom. My baptismal certificate is proof of my citizenship. Just wait till in heaven I share with that eternal, immortal King fully in his realm.

What a name, *King,* my Savior-God has, one that deserves my praise all my days!

Eternal Lord, thank you for coming as my King to make me a citizen of heaven. Amen.

PRAISE FOR HIS NAME— ALPHA AND OMEGA

I am the Alpha and the Omega, the First and
the Last, the Beginning and the End.
Revelation 22:13

The book of Revelation calls him "the Alpha and the Omega"
four times. We'd probably say "*A* and *Z*." Just as those two
letters are the first and last in our alphabet, so Alpha and
Omega are in the Greek.

Why is this a good name for Jesus? First of all, because he's
our eternal Savior. His salvation is forever. Nothing new will
ever take its place. Unlike the automobile with new models
every year or the computer where hardware and software are
obsolete almost before we buy, Jesus' salvation stays the
same. There is no Savior before him, nor any after him. He
truly is the First and the Last.

Jesus is also the Beginning and the End. In a Canadian city
where I once lived was a department store named A to Z. Its
motto was, "If we don't have it, you don't need it." I don't
know how often that store had to eat its words. But I do
know that Jesus is all-sufficient. His salvation offers my soul
all it ever needs. Nothing ever has to be added. No updated
part will ever have to be attached. His words on Calvary's
cross, "It is finished," still mean that sin is canceled and salvation is complete. Whether I call him Alpha and Omega or *A*
and *Z*, Jesus is all I'll ever need.

What a name, *Alpha and Omega,* my Savior-God has, one that
deserves my praise all my days!

Lord Jesus, thank you for being my one and
only, all-sufficient Savior. Amen.

PRAISE FOR
HIS NAME—CARPENTER

Where did this man get these things? . . . Isn't
this the carpenter? Mark 6:2,3

They called him "the carpenter" that day to belittle him. Yet
when we stop to think, isn't that a good name for Jesus? He's
the heavenly Carpenter.

Just think what a carpenter does. He builds and fixes. At
time's start, Jesus was busy building. "Through him all
things were made," John 1:3 reminds me. Till time's end,
he's still busy. "On this rock I will build my church," he said
(Matthew 16:18). With his gospel this Carpenter adds people
to his invisible church of believers that reaches into eternity. Best of all, he's *my* Carpenter. Not only did he make me
through my parents. He also remade me, turning the sinful
wreck I was from my mother's womb into a believer and fix-
ing every day the dents sin still gouges into my faith.

And just think how this Carpenter died. How often did he
carry a tree back to the carpenter shop to turn it into useful
lumber? How many times did he pick up hammer and nails to
make something useful out of those boards? Now others use
the tools of his trade to nail him to a tree. And I know why
my Carpenter let them do it. It was because of his love for
me—love that wanted to make me one of his creations to
adorn his Father's house forever.

What a name, *Carpenter*, my Savior-God has, one that
deserves my praise all my days!

Lord, thank you for crafting and keeping me as
something precious for your Father's house. Amen.

PRAISE FOR
HIS NAME—THE WAY

I am the way. . . . No one comes to the Father except through me. John 14:6

"Which way do we go?" I asked, approaching Atlanta. Hopefully my wife had read the map correctly. Or else we'd miss the bypass and waste some time. When the way to heaven is involved, we'd better have the right road, or we'll waste more than time.

Jesus knows where we want to go. Ever since sin slammed shut not only the door to Eden but also to heaven, man's been looking for the road back. Like some prodigal son, he's been roaming far from home, but unlike that boy, he doesn't know the way back. Though he tries to push his anxious concerns about eternity to the back of his mind, they still sit there bothering him.

We know the way. Jesus has told us. "I am the way," he said. He's not just some highway marker like the one pointing to the bypass around Atlanta. He's the road itself. And what a highway he is! Straight as an arrow. Smoother than freshly cured cement. Never a detour and not one orange barrel. No toll booths to clog up the traffic flow and collect our cash. He is the way, the only way to the Father's house above. With his death and resurrection as payment for all sin, he made himself the *freeway* to heaven, one that asks nothing from us, because it took everything from him.

What a name, *the Way,* my Savior-God has, one that deserves my praise all my days!

> Lord, direct and keep my feet in faith on you
> as the only way to the Father's house. Amen.

PRAISE FOR
HIS NAME—THE TRUTH

I am . . . the truth. . . . No one comes to the
Father except through me. John 14:6

The world is filled with all kinds of truth. People have rummaged in the ruins of the past, worked at classifying the animal, vegetable, mineral kingdoms, split atoms, and orbited satellites. Yet none of these so-called truths can answer the question, What must I do to be saved?

There only Jesus will do. That's his claim when he says, "I am the truth." Notice what he says. It isn't "I am truthful." Of course, he is. The sinless son of God cannot lie. Nor does he say, "I'll tell you the truth." The prophets and apostles did that. They were only mouthpieces, proclaiming truths that were given to them. Jesus is so much more.

Jesus is truth itself. If this were mathematics, we'd say, "Jesus = Truth" or "Jesus = Salvation." He is truth in action. He stepped from eternity into time, clothed divinity in humanity, slept in a cradle, suffered on a cross, shed his blood as the God-man to make himself the truth of our salvation. If I want to know how to be saved, there is only one answer—Christ. If I want to tell others how to be saved, there is only one truth to speak—Christ. I can live without many of the truths the world puts forward, but I cannot be saved without Christ.

What a name, *the Truth,* my Savior-God has, one that deserves my praise all my days!

> Lord, fill my heart with you as my Savior, for
> then I'll know the way to my Father. Amen.

PRAISE FOR
HIS NAME—THE LIFE

I am . . . the life. . . . No one comes to the
Father except through me. John 14:6

Do you know CPR? Some years ago, along with our parochial
school teachers, I attended a class where we learned this life-
saving technique. So far I haven't had to use it, but it's good
to know.

What about spiritual life? How much do I know? When Jesus
said "I am the life," he was referring to spiritual life. He was
making the point that without him, people are dead beyond the
point of resuscitation. True, millions exist each day without
him. They walk and talk, work and play, marry and bury, but
as dead people. When God looks at them, he sees only spiritual
corpses bound only for hell's bonfire. No wonder Scripture
describes hell as everlasting death. It's the dead end for souls
that without the Savior can only be dead in unbelief.

Thank God I know about spiritual life. With Peter I can say,
"You have the words of eternal life" (John 6:68). With the
hymn writer I can sing, "Chief of sinners though I be, Jesus
shed his blood for me, Died that I might live on high, Lives that
I might never die" (CW 385:1). Only in Jesus am I alive because
only in him is sin's pardon and heaven's hope. As one church
father put it, "Without the Way, there is no going; without the
Truth, there is no knowing; without the Life, there is no living."

What a name, *the Life,* my Savior-God has, one that deserves
my praise all my days!

Lord, you've made me alive through faith. Keep
me alive till I reach heaven's shores. Amen.

LOVE IN GETHSEMANE

Being in anguish, he prayed more earnestly, and his sweat was like drops of blood falling to the ground. Luke 22:44

Places are important to us. Like our homes, however humble but filled with love. Like our churches, whatever their styles but filled with love. Even more so with the places of the passion. Those spots where Jesus suffered and died are important to us because they are filled with the greatest love of all.

What's going on? What crushes our Savior to the earth in Gethsemane and causes him to beg? What's this cup he dreads to drink? We know because we've heard the answer in other Lenten seasons. That cup was filled with the bitter potion of hell's punishment for sin. No wonder Jesus turns to his Father pleading, "Take this cup from me." Sin must be serious. Look at what it does to Jesus. Each of my sins was a drop of poison in that cup. Each one brought drops of blood to Jesus' scalp.

His love must be serious too. Three times he looked his Father in the eye and asked, "Can I pass?" And when the answer was no, look at Jesus' response. There was no murmuring against the Father's will or questioning about the Father's way. Instead, it was "Not my will, but yours be done." How Jesus must love his Father to follow that will even to that horrible cross! How Jesus must love me to be willing to do this for a sinner like me! Gethsemane was only an olive tree garden in those days. But I remember it because of Jesus' wondrous love.

Lord, when my sins give me alarm, show me again your love in Gethsemane's shadows. Amen.

LOVE IN THE COURTYARD

The Lord turned and looked straight at Peter.
Luke 22:61

In life the greatest hurt comes often from one we love. So also with Jesus. Some of his greatest sorrows came from those closest to him. Like from Peter that night in the high priest's courtyard.

How could Peter forget? He had seen and heard so much at Jesus' feet. At Jesus' command he had even walked on water, though not all that long or well. Of no other disciple did the Master ever say, "I have prayed for you, . . . that your faith may not fail" (Luke 22:32). Yet Peter forgot. That night in the high priest's courtyard, he whose name meant "rock" showed himself to be only crumbling sandstone.

Point the accusing finger at Peter? Not unless I'm ready to see the other four pointing at me. What special days with Jesus I too have enjoyed! Like my baptism and confirmation days, my Communion days, my wedding day, all those days of his help with my problems. And yet like Peter I'm ready to chuck it all away the first time the feet of faith get close to the fire.

Why did Jesus remember even though Peter forgot? Why did he recall Peter with a look? I know the answer. And I pray God's love will keep looking at me. "Preach not because you have to say something, but because you have something to say," said a professor. Lent is the best time to preach and to listen. And the message? Always the news of his wondrous, redeeming, and recalling love.

Lord Jesus, look on me, and with your love
reclaim me when I stray. Amen.

LOVE IN THE COURTROOM

From now on, the Son of Man will be seated at
the right hand of the mighty God. Luke 22:69

The accused was totally innocent and yet completely guilty.
The impartial eye could pick out the flaws in his trial. Jesus
was standing before a kangaroo court that only needed an
appropriate charge for the verdict already decided. "Guilty,"
the court judged him, though he was totally innocent.

Or was he? In heaven a higher judge was on the bench. And
he had already declared his sinless, perfect Son guilty, horribly guilty, because of the load he was carrying. Remember
what the load was? "We all, like sheep, have gone astray,"
Isaiah wrote (53:6). Remember how he continued, "And the
LORD has laid on him the iniquity of us all." How do we begin
to describe the guilt the holy Father saw when he looked at
our substitute in that courtroom? Even more, how do we
begin to explain the love that made it happen?

Someday it'll be my turn in court, and I, who am completely
guilty, will be declared totally innocent. Let the unbelievers
shiver at the thought of standing before the righteous judge
on that Last Day. For me it's a great day coming. Because of
the innocent Jesus who took my guilt, I can join the apostle even now in rejoicing, "Who is he that condemns? Christ
Jesus, who died—more than that, who was raised to life—
is at the right hand of God and is also interceding for us"
(Romans 8:34).

Lord Jesus, thank you for taking my guilt and
giving me your innocence. Amen.

LOVE BEFORE THE JUDGMENT SEAT

He [Herod] plied him with many questions, but Jesus gave him no answer. Luke 23:9

We just aren't used to Jesus being silent. Isn't this the same Jesus who went everywhere preaching the gospel? Yet before Herod's judgment seat, the Savior remained silent.

Peter tells us why, "When they hurled their insults at him, he did not retaliate; when he suffered, he made no threats. Instead, he entrusted himself to him who judges justly" (1 Peter 2:23). Did you hear that? Jesus' silence was dictated by his love. Instead of striking back at his enemies, he said nothing. His love wouldn't let him hurt them. Instead of hurling even greater insults at them, he was silent. His love for his Father wouldn't do what his Father said was wrong. Love dictated his silence.

Not only was Jesus silent lest he sin but also because of our sins. Isaiah, some seven hundred years earlier, wrote, "He was led like a lamb to the slaughter, and as a sheep before her shearers is silent, so he did not open his mouth" (53:7). The Savior stood there saying nothing, doing nothing, because he was there to pay for our sins. What love that says everything about him, my beautiful Savior!

But what words he has for me. "Go in peace," he says when I haul my tonnage of sin before him each day. "Plunged into the depths of the sea," he comforts me when those "special" sins rub my conscience sore. From his silence before Herod come words of wondrous love for me.

Jesus, ever tell me of your saving love and keep my heart listening. Amen.

LOVE ON THE STREETS OF JERUSALEM

Jesus turned and said to them, "Daughters of Jerusalem, do not weep for me; weep for yourselves and for your children." Luke 23:28

Wouldn't we have cried too if we had been standing with those women? And wouldn't you think that Jesus would have wanted our tears? When we suffer, we appreciate sympathy. But not our Lord Jesus. Dragging his cross through the streets of Jerusalem, he says, "Do not weep for me."

Why not? Because all was well with him. He knew that the way his Father had chosen to free the world from sin's hellish curse was by his making those bloody footprints to a hill called Calvary. As the loving Son of the eternal Father and as the ever-loving friend of sinners, he was willing to walk that path.

But all was not well with those women. So the Savior warned them, "Weep for yourselves and for your children." In divine wisdom he could see the horrible days of destruction coming for Jerusalem. He could see even farther to how God's righteous anger would shatter unbelievers into kindling for the fires of hell. And the same love that made him walk to Calvary compelled him to caution them.

Time to check my heart and life again, isn't it? Any sin there that I've become comfortable with? Any sin that I've willingly made my bedfellow? Any sin that I've told God to keep his fingers off? Then perhaps it's time to hear his words of love warning me, even as he seeks to call me back.

Savior, in my weakness and with my sins, help me hear your loving voice calling me. Amen.

HOSANNA TO OUR KING

Say to the Daughter of Zion, "See, your king comes to you, gentle and riding on a donkey, on a colt, the foal of a donkey." Matthew 21:5

What kind of parade was that? Wouldn't you have expected better for a king like Jesus? The best of chariots with an armed guard? Marching bands and prancing steeds? Kings rode the finest horses, not borrowed donkeys. "Hosanna," they shouted to him, but what kind of king was he?

That's just the point. Yes, Jesus is the eternal God whose throne fills the heavens and whose scepter casts its shadow over all the earth. But he rides into Jerusalem in all lowliness to show that he's also man. He became one of us, took on our flesh to do what none of us could do, to carry out the heavenly mission of salvation. Because he came in such humble form, many missed him. Oh, they cheered when that strange parade went by, but then they went home and forgot all about him.

During one of his campaign speeches, an older woman shouted out at Ronald Reagan, "Everything you've said sounds just fine. But haven't you forgotten us old folks?" The man who was to become the oldest president of the United States replied with a smile, "Forget you? How could I ever forget you? I'm one of you." Don't I get it? God has not forgotten me. His coming into the flesh and his humble entrance into Jerusalem were his way of saying, "How could I ever forget you? I've become one of you. I came to be with you and to die for you on Calvary's cross."

Lord, help me to see the reason behind your humility, and then ride on into my heart. Amen.

HOSANNA TO OUR SAVIOR

Hosanna to the Son of David! Blessed is he who comes in the name of the Lord! Hosanna in the highest! Matthew 21:9

Don't you wonder what Jesus' thoughts were as he rode in that Palm Sunday parade? He had no false dreams about where that ride was taking him. All the palm waving and hosanna shouting didn't fill him with delusions of grandeur. Earlier, on the way to the parade, he had told his disciples exactly what lay ahead of him. Not the keys to the city, but a cross outside it. But that cross would unlock the doors to the heavenly Jerusalem. With his crown of thorns and his throne of pain, he would pay for the world's sin. From this Savior-King would come a victory such as the world has never seen and will always need.

Thank God I know the purpose of that Palm Sunday parade. Because of his grace I can hold my sin-stained heart up to this heavenly King and sob with the tax collector, "God, have mercy on me, a sinner" (Luke 18:13). I can hold my flickering faith up to him and cry out with the nobleman, "I do believe; help me overcome my unbelief" (Mark 9:24). Finally, I can hold my dying heart up to him and exclaim with David, "I will fear no evil, for you are with me" (Psalm 23:4).

The more I see in this King, the One who came to die for my sins and prepare eternal life for me in heaven, the more I'll shout my hosannas to him today, tomorrow, and in eternity.

Lord, show me your cross' victory over sin so that I shout hosanna all my days. Amen.

HOSANNA WITH OUR LIPS AND LIVES

They brought the donkey and the colt, placed their cloaks on them, and Jesus sat on them. A very large crowd spread their cloaks on the road, while others cut branches from the trees and spread them on the road. Matthew 21:7,8

They praised Jesus with their lips and hands that first Palm Sunday. The disciples did it by following Jesus' orders and fetching the donkey. The people did it by rolling out the red carpet of their own cloaks and palm branches. Eagerly they praised him, though few fully knew the right reasons why.

We do. We praise him because he is our Savior and our King. He came down to our earth to raise us up to his heaven. He came to take our sins and give us his holiness. He rode on to a cross of pain so that we might end up with his crown of glory. What beautiful reasons we have to praise our King!

In England, on the base of a statue of Jesus with arms out-stretched were the words "Come unto me." After the war, an artist was hired to restore that statue shattered by German bombs. But he couldn't find Jesus' hands. So he left the statue without them and changed the wording on the base to read, "Christ has no hands, but ours."

I can't wave palm branches or spread a topcoat in his path. But I can praise my King. Paul had it right, "Whatever you do, whether in word or deed, do it all in the name of the Lord Jesus, giving thanks to God the Father through him" (Colossians 3:17).

God, help me live my hosannas. Amen.

HE REMEMBERS ME

He took bread . . . and gave it to them, saying,
"This is my body given for you." . . . He took
the cup, saying, "This cup is the new covenant
in my blood, which is poured out for you."
Luke 22:19,20

That Thursday evening as Jesus ate the Passover meal with
his disciples, he had plenty on his mind. Ahead of him lay a
night and a day packed with the worst men could ever
invent. Who could have blamed him if he had told those disciples to leave him alone? But he didn't. His love for sinners
wouldn't let him. That love even moved him to leave a parting gift for them, a blessed inheritance that would help them
through the ages. Looking at his disciples, then and now, he
saw how they would need assurance of sin forgiven, how
often their wounded hearts would need special healing.

And in love he gave them a miracle. He left them the treasure of his Holy Supper, in which he gives his true body with
the bread and his true blood with the wine so that penitent
sinners might be assured of forgiveness. "Go in peace," he
tells the penitent, "your sins are forgiven as surely as my
body and blood prepared that forgiveness which you now
have just received."

Thank God he remembers me! Now pray God helps me never
forget what he offers me in his Holy Supper. Someone once
said that this sacrament takes the first Good Friday and
moves it down to us today. In his Holy Supper, Jesus comes
to me, the sinner, and says, "Take eat, my body given for *you*.
My blood poured out for *you*. *You* go home in peace."

God, help me remember what a Savior I have
and what he offers me in his meal. Amen.

A WORD
OF FORGIVENESS

Father, forgive them, for they do not know
what they are doing. Luke 23:34

Last words of loved ones are important. We bend closer so as
not to miss them. We treasure them when our loved ones are
gone. So also with Jesus' words from the cross. They are like
windows through which we can look into his soul and see his
great love for sinners.

The sound of the hammer had barely faded when the Savior
spoke. His first sentence from the cross was not a cry of pain
or a curse of hatred. It was a prayer asking his Father to forgive those who crucified him. "Father," he prayed. That word
speaks of the enormity of their crime. They were killing God's
own Son. Should not his holy hand be already streaking down
to seize the guilty and grind them into pieces? "Forgive,"
Jesus continued, using a word that meant to dismiss, to send
out of sight. His Father knew why Jesus prayed this. His Son
was on that cross paying for the sins of these people too. His
sacrifice made his prayer the mightiest ever spoken. "Them,"
Jesus said. He mentioned no names so I can put mine there.
He had Luke record it so I could read it.

"They do not know what they are doing," Jesus went on.
What they did was wrong, but they didn't know to whom
they were doing it. Christ was asking his Father to grant
them a time of grace in which to learn that they had crucified his own Son sent to be their Savior. What love! Even as
he dies to prepare forgiveness, he prays that those who crucified him would come to faith and benefit.

Lord, help me appreciate that you were praying
about me. How I need your prayer daily! Amen.

A WORD OF PROMISE

I tell you the truth, today you will be with me
in paradise. Luke 23:43

Two men were crucified with Jesus. We don't know their
names. The best we have is "criminal." Though they admitted
their guilt, we don't know their crimes. But we do know what
Jesus promised one of them. And we pray that Jesus would
make the same promise to us.

"I tell you the truth," Jesus told that penitent criminal.
When he who owns the heavens and earth uses such words,
it's as good as done. "Today," the Savior continued. For three
to four hours more the thief would draw his ragged breath,
but that very day his cross would be exchanged for a crown
and his soul would be lifted up to heaven's glory. "With me,"
the Lord went on. All heaven is in those two words. The best
we know about heaven is that it means to be with Christ and
share eternally in his love. "In paradise," the Savior ended.
That morning saw the thief being led out of his prison cell to
pay his debt to society. That afternoon saw his life fading
away on a cross and his soul facing hell's gaping doors. But
that evening saw him walking hand in hand with his Savior
in heaven. What love! It gave the undeserving thief the
whole loaf instead of the crumbs he had asked for.

On the gravestone of Copernicus, the famed astronomer and
faithful believer, are the words "Not for the grace of Paul do
I ask. Nor for the pardon once shown to Peter. Only for the
forgiveness bestowed upon the thief on the cross do I petition." Me too! When my time comes, my ears of faith need to
hear my Savior say, "Today you will be with me in paradise."

Lord, please, in your grace, so promise
me. Amen.

A WORD OF CONCERN

He said to his mother, "Dear woman, here is your son," and to the disciple, "Here is your mother." From that time on, this disciple took her into his home. John 19:26,27

In the small group huddled beneath Jesus' cross were his mother, Mary, and his dear disciple John. In the midst of his suffering and their grief, the Savior spoke to them. What did he have to say?

Most in Jesus' shoes wouldn't have thought about their mothers or would have pleaded for their help. But Jesus turned to his mother with a word of concern. She needed a place to live and something with which to live. Jesus had no home, no money, not even any clothes. But he could give her his dearest friend John as a son to care for her. In the word by which he called her, he indicated even a greater gift from his hand. "Woman," he said, reminding her that he was more than her Son. He was her Savior, who was dying on the accursed tree also for her.

Does his caring love reach wider than those two beneath his cross? I have to know! And with this third word from the cross my Savior answers me. Hasn't he said, "Whoever does the will of my Father in heaven is my brother and sister and mother" (Matthew 12:50)? As a believer I am a member of his spiritual family. He cares as much for me as for his mother huddled beneath his cross that Good Friday. There's nothing in my life his love doesn't touch. Even as he dies to take care of my sin, he speaks this third word to assure me that the rest is covered too.

Lord, remind me that you daily care for me as your family member. Amen.

⌐A WORD OF ANGUISH

My God, my God, why have you forsaken me?
Matthew 27:46

"God forsaken of God—who can understand it?" Luther once asked. Jesus' cry of anguish from the cross is far too deep for our little minds. But from it comes rich comfort for us.

How could God forsake God? How could the only Son be abandoned by the One who sent him? There's only one answer. When God looked at Jesus on that cross, he saw only the ocean of guilt, the mountain of iniquity, the desert of transgression committed by man. From such a sin-laden Son, the holy Father could only turn aside. He plunged that Son so dear to him into the depths of hell to suffer the punishment for the world's sin. What anguish of hell Jesus endured that day we can't even begin to imagine. But why he did so, we had better never forget. It was because of sin—mine included.

Can I hear Jesus' cry of anguish and ever again think lightly of sin? Can I ever again fool myself into thinking that God might deal more lightly with me than with his Son? Better still, do I find rich comfort in Jesus' cry of anguish? Do I hear my Savior saying: "Because God forsook me, he won't forsake you. Because God punished me, he won't punish you. Because God crushed me under his anger, he will raise you up in love. Because God rejected me, he will receive you as his very own"?

> Lord, like Luther, I'll never be able to grasp the anguish in your cry. But please, Lord, use it to comfort me daily. Amen.

A WORD OF PAIN

Jesus said, "I am thirsty." John 19:28

Jesus' fifth sentence from the cross is one of the shortest. In the original it isn't even a sentence, just one word of four letters. Yet we dare not pass it by lightly. There's much we can learn from it.

First of all, I learn that Jesus was true man. How can I doubt that fact when I hear him whisper through cracked lips, "I am thirsty"? He left the company of angels, entered a mother's womb, took on my flesh so that he could thirst upon that cross. Totally like me, except without sin, he hung there.

Any comfort for me in this truth? Do I think that Jesus doesn't know what living on earth is like? That he doesn't know the pain I have, the sorrows, the heartaches, the troubles? He knows exactly what I go through and the help I need. He tasted trouble, knew sorrow, felt pain. He wept, slept, and thirsted. As one who shared my life, he sympathizes with me and, more important, can help me.

Nor should I forget why he thirsted. His soul suffered the agonies of hell because of my sins. His body endured physical pain, including thirst, also because of my sin. I might even say that my thirst caused his thirst. My inborn thirst for the things displeasing to God caused his pain. My unquenchable thirst for sin smashed his hands, bruised his body, and parched his throat. On the cross he endured physical and spiritual agony that he might be the fountain that can quench my spiritual thirst forever.

Lord, give my thirsty soul to drink of your
water of life daily. Amen.

A WORD OF COMPLETION

When he had received the drink, Jesus said, "It is finished." John 19:30

Does anyone leave this world with everything done? With every word written and every goal reached? Part of death's frustration is the sense of incompleteness it brings. Not so with Jesus. When he breathed his last, he could shout triumphantly, "It is finished."

What did he mean? Just as the Greeks stamped these words on tax bills to show they were paid in full, so Jesus now wrote them with the red ink of his blood on the bill of our sins. "Finished, paid in full," he said. "Not one more penny needs to be added. I have paid for all sins; not one is left. I have shed my precious blood to redeem every sinner. And now it, my work of salvation, is finished." From his cross Jesus turned his gaze from the first sinner to the last and saw none for whom he had not paid.

What joy there must have been in heaven when Jesus spoke this word! The Father must have said again, "This is my Son, whom I love; with him I am well pleased" (Matthew 3:17). The angels must have sung again, "Glory to God in the highest, and on earth peace" (Luke 2:14)—peace made possible by the blood of God's Son. And I, for whom it all took place, how should I feel? When my sins cause me alarm, the voice from Calvary answers, "It is finished." When Satan tries to lead me around by the nose, the voice from Calvary answers, "It is finished." When death chills me with its icy breath, the voice from Calvary answers, "It is finished." My Jesus has won, and I share in his victory. What joy is mine!

> Lord, in this incomplete world, assure me daily of my complete forgiveness in you. Amen.

A WORD OF CONFIDENCE

Father, into your hands I commit my spirit.
Luke 23:46

A sudden thunderstorm sends the fearful child crawling into his or her parents' bed. How much worse the storm of death would be if it weren't for the Savior's final sentence from the cross.

"Father," he began, speaking confidently as a Son to his Father. In the afternoon darkness, when the battle was completed, Satan's head crushed, hell conquered, Jesus turned to his loving Father. What assurance for me! Sin may at times turn me into a prodigal and trouble make me doubt, but Jesus' last word comforts me. In spite of everything in me or about me, God is still my Father.

"Into your hands I commit my spirit," Jesus went on. I die because I can't prolong life one half second. Not with Jesus. When his work of salvation was done, he laid his soul into his Father's hands. What assurance for me! With sin's debt paid, death is now a bee without a stinger. When my moment comes, I can pillow my head on that prayer, "Father, into your hands I commit my spirit."

At Jesus' last moment, his soul entered paradise to be safe at his Father's side. On Easter the stone was rolled away to show the Son of God risen with body and soul forever and gloriously joined. What assurance for me! Those are the warm, loving hands of my Father that stretch down to carry my soul to his house and to raise my lifeless clay from its resting place on the Last Day.

Lord, keep me safe through faith in you and
carry me home when it is time. Amen.

EASTER'S ALL-OUT VICTORY

But Christ has indeed been raised from the
dead. 1 Corinthians 15:20

On Good Friday the battle seemed lost. The promised "Seed of
the woman" had breathed his last. Secret followers hurriedly
deposited his lifeless body in a cold tomb. And hell's victory
bash began.

Until Easter Sunday! The Champion sent by a loving God to
fight for us is no longer dead. "Christ has indeed been raised
from the dead." The din of hell's victory celebration
dimmed—replaced by the moans and groans of those eternally damned. But you and I celebrate with holy joy.

Yes, we still fall into sin. Satan still sends out his sneaky
patrols to identify and bloody us in the weak spots of our
faith. But not to worry, Easter victors! Like a reader who has
skipped to the last chapter, we know the outcome. Christ has
been raised from the dead. He has paid for our sins.

Yes, we still lose loved ones. Death still swings its scythe, mow-
ing down old and young alike. But not to worry, Easter victors!
"Christ has indeed been raised from the dead." Now our graves
have two doors, one marked "entrance" and the other "exit."

Yes, we still suffer the bumps and bruises of daily life. Sickness
still invades, hurts still happen, people still disappoint. But not
to worry, Easter victors! "Christ has indeed been raised from the
dead." "He lives to silence all my fears; He lives to wipe away
my tears" (CW 152:5).

Lord, help me to live in the assurance of
Easter's all-out victory every day. Amen.

LIFE TO THE FULL

I have come that they may have life, and have it to the full. John 10:10

So swiftly life speeds by. So quickly it carries us to that gravestone with our names and two dates on it. And between those two dates, only a dash to represent the short interval called life. Is that all there is? If so, life's nothing more than a cruel joke, some dismal hoax, played on helpless mortals by an unfeeling deity. If so, then better to have it over quickly or never to have lived at all.

Is that all there is? Easter with its glorious message of the risen Christ shouts out otherwise! "He is risen," Easter says. Life never ends but leads to heaven where a loving Father waits for his children. Life's short chapter is written on earth, but heaven's final chapter has no concluding sentence.

"He is risen," Easter says. The grave is only the station where the believer's soul catches the early train while the body waits for the final train on the Last Day. It's not "good-bye" but "see you later" we speak to departing believers as we await the reunion with them in heaven.

"He is risen," Easter says. But while he leaves us here on earth, it's not just that we might earn and eat, entertain and enjoy ourselves. Our daily, joyful mission is to live for him and to shine with the light of Easter that others might stand in the light also.

Life on earth speeds by, but life in heaven lasts forever. And it's mine through the risen Jesus.

Thank you, Lord, for showing me the full life in the risen Savior. Amen.

AFRAID? JESUS SAYS, "IT IS I MYSELF"

He said to them, "Why are you troubled,
and why do doubts rise in your minds? Look
at my hands and my feet. It is I myself!"
Luke 24:38,39

Talk about fear! It was so real behind those locked doors that first Easter weekend in Jerusalem that you could almost smell it. Just when the disciples were convinced that Jesus was the Son of God, the bottom had dropped out. They had walked with him and witnessed his words and works. Twice they had even heard the Father call him "my Son" and seemed to have their answer as to who he was. But then the stone had been rolled before the tomb, shutting in Jesus' lifeless clay. And another stone, one of fear, had rolled before their hearts, shutting out their trust that he was the Son of God.

Until that first Easter Sunday evening! There the risen Jesus stood right before them. First came his question, "Why are you troubled?" And then his answer, "It is I myself." Gone were their doubts and fears. He was alive and standing as the living Son of God before them.

I believe that Jesus is true God from all eternity, don't I? Then why am I so often afraid? Why do I so often act as if Jesus were still lifeless in the tomb and powerless to help in life? Why do I so often weary under burdens and wipe at tears as if I had no living Son of God to help in time of need?

To me too the risen Savior comes again with his gentle question, "Why are you troubled?" For me too he repeats his reassuring answer, "It is I myself."

Risen Savior, eternal Son of God, help me see
you with your power always at my side. Amen.

AFRAID? JESUS SAYS, "PEACE BE WITH YOU"

While they were still talking about this, Jesus himself stood among them and said to them, "Peace be with you." Luke 24:36

How those disciples had sinned against their Lord! They had littered the days of Holy Week with broken promises and boastful pride, dirty cowardice and dismal lack of love. Who would pull sin's burning arrows out of their souls? Who would patch sin's seeping wounds in their hearts? Hope of forgiveness seemed as dead as the Master. No wonder they huddled in fear behind locked doors.

Until that Easter Sunday evening! There the risen Jesus stood right before them. His first words were not "Shame on you," or "How could you?" but "Peace be with you." Then came the sight of his nail-pierced hands and feet, vivid reminders of the cost of forgiveness and yet solid assurance that forgiveness was real. For those wounds were found not on a dead but a living Lord. Sins were gone as surely as the risen Lord stood before them.

God knows what the ledger would look like and how long the library shelf would have to be if all my sins were recorded. Just a brief flipping through the pages would fill my soul with mortal dread and the bitter prospect of an eternity in hell. Such a thought ought to alarm me, and when it does, the living Redeemer's words will take on new meaning for me. "You don't have to be afraid," he reminds me gently, "there's peace and pardon in my name."

Risen Savior, living Redeemer, help me see you with your forgiveness always at my side. Amen.

AFRAID? JESUS SAYS, "LOOK AT MY HANDS AND MY FEET"

Look at my hands and my feet. It is I myself! Touch me and see; a ghost does not have flesh and bones, as you see I have. Luke 24:39

For the disciples, as for all people, the question wasn't whether but when they would die. Then had come a glimmer of hope. One came among them who claimed, "He who believes in me will live, even though he dies" (John 11:25). But he too had died and his grave seemed a grim preview of what awaited them. Until that Easter Sunday evening, when the risen Jesus stood in their midst with his living hands and feet as the guarantee behind his promise.

Do I wrestle with physical difficulties? Do I weary under life's relentless march and the ravages of pain? "Look at my hands and my feet," my glorified Lord says, giving me a preview of what awaits me in heaven and also giving me strength for my journey along the way.

Have I left a loved one behind in the cemetery? Is that mound of dirt a stark reminder of death's reality and inevitability? "Look at my hands and my feet," Jesus says, assuring me that those who have fallen asleep in him will rise just as he did.

Do I dread that day when my heart will stop and my breath cease? Think how horrible it would be not to hear Jesus saying, "Look at my hands and my feet." Because he lives, I also will live.

Risen Savior, Conqueror of death, help me live and die assured of eternal victory. Amen.

RESURRECTION MEDICINE

The disciples were overjoyed when they saw the Lord. John 20:20

How afraid we can be of death! We don't like going to the doctor because we're afraid he might find something that will end up killing us. We don't like to talk about diseases such as cancer or heart trouble because they can so often be fatal. Medicine that comes from a syringe or in a bottle may help keep us alive, but not forever. We need resurrection medicine.

Where can I find it? The same place the disciples did that first Easter. "[They] were overjoyed when they saw the Lord." For them resurrection medicine came in the form of the living Lord. For me it's the written Word. They saw the risen Jesus in person; I see him with the eyes of faith. Through the Word he stands before me, just as surely today as he did before the disciples in the locked room. Through the Word he speaks his promises of sin pardoned, death put to flight, and heaven flung wide open just as surely to me as to those first believers. I can get his very necessary resurrection medicine through regular dosages of his Word.

"Pastor, I can't lose," said the hospitalized Christian facing serious surgery. "Either the surgery will be successful and Jesus will let me live a bit longer for him. Or he'll take me to live with him forever." She knew about resurrection medicine. For her it made all the difference in life and death. Time to shake the bottle of his Word and use the only medicine that can make me live forever.

Lord, fill me regularly with your life-giving Word. Amen.

TIME TO TELL OTHERS

Mary Magdalene went to the disciples with the news: "I have seen the Lord!" And she told them that he had said these things to her.
John 20:18

We can almost hear Mary sobbing at Jesus' tomb that first Easter. We can almost taste her bitter disappointment over what seemed to have been hopes misplaced in him. We can almost feel the joy that flooded her heart when the risen Savior called her by name. But do we remember what she did after the risen Savior left her that day?

Can we even faintly imagine how her steps flew back to Jerusalem? How she pounded on the locked doors of the disciples' room? How her words tumbled out: "He's alive. I've seen him. He's our risen Jesus, our eternal Savior, our everlasting King"? Joyfully she must have repeated every treasured word the risen Lord had spoken to her.

So whom have I told? With whom will I share the joyous news of Easter? My family? Hopefully, how can I not tell them about their only hope for heaven? My neighbors? They need more than my "Hi, how are you?" They desperately need the good news about the risen Savior. People across my country and across the world whom I have never met but want to meet in heaven? I have such good news, and there are so many who still need to hear it.

But before I can tell others, I need the joy Mary felt when she saw her risen Jesus.

Lord, fill me with such joy again this blessed Easter season. Amen.

TEACH ME TOO LORD

And beginning with Moses and all the Prophets, he explained to them what was said in all the Scriptures concerning himself. Luke 24:27

What a Bible class that must have been! The teacher was the Lord Jesus. The students—two Jewish peasants. The time—the first Easter afternoon. The theme—Jesus Christ is the heart of all of Scripture. The risen Savior walked those two Emmaus disciples through the Old Testament Scriptures. Everywhere he led them, they found his redemption of sinners. "These are the Scriptures that testify about me," he once said (John 5:39). Now he taught those disciples how the humility of Christmas, the pain of Calvary, and the victory of Easter had been foretold by Moses and all the prophets.

Do I wish that I could have been in his Bible class that Easter afternoon? Or do I realize how good I already have it? The risen Savior walks with me and teaches me just as wondrously as he did those two Emmaus disciples. "Come," he says, leading me into the New Testament. "Let me show you how I was born, crucified, and rose just as foretold so that your sins may be forgiven. Come, let me show you how my love for sinners like you made my death and resurrection necessary."

Why did the risen Savior use the Scriptures that day with those disciples? Why didn't he just point to himself and ask them to believe? Don't you think he was trying to tell me something? "Do you want to sit in my Bible class?" he was asking. "Then go to my Word. It testifies about me."

Risen Lord, take me deeply into your Word so that I always know you as my Savior. Amen.

BELIEVING IS SEEING

Blessed are those who have not seen and yet have believed. John 20:29

Jesus' words about believing without seeing didn't apply to Thomas. That once-doubting disciple believed because the risen Savior, wounds and all, stood before him the Sunday after Easter. Strictly speaking, those words didn't apply to the other disciples either. They too saw their risen Lord. No, this beatitude is meant for people like me.

Have I ever wished like Thomas to see Jesus in person and touch his wounds? To know what Jesus looks like and what he sounds like as the other disciples knew? Obviously that's not possible, at least not on this earth. Nor is this a disadvantage for me, as Jesus reminds me. Whether he stands before me in person or on the pages of his Word, whether I hear the sound of his voice or read his recorded words, it's not the seeing but the believing that counts.

Luther wrote, "We should be careful not to follow our eyes. We should rather close our eyes and open our ears and hear the Word." Paul put it even better, "We live by faith, not by sight" (2 Corinthians 5:7). And Peter put it perhaps best of all, "Though you have not seen him, you love him; and . . . believe in him and are filled with an inexpressible and glorious joy" (1 Peter 1:8).

Isn't that what the risen Lord was telling me that Sunday evening? Believing *is* seeing!

Lord, give me the eyes of faith to see you
in your Word as my living, all-sufficient
Savior. Amen.

THE SAVIOR AND ME ALWAYS

And surely I am with you always, to the very end of the age. Matthew 28:20

What a promise the risen Savior left us. *"Surely,"* he began, meaning, "Note this and note it well." *"I am with you,"* he went on. Not just his words or his memory, but he himself, the risen Conqueror of sin and death, will be at our sides. Note also that little word *"am."* Not "I was with you, but that may change," but "am, right now and always." *"With you,"* he went on. With whom? Believers, of course, his disciples of all times, as his next words show. *"With you always,"* he promised, not just today and tomorrow, but each day as he would give it. *"To the very end of the age,"* he concluded. His promise and presence will hold true until the end of history.

With such a promise, I can live while the world around me struggles just to exist. Morning comes, and as I open my eyes, I pray, "Thank you, Lord Jesus, for having kept me safe through the night." Trouble comes, and I can say, "Help me, Lord Jesus, to carry what I can and cast the rest on you." Temptation comes, and I reach out, "Lord, I'm so weak, but you can strengthen me." Sin overcomes, and I confess: "I've done it again, Lord Jesus. Do not leave me, but for your love's sake forgive me." Blessings come, and it's not "I had it coming, or I deserved more," but rather, "Thank you, Lord Jesus, for being so kind when I'm so undeserving." Night, eventually the night of death, comes, and it's "Now I lay me down to sleep. I pray the Lord my soul to keep."

But only because of my risen Savior's promise.

My Savior, stand at my side and keep me standing beside you every one of my days and in your eternal day. Amen.

MY BLEEDING SHEPHERD

> I am the good shepherd. The good shepherd lays down his life for the sheep. John 10:11

The pastor was calling in his sermon theme for the church notice in the newspaper. He dictated, "The Lord's my shepherd."

"Is that all?" asked the secretary on the other end of the line.

"That's enough," replied the pastor. Imagine his surprise when he opened the Saturday newspaper and read his sermon's theme: "The Lord's my shepherd. That's enough."

How true! Jesus is the only shepherd I ever need. No one else can do what he did. He laid down his life for me. Of me he thought when the agonies of Gethsemane pushed his soul into the dust. Of me, when the scourge plowed his back. Of me, when the crown of thorns was pounded down upon his brow. Of me, when the nails pinned him to the tree. Of me, when he said of sin's payment, "It is finished." For me he bled that I might live. His blood paid for my sins completely, and his heaven is now opened to receive me.

It's not enough for me simply to say, "Jesus is a good shepherd." Not even enough to state, "Jesus is *the* Good Shepherd." When I by God's grace can say, "Jesus is *my* Good Shepherd," then I really have something. Then I have the gigantic difference between peace and turmoil, salvation and damnation, heaven and hell. Then I have the only shepherd I ever need.

> Loving Savior, thank you for bleeding and dying for me. Thank you for giving me the faith to call you my Good Shepherd. Amen.

MY SEEKING SHEPHERD

Does he not leave the ninety-nine in the open country and go after the lost sheep until he finds it? And when he finds it, he joyfully puts it on his shoulders and goes home. Luke 15:4-6

"I am Jesus' little lamb, ever glad at heart I am," sang the elderly grandma. Every time I visited her in the nursing home, she used those words. Was she back somewhere in her childhood? Back to her early Sunday school days? No matter! At 91 years old she was still Jesus' little lamb.

So am I! And not because of my doing. There was nothing in my sin-scarred soul and sin-stained life that deserved consideration by the Good Shepherd. Nothing in me at all that caused him to seek me out and raise me up into membership in his flock. All this and much more, Jesus, my Good Shepherd, has done for me because of his amazing grace and astonishing love.

At the baptismal font, he found me and folded me to his breast. Through his Word as I learned it on my mother's lap, in my Sunday school days, in the church service, and my own readings, he wrapped his caring arms closer around me. When at times in my life I tried to avoid him, he sought me. When I would have hidden from him, he found me. When I turned away from him, he returned to help me. Always he was there, seeking and inviting, "Come back and be reconciled to God."

Not only does my Good Shepherd have joy when he carries me home on his shoulders. So do I!

Good Shepherd, thank you for love that found me when I sought you not. Amen.

MY FEEDING SHEPHERD

He makes me lie down in green pastures, he leads me beside quiet waters. Psalm 23:2

"That's me," said the first grader, holding up a picture of Jesus with a child in his arm. I had asked, "Do you know who that is?" Quickly, joyously he tumbled out the answer, "That's me." Me too! The Good Shepherd holds me in his arms and takes good care of me, whatever my age might be.

What a beautiful picture the psalmist paints. It's not on the brown grass of Montana in the height of summer where my Shepherd feeds me, but on the first sprouts of spring, lush with sweetness. It's not from the swift currents of some rushing river where he would have me drink, but from the crystal clear water of some quiet pool. As a result, I can "lie down," that is, stretch out in complete contentment like some sheep chewing its cud in the peaceful shade.

Get the picture? Those age-old questions "What shall I eat? What shall I wear? With what shall I be clothed?" may cause others anxious moments. But not me. "When the woes of life o'ertake me, hopes deceive, and fears annoy," I can feel the Shepherd's arms tightening around me. "Don't worry," he says. "The green pastures and quiet waters are still there, and I'll lead you to them." Better still, my Good Shepherd feeds my soul. When sin swamps me, temptation tricks me, death frightens me, he whispers to me, "Don't worry. The lush grass of my Word and the peaceful waters of my Holy Supper are still there to feed your soul and cause you to lie down in contentment."

Please, Lord, help me say, "The Lord's my Shepherd. That's all I want." Amen.

MY LEADING SHEPHERD

Surely goodness and love will follow me all the days of my life, and I will dwell in the house of the LORD forever. Psalm 23:6

"Read me the Good Shepherd psalm," he asked from his hospital bed. When I got to the last verse, softly he whispered the words with me. The future was bleak, but how could he go wrong if his Good Shepherd was leading him?

Did I notice how David viewed the future? He spoke not in years, but days. Day by day he saw God's goodness and mercy following him. Actually, the Hebrew word he used for "follow" was much stronger. It meant to pursue, to chase after, catch up to, and clutch him. Twin traveling companions he saw constantly at his side. With *goodness* David referred to his Shepherd taking care of his bodily needs. With *love* he pointed to the Shepherd's abiding love that provided forgiveness and strength for his soul. Though David didn't know what the future held for him, he knew who held the future. Wherever his Good Shepherd led, he could safely follow.

So can I. Even when my last moment comes, I can follow his leading to the Father's house above. There I will be home forever with him. On the world's last day, he will call my body home too, regardless of how long it has slumbered in some grave. Then I won't need to hear the Good Shepherd psalm any longer. Instead, I'll be able to look right at him and thank him for his gracious leading.

Good Shepherd, surround me with your goodness and mercy each day till you take me home. Amen.

JUDGMENT DAY TODAY

Whoever believes in him is not condemned, but whoever does not believe stands condemned already because he has not believed in the name of God's one and only Son. John 3:18

Judgment day—that's what some call April 15. Today's the day to file our taxes or face the penalty. Some pay ahead of time; others petition for an extension. But sooner or later, we have to pay up.

April 15 isn't even a faint picture of the real judgment day. For sinners that day comes at death, when the soul heads either to heaven or to hell. On the Last Day the Lord Jesus will raise all the dead to stand reunited with their souls in the final announcement of what their judgment was. If there's a judgment to be feared, here's the one. At stake aren't dollars for taxes, but my eternal future.

Afraid of that day? Not when God's grace has brought me to faith in his one and only Son. Those who know Jesus as their only Savior have already been judged. They have been declared free from sin and fit for heaven. Jesus' blood and righteousness are their beauty and glorious dress. "Come, inherit the kingdom prepared for you," will be his welcome to believers at the moment of their death and on the last great day.

Actually judgment day is already past for me. At the baptismal font, the Holy Spirit placed the sign of Jesus' saving cross not only on my forehead but in my heart. God has already declared me his child and promised me his heaven. Now I need to pray daily that the Savior keep me safe and sound for eternity.

Lord, please hear me for your mercy's sake. Amen.

WHO'S THE PREACHER?

Jesus said to her, "I am the resurrection and the life." John 11:25

In my experience, the funeral sermon text most frequently requested is Psalm 23. A close second is John chapter 11, verses 25 and 26. Someone even called these words the best funeral sermon ever preached. Why? Because of the preacher! Normally not the preacher but his message is important. How different with the funeral sermon in John chapter 11! It's the best ever because its preacher was also the message. "I am the resurrection and the life," Jesus told Martha, who was grieving at the grave of her dear brother Lazarus. Death and burial had brought them together, but Jesus preached about resurrection and life.

Note that he didn't try to wipe away Martha's tears with "I hope there is resurrection and life." Simply and comfortingly he stated, "I am the resurrection and the life." Both are so closely bound up with him that he calls himself by their names. Outside of him these precious commodities can't be found.

Why? His filled cross and emptied tomb shout out the answer. He is resurrection and life because he paid for all sins and pulled all of death's teeth. Because he rose from the grave to show it can't hold us either. Because as Paul put it, "[He] has destroyed death and has brought life and immortality to light through the gospel" (2 Timothy 1:10). What a preacher! And because of him, what a sermon!

Risen Savior, remind me as I journey toward death that you are my resurrection and life. Amen.

WHO'S THE DECEASED?

Jesus said to her . . . "He who believes in me
will live, even though he dies." John 11:25

Martha was crying. The tomb held her dear brother's decaying
body. As true man, Jesus joined in those tears, because Lazarus
was also his dear friend. What made Lazarus so close to Jesus?

Was it that Lazarus had opened his home at Bethany to Jesus
on his journeys? That both had many things in common?
That a close friendship had developed over a period of time?
Jesus pointed to much more with the words "He who believes
in me." By God's grace and the Spirit's working, Lazarus
believed in Jesus. He looked to Jesus as the Savior who was
to come, indeed, as his personal Savior. Through God-given
faith, Lazarus was not just Jesus' friend but a brother in God's
heavenly family.

Of his believing friend, Jesus said, "[He] will live, even though
he dies." What a comforting promise! "Martha," Jesus was saying, "yes, your brother, my friend Lazarus, is dead. That is, if
by that term you mean his soul has left his body. And yet he
is alive. His soul lives on in heaven with our Father. And his
body will also one day be raised from the tomb and be rejoined
with his soul for eternity in heaven. So it will happen for all
who believe in me as the resurrection and the life."

When I weep before the casket of my loved ones, that's the
message I need to hear. Better than wishing my loved ones
back to this vale of tears is being assured they are living
with the Lord.

Risen Savior, dry my tears with your sermon
that those who die in faith in you still live.
Amen.

WHAT ABOUT
THE MOURNERS?

Jesus said to her . . . "And whoever lives and believes in me will never die." John 11:26

What about those who join Mary and Martha on the mourners' bench at a funeral? Has Jesus, the resurrection and the life, anything to offer us who are still alive and in this world? Listen to this heavenly preacher some more. He says, "And whoever lives and believes in me will never die."

Don't those words seem to contradict all human experience? Certainly Lazarus, though brought back to life that day, had to face death again in the future. Mary and Martha had to die too. So do all of Jesus' friends sooner or later. Yet the Savior promises that we shall never die. His words are meant for believers and believers only. To the unbeliever, death is death indeed. It plummets him or her into the eternal dungeons of hell where punishment for sin never ends.

But for those who have been brought to the faith that their sins are forgiven through Jesus' suffering and death, life's end has lost its terror. For them, physical death is the doorway to heaven. Their last faint heartbeat is the gentle tapping at heaven's door, which opens to the life that never ends.

The dutiful son who had hurried from miles away to his dying father's bedside just had to return home. "Go back and take care of your business," his father told him. "If I should slip away while you're gone, you'll know where to find me." He knew and so do I that God's children never die.

Jesus, my resurrection and life, help me to live and die with your promise in my heart. Amen.

HEADING HOME

In my Father's house are many rooms. . . .
I am going there to prepare a place for you.
John 14:2

King Louis XV of France strictly forbade the use of the word *death* in his presence. It is said that he punished anyone who brought morose thoughts to his attention. And yet such action couldn't conquer his fear of death or stop death from claiming him.

Listen to Jesus' answer for our fear of death. "In my Father's house," he starts out, "are many rooms." What comfort, what joy are mine in the knowledge that beyond the gates of death lies a friendly Father's house. When I was a child, I found warmth and security in the home of my parents. When I went away to school, nothing was better than getting back home. Soon the time will come when I will head back home again— this time to the house of my loving Father.

In that house Jesus said "are many rooms." This earth is only the motel I use on my way to heaven. My life is just the travel time allotted. But in my Father's house are permanent rooms where I will live forever. When Jesus said "many rooms," he surely was indicating there's one for me too. His blood, shed on Calvary's cross, has written my name on one of the doors. With his payment for sin he has signed a permanent lease for me. Now he holds open the room he has already claimed for me.

Thoughts of death may not be my most favored ones. But think what it would be like without Jesus.

> Loving Savior, remind me of your Father's
> house above when thoughts of death trouble
> me. Amen.

REAL PEACE

Peace I leave with you; my peace I give you. I do not give to you as the world gives. Do not let your hearts be troubled and do not be afraid. John 14:27

"Real cheese," the little sticker on the frozen pizza said. Being from Wisconsin, the nation's dairy state, that's what I want. Even more so, when it comes to peace, I suppose I can live and die without real cheese but not without real peace.

The world uses the term *peace* rather frequently. Members of the United Nations dispute at great lengths and costs about peace for all countries. Candidates for office promise the end of war and the certainty of peace if elected. Books and magazine articles offer peace of mind and serenity of life. TV and newspaper ads propose peace for my pocketbook, my headache, my this, and my that.

When Jesus speaks of peace, he has none of the above in mind. "My peace I give you," he says. At once my eyes are lifted to his cross. In him, the crucified Savior, I have the real thing. That is, peace in the truest sense of the word when I know that because of Jesus' payment for sin, all is well between God and me. When with God-given faith I know he has opened the door to heaven for me and now lovingly leads me through life to that door. This peace surpasses all understanding and comes only from Christ. Notice that's what he said. Not "my peace I *wish* for you," but "my peace I *give* you."

Real cheese—sure, if I can get it. Real peace—that I must have, and it's found only in Jesus.

Lord, through your Word remind me constantly of your forgiveness so that I have peace. Amen.

SOMETHING TO GET EXCITED ABOUT

How great is the love the Father has lavished on us, that we should be called children of God! And that is what we are! 1 John 3:1

The game was over. The championship was theirs. "We're number one," they shouted excitedly as the cameras flashed. My granddaughter's team had something to be excited about.

So do we. We have different occupations, live in different locations, come from different generations, but one blessed name covers us all. "Children of God," John calls us, members of God's family, heirs of his heaven. That's not what we were by nature. "We were by nature objects of wrath," the sacred writer reminds us (Ephesians 2:3). At conception the labels "children of the devil" and "heirs of hell" were pasted on us. Because of sinful parents we were God's enemies, not his children. Yet look at what we have become. That's something to get excited about!

How could such a transformation take place? John tells me so excitedly, "How great is the love the Father has lavished on us that we should be called children of God!" God's amazing love did the impossible to me. It punished his Son for my sins. It sent his Spirit to seek me out in the surging sea of unbelieving mankind. It brought me through Word and sacrament to faith in his Son as my Savior. "My son, my daughter," God now calls me, but only because of his amazing love in Jesus. Winning a championship can be exciting, but nothing like being called God's child and knowing that because of his amazing love, it's true.

Lord, keep me excited till I can praise you in heaven. Amen.

I CAN HARDLY WAIT

What we will be has not yet been made known. But we know that when he appears, we shall be like him, for we shall see him as he is. 1 John 3:2

Out to sea in the service of his country, he had not yet seen his four-month-old son. Mail brought pictures, but how that sailor wanted to see his loved one face-to-face! As children of God, we know the feeling. We have mail about Jesus in Scripture but can hardly wait to see him in person.

That day is coming, either at my death or at the end of the world. And what a day it will be, so full of blessing that it's hard to describe. All we can do is repeat what John has written. "We shall be like him," he says. In heaven I will be holy like my Savior. All my sin, temptation to sin, consequence of sin will be removed. What that means I can only faintly imagine as I slough my way through this world of sin. But I know it's coming. Also, I know how such holiness is possible, only because of God's saving love for me in Christ. And I can hardly wait!

"We shall see him as he is," John also writes. With eyes of faith I see my Savior now on the pages of his Holy Word. With the eyes of my heart, I have imagined what he looks like. But in heaven I'll know. In heaven I'll see him face-to-face. What a sight that will be—that first full look at his spotless purity, his splendid power, and especially his saving grace. And that sight will be mine because of the great love the Father lavished on me when he made me his child.

Lord, thank you for making me your child through Jesus. Keep me as your child forever. Amen.

REMEMBER JESUS CHRIST

Remember Jesus Christ, raised from the dead, descended from David. 2 Timothy 2:8

Are you a member of the "Hereafter Club"? That's reserved for people who at a certain age walk into a room to get something and then stand there wondering, "What am I here after?" As the years increase, it happens that memory decreases. Hopefully, though, we'll never forget Jesus Christ.

"Remember Jesus Christ," Paul urged Timothy, "raised from the dead, descended from David." What a succinct summary of God's salvation as promised in both the Old and New Testaments. Jesus Christ was descended from David. He was the promised one for whom believers were waiting. With faith in him, Abraham crossed the wilderness to a new country. With faith in him, Noah entered the ark with the animals. With faith in him, David strummed his lute and composed psalms to him. With faith in him, Isaiah wrote his prophecy and Malachi said he was coming soon. They all longed to see the day when God's promised Savior would come to free them from their sins.

And he did come. "Remember Jesus Christ raised from the dead," Paul also wrote. In these words we see our Savior's Godforsakenness because of our sin's burden. In these words we see tender hands take him from the cross and deposit him in a tomb. And then on Easter we see his triumphant resurrection, God's stamp of approval on all that his Son had done. Yes, remember Jesus Christ raised from the dead. My sins are gone. My grave will open. Heaven is my real home.

Lord, let me always remember Jesus so that I can share heaven's hereafter with him. Amen.

THE MOST WONDERFUL SEED EVER PLANTED

I tell you the truth, unless a kernel of wheat falls to the ground and dies, it remains only a single seed. But if it dies, it produces many seeds. John 12:24

By now serious gardeners have planted their seeds. The containers stand on the windowsills, soaking up the sun, while the seeds sprout and grow. What a miracle is packed into each seed.

Everyone knows that a seed produces nothing if left in the package. It has to be planted in the ground. There it first dies in germination. But out of that decaying seed comes a sprout. That sprout becomes a plant and then a ripening stalk with many kernels. But first the seed must die.

"I tell you the truth," Jesus said about these words, so they must be important. Looking more closely, I realize he was referring to himself. He was like a seed. If he would not die, he could produce no fruit. If he were not slain for the sins of the world, he could not save the world. Then he alone would return to heaven, taking no souls with him. But plant Jesus in the ground—nail him to the cross, bury him in the tomb— and many kernels of wheat would come from him. Then all who believe in him as their only Savior—the wheat he produced—would be with him in heaven.

Now I understand why the pastor in every sermon preaches about Jesus' death for sinners. Now I realize why Scripture again and again points to his atoning cross. Like a seed, Jesus had to die so that I could be like a kernel of wheat, reserved for heaven's granary.

Lord, make and keep me one of those kernels reserved for heaven by your death. Amen.

GRAFTED INTO THE VINE

I am the vine; you are the branches. John 15:5

Scripture uses many pictures to describe the close, intimate relationship between Christ and those who believe in him. But this one of a vine and branches ranks near the top.

"I am the vine," Jesus said. I don't have to be a gardener to understand him. I can almost see that strong vine coming up out of the soil, bringing life to the branches attached to it. With eyes of faith I can see how God planted Christ as a life-giving vine into this world at Bethlehem. How this vine grew from Bethlehem to Calvary, from a manger of poverty to a cross of pain, to bring eternal life for people like me. Can anyone else but Jesus lay claim to this title of life-giving vine?

"You are the branches," Jesus goes on. "You," he said, looking at people like me. Those who have been brought to faith in Jesus as their Savior are as closely connected to him as branches to a vine. They are grown tight to him, eternally alive in him, and draw spiritual strength from him.

God's grace does this grafting. Through the gospel in Word and sacrament, God's grace sweeps the unbelief out of my heart and there creates faith in the Savior. My attachment to Christ the vine is God's gracious gift. How wonderful and how necessary to be able to say with God-given faith, "As the branch is to the vine, I am his and he is mine!" (CW 385:1).

Lord, ever keep me attached as a branch to
Christ, the life-giving vine. Amen.

NO GOOD IF DETACHED

> Remain in me, and I will remain in you. No branch can bear fruit by itself; it must remain in the vine. Neither can you bear fruit unless you remain in me. John 15:4

One night lightning hit our black walnut tree, stripping the bark from one of its branches and all but severing it from the tree. Sure enough—it wasn't long before the leaves on that branch dried up. Nor were there any walnuts on it later. Disconnected from its source of life, it was dead.

Jesus speaks of the same phenomenon in our verse, only in spiritual terms. Three times he uses the word *remain*. "*Remain* in me," he says. "No branch can bear fruit by itself; it must *remain* in the vine." "Neither can you bear fruit unless you *remain* in me." How much more emphatic can he be about the importance for believers to be connected to him as the life-giving Vine? No connection to him means no nourishment for faith. No nourishment leads to faith drying up and, of course, no fruit of faith in daily life. Disconnected from the source of life, a person can only be dead.

"Remain in me," Jesus commands. That's not as simple as it sounds. Staying attached to Christ the Vine through faith is not my doing, but the work of the Holy Spirit. Through Baptism he grafted me as a branch in the Vine. Through the gospel, as I use it or hear it, he strengthens my attachment to Christ. Through the Lord's Supper he bandages my faith. Only as he, through these blessed means, pours his pardon and power into my faith can it remain alive and grow fruit in daily life.

> Precious Vine, keep me close and let nothing sever me from you. Amen.

PRESSURED FROM WITHIN

If a man remains in me and I in him, he will bear much fruit. John 15:5

Those who drill for oil tell us there are three kinds of wells. There's the dry well that is just a hole in the ground producing nothing. The pumper is a well that has oil, but needs a pump to force the oil to the surface. The gusher is a well with pressure enough to bring the oil up by itself.

Which of these wells describes the life of a believer? Jesus makes it clear when he says, "If a man remains in me and I in him, he will bear much fruit." People who are connected by faith to Christ the vine show this by producing fruit. They don't stand there empty. Nobody has to force them. Christ in their hearts makes for fruit in their lives. The Savior's love within pressures them.

What do they produce? Paul in Galatians chapter 5 speaks of "love, joy, peace, patience, kindness, goodness, faithfulness, gentleness and self-control" (verses 22,23). These are no rare, exotic fruits, but ones found in daily life. The way I conduct myself at home, in the classroom, out in the community, at the plant, in the office are fruits that grow upon branches attached to the vine.

But all is due to the vine. I have no sap or life of my own. My life as a Christian comes not that I might be, but because I am attached to him. I live the Christian life not to gain salvation but to show I already have it. Christ's great love living within makes me into a gusher kind of well.

Lord, help me show my faith by the fruit in my daily life. Amen.

WITHOUT HIM—NOTHING

Apart from me you can do nothing. John 15:5

One morning little Julie wanted to surprise her mother with breakfast in bed. So she got out the breakfast tray. She put the orange juice in the glass, the cereal in the bowl, the bread in the toaster. But the toast wouldn't pop up. She had forgotten to plug the toaster into the outlet.

No toast from a lifeless toaster—that's understandable. But no fruit without Jesus—that I may have trouble with. Yet Jesus makes it clear. "Apart from me you can do nothing," he says. If I'm not connected to him in faith, I can do what I want but it will be nothing in his eyes. My charitable deeds, my gifts of money, my daily conduct, though outwardly splendid and worthy of people's applause, will be so much rotten fruit, fit only for the garbage disposal.

Because Jesus looks beyond the what to the why, he asks, "Why were these things done? Were they done out of a heart of faith to my glory and for the welfare of your fellowman? Were they done by a believer, attached to me, the vine, using my strength and seeking to say Thank You to me?" If not, then even those deeds that people praise highly are nothing but sin and shame in his eyes.

No connection to the outlet—no toast. It's no different with the Vine and the branches. Apart from him—nothing. With him—much fruit. Or to put it another way—branches severed from him can never be fruitful. Branches rooted in him can never be fruitless.

Lord, through the power of your gospel, keep me connected to you and fruitful. Amen.

HE KNOWS
HOW TO PRUNE

My Father is the gardener. He cuts off every branch in me that bears no fruit, while every branch that does bear fruit he prunes so that it will be even more fruitful. John 15:1,2

"To raise good tomatoes, you have to pull off the suckers," my father used to say. Those wild branches on the bottom of the plant would sap its strength and slow down the production of fruit.

In our verse, Jesus speaks of pulling off the suckers. God the Father is the gardener who prunes the branches on the vine. The dead branches he cuts off and throws way. The living branches, those who have been made clean by the Word of salvation, he does not leave by themselves to grow wildly. They need his tender, loving care. They need constant pruning so that some wild growth of sin doesn't sap their strength and slow down their fruit production or even turn them into dead branches.

My Father knows exactly how to prune. The shape of his shears may vary and their snips hurt at times. But every bit of his pruning has in mind my betterment as a branch grafted to Jesus. Through the preaching of his Word, he may snip away at my sins and draw me closer to him. Through the adversity that he allows, he may prune away my faults and tie me closer to him. Through a sudden accident, for example, he may cut away my self-reliance and lift my eyes up to him. In his loving wisdom, the heavenly gardener knows when and how to prune that I might become more fruitful as a branch on the vine.

Lord, prune from me the shoots of sin and the suckers of this world that I might be a strong branch producing more fruit for you. Amen.

FIT ONLY
FOR THE FIRE

If anyone does not remain in me, he is like a branch that is thrown away and withers; such branches are picked up, thrown into the fire and burned. John 15:6

Early each spring the trees in the orchard are checked. Dead branches are sawn off, piled up, and then ignited. What a sad sight those brush piles burning at the edge of the orchards are.

Can't you almost see the heavenly gardener at work? Carefully he checks each branch. One appears to be dying, but he doesn't saw it off at once. Patiently he waits and tries repairing it. But finally the last trace of life is gone, and he saws off the dead branch. To the fire it goes.

Note carefully, though, how Jesus describes those dead branches. He doesn't say, "If anyone has no fruit," but "if anyone does not remain in me." The lack of connection with the Savior makes one a dead branch in the eyes of the heavenly gardener. The dead branches are those in whose hearts is no faith in Christ. His life-giving sap doesn't run through them, and as a result there can be no fruit in their lives. The fault lies not with the Vine, but with the branch and its connections to the Vine. I may not always be able to spot the dead branch, but the gardener knows. He who sees the heart makes no mistakes. He knows which branches are dead and saws accordingly.

How sad that brushfire in hell will be. On the other hand, how thankful I should be that God has grafted me in faith to Jesus and made me a living branch in the Vine.

Please, Lord, for your love's sake, always keep me there. Amen.

THIS I ASK
FOR JESUS' SAKE

I tell you the truth, my Father will give you
whatever you ask in my name. John 16:23

Picture yourself before heaven's door. You have a request to
make of the heavenly Father. You knock, and he opens it.
"Lord," you begin, "I'm so and so, and I've come to request
such and such." The words are barely off your tongue when
he shuts the door in your face. What else could you expect?
What right do sinners have to approach a holy God, much less
to make demands on him?

You pick yourself up and try again. Once more you knock.
And once more the door opens. "Lord," you pray, "I'm your
child. See, I wear the robe of righteousness woven by your
Son on the loom of the cross. The stains on this robe are real;
that's his blood that covers all my sin. He has told me that
he has made me your forgiven child and that whatever I ask
in his name, you will give to me."

The door opens wide; the Father's arms reach out. Lovingly he
lifts me up on his knee. Tenderly he encourages me to speak.
Why is it that I, an unworthy sinner, can come to God at all
with my prayers? It's because of my risen Savior. Before the
Father's throne he points to his love that paid for my sins and
his grace that made me a believer. And then he pleads that God
hears my prayer for his sake. So it is possible for me in Jesus'
name, only because of Jesus' full payment for my sins, to come
to God and find a loving Father who will both hear and answer
all such prayers. I don't have to add the words "this I ask for
Jesus' sake" to each prayer, but I do need to believe them.

Lord, help me use the privilege only believers have
of calling on you in my Savior's name. Amen.

IT'S THE SPIRIT THAT COUNTS

When the Counselor comes, whom I will send to you from the Father, the Spirit of truth who goes out from the Father, he will testify about me. John 15:26

A new manager takes over a faltering team, and by season's end they're in the playoffs. It's the spirit that counts. So also with my faith. It's the spirit that counts, that is—the Holy Spirit.

Many questions nagged at the disciples' minds. When they inquired about greatness in God's kingdom, Jesus washed their feet. When they questioned, "Lord, we don't know where you are going so how can we know the way," Jesus replied, "I am the way, no one comes to the Father except through me." When they asked, "Lord, show us the Father," Jesus corrected them with "anyone who has seen me has seen the Father." For so long Jesus had been among them, but so many questions remained. Who would dispel their doubts and strengthen their faith when he was gone?

Jesus' answer is also for me. He promises to send the Holy Spirit to stand at my side as a Counselor. This Spirit of truth opens my heart to receive and retain the truth. And the greatest truth the Spirit brings me is the truth of salvation through Jesus. What a promise Christ gave those disciples and me, the promise of the Spirit to create and continue faith in us through the Word. "It's the Spirit that counts," Jesus tells me, "the Spirit who works faith in me as your Savior." My faith is the Spirit's miracle. Its continuation is his work.

Thank God for the work of his Spirit through his Word. Amen.

ORPHANS NO LONGER

I will not leave you as orphans; I will come to you. Before long, the world will not see me anymore, but you will see me. Because I live, you also will live. John 14:18,19

What a sad sight! A tragic car accident had snuffed out their parents' lives. At their parents' funeral the young children sat, not even knowing yet how alone they were. Much like those first disciples.

That Maundy Thursday evening seemingly bitter tragedy would take Jesus away from them. He would begin the road to the cross and tomb. His blood would run, and his heart would stop. A stone would secure him in a grave; he was never to be with them again. How much like orphans they felt.

But not for long. Jesus promised that he would come to them again. Their sorrow would turn into joy. His crucifixion was in payment for their sins. His resurrection was proof that his payment was sufficient. It was also the guarantee that they too would live. Just as his death counted for them, so did his resurrection. The sight of the living Lord assured them that they were orphans no longer.

I've seen him too. Just as Jesus promised, he sent his Spirit to work faith in me to see him. At my baptism, through the Word, at the Communion Table, the crucified and risen Savior comes to me and tells me, "You're not alone. I am with you with my pardon, my peace, and my promise of heaven. You're no orphan, so don't act like one. You're mine, so rejoice that you are."

Lord, thank you for sending your Spirit
to assure me that I am yours and you are
mine. Amen.

STOPPING FOR
HIS ASCENSION

After he said this, he was taken up before their very eyes, and a cloud hid him from their sight. Acts 1:9

"Scenic view ahead," says the road sign. You're in a hurry to find a motel, so you don't pull off, only to miss one of the better sights. We can learn much from stopping to view Jesus' ascension.

Now, 40 days after Easter, the risen Savior stands with his followers on the Mount of Olives. The Scriptures have been fulfilled. The cross has been erected and bloodied. The tomb has been filled and emptied. Jesus has finished his mission of salvation and is ready to return to a glorious heaven.

What does the sight of the ascending Savior show me when I stop to look? He leaves, not with half a sacrifice for sin, but a complete one. His work of salvation requires no finishing touches, no loose ends to be tied together by me. His ascension shows me that I "have been made holy through the sacrifice of the body of Jesus Christ once for all" (Hebrews 10:10). Jesus' mission is done!

Before Jesus "was taken up before their very eyes" that first Ascension Day, he told his followers, "You will be my witnesses in Jerusalem, and in all Judea and Samaria, and to the ends of the earth" (Acts 1:8). That's my mission too—to tell needy souls about the Savior's finished work of salvation. The ascending Savior reminds me that as long as one soul still hasn't heard, my mission is not done!

Lord Jesus, let your ascension remind me your mission is done while mine is only begun. Amen.

THE TRIUNE GOD'S BLESSING OF PRESERVATION

The LORD bless you and keep you. Numbers 6:24

How do we even begin to explain the mystery behind the triune God? That he can be three distinct, entire, equal, eternal persons and yet one God lies far outside the grasp of my human mind. Better for me to look beyond the mystery of the triune God's being to the blessings he brings me.

Do I hear what he promises *me?* Just think of it! He, who keeps the whole world running and the whole human race alive, promises that he will especially bless and keep me. I am "the apple of [his] eye," he reminds me (Psalm 17:8); "the sheep of his pasture"(Psalm 100:3). What can be more precious to him than those whom he has made his beloved children in Christ?

Do I hear *what* he promises me? The bread on my table and the butter to put on it; the anxious trip to the hospital and the happy return; the job I still have and the children kept safe from harm are just samples of what my preserving Father sends my way. But why stop with such nickels and dimes? He has tens and twenties for me too. What happened when sin chewed at my soul? When my faith flickered like some match in the wind? When the temptation before me seemed like Mount Everest? Wasn't he there to preserve me? Didn't he mean it when he said he would bless and keep me? Lesser blessings for my body and greater ones for my soul he sends my way daily. This, the wonderful triune God offers me as God the Father promises, "[I will] bless you and keep you."

> Lord, thank you for watching over and providing for such an unworthy creature like me. Amen.

THE TRIUNE GOD'S BLESSING OF PARDON

The LORD make his face shine upon you and be gracious to you. Numbers 6:25

When a new mother gazes down at the little miracle asleep in her arms, or when a young man looks over at his beautiful bride, what does the look spell? Love, of course. That's love shining on those faces, and that's love God promises me when his blessing says, "The LORD make his face shine upon you and be gracious to you." Only here's a love far more dear than any human could ever muster. He who is the source of all love promises to look on me with the most tender and touching love I can ever experience. Not only that, it's a love that I just have to have daily.

Is it love that I deserve? Shouldn't God be sending my way the flashing look of righteous anger and the snapping of eyes full of holy wrath? How come punishment, well deserved because of my sins, becomes pardon, freely given? Because of God the Son, the second person of the wonderful Trinity. He came to earth to fully bear the wrath of God over my sins so I can bask in the sunshine of his forgiveness. Because the lightning bolt of God's righteous anger over my sins struck Jesus, I can see him looking down on me with his marvelous love.

As the denials of a Peter and the betrayals of a Judas, the common sins and the peculiar temptations of my life arise to blacken my soul and bring penitent tears to my heart. I know what a blessing the pardon earned for me by God the Son is.

Lord, shine upon me with the pardon purchased by your love. I need its sunshine daily. Amen.

THE TRIUNE GOD'S BLESSING OF PEACE

The Lord turn his face toward you and give you peace. Numbers 6:26

A third blessing, equally marvelous, the wonderful triune God has for us. In his benediction he calls it peace, a blessing we usually associate with the work of the Holy Spirit.

Peace! That's what brought Christ down from a throne of glory to a cross of shame. Peace! That's what Christ has prepared for all people. No, not peace as the world understands it. Not an end to rocket rattlings and nuclear threats. Not an end to racial tensions and relatives' bickerings. Not an end to cold-blooded killings in the street or more sanitary murders of the unborn in the womb. Such outward peace could indeed come if everyone had God's true peace in his or her heart.

When the Lord promises peace, he means the real thing—peace with him. He means the peace I have when I see God's face turned toward me instead of away from me. The peace I have when I see his love smiling on me and forgiving me in Christ. The peace I have when I know and believe that he is my loving Father who guides me every stumbling step I take as his child. The peace I have when I know and believe that when I step out of this life, he will take me to heaven.

Every believer is the work of the Holy Spirit. So am I. As Martin Luther stated, "He has called me by the gospel, enlightened me with his gifts, sanctified and kept me in the true faith." When the Spirit brings me to faith, he gives me the peace I need in life and death.

Lord, give me your peace for Jesus' sake and through the Spirit's work. Amen.

HANG ON

Hold on to what you have, so that no one will take your crown. Revelation 3:11

"Hang on to my hand," a mother invites her toddler. "Hang on" is one of those frequent bits of advice in life. So also for young believers being confirmed this month in many congregations. And for me!

Whenever anyone says, "Hang on," I tend to listen. How much more so when those words come from the Lord Jesus. Actually he said to keep holding on. To what? "Your crown," he replies, using a picture from the athletic contests. Today we'd probably talk about the gold medal at the Olympics. Jesus points me to the finish line of life and the gold medal waiting for me in heaven.

What crown? It's the pure gold of God's pardon for all my sins, forged for me when Jesus shed his blood on Calvary's tree. It's the sterling silver of a sure hope for heaven, given me when the Spirit brought me to faith in the Savior. It's standing in the victor's circle in heaven forever next to Jesus. Everything else is trash compared to this eternal crown.

But the fingers of my faith are so weak. Some days even weaker than others. How can I hang on till eternity? "Faith comes from hearing the message, and the message is heard through the word of Christ," Scripture reminds me (Romans 10:17). If I want to hang on to the crown, I need also to hang on to God's Word through which his Spirit strengthens the grip of faith.

Lord, strengthen my faith through your Word so that I can stand in heaven's victory circle. Amen.

DEFINITELY DIFFERENT

Therefore, I urge you, brothers, in view of
God's mercy . . . do not conform any longer to
the pattern of this world, but be transformed
by the renewing of your mind. Romans 12:1,2

If I could speak to those young believers who are being confirmed or are graduating these weeks, what would I say? Would I join the apostle Paul in urging them to be definitely different?

It's difficult to be different. Everyone wants to be part of the "in" crowd. When Paul says, "Do not conform any longer to the pattern of this world," he has more in mind than designer clothing and digital recordings. He means my life as God's child. For me, life leads to heaven and is not just to be lived out on earth. My talents are for serving Christ, not just for making a living. God's commandments are guidelines for peaceful living, not the police officer's rules to squeeze me in or close me out. As God's child, I'm different and my Lord expects me to show it, difficult as it may be.

With one short phrase Paul points to the motivation. "I urge you," he said, "in view of God's mercy." That phrase takes me to Bethlehem where I see God's loving heart beating in the chest of his Son. Next, it leads to Calvary where I see his loving heart stop beating because of my sins. Then it directs to the Word, the baptismal font, the Communion altar, where his loving heart invites me to come and gives me faith to respond. Finally it points me to heaven, where I will be clasped close to his loving heart forever. Only such redeeming love can make me want to be definitely different.

Lord, fill me with your precious love in Christ so
that I am powered to live as your child. Amen.

A DOCTOR ON BOARD

He [Jesus] said to the paralytic, "Son, your sins are forgiven." Mark 2:5

"Is there a doctor on board?" asked the flight attendant over the intercom. A passenger had fallen sick on the cross-country flight I was on and needed immediate care. Fortunately a doctor came forward.

The paralytic needed immediate care. That's why his friends lugged his stretcher up on the roof and lowered him down before Jesus. Unable to make their way through the crowd, they pulled aside the roof tiles in their determination to get to the healer. First Jesus cured that man's most serious ailment. "Your sins are forgiven," Jesus told him. And it was done. Here was a doctor who not only prescribed medicine but was the medicine itself. Jesus offered the paralytic the forgiveness he needed—the forgiveness that Jesus had come to prepare on Calvary's cross. Then the Savior turned to the lesser problem. "Take your mat and go home," the divine physician told the man. And again it was done.

Of course, Jesus wants me to see his healing hand behind the doctor's knowledge, the prescription bottle, and the surgeon's skill. But he especially wants me to know who takes care of the needs of my soul. Only his pardon prepared on Calvary's cross can stitch up sin's wounds on my soul. Only his power can accomplish the heart transplant I need, replacing the one dead in unbelief with one beating in faith. Only his skill can correct the rhythm of my heart so that it matches what he wants. Such a doctor I need on board life's flight all the way.

Divine Physician, dispense the medicine of your forgiveness and heal my heart every day. Amen.

HIDDEN MANNA
AND A WHITE STONE

To him who overcomes, I will give some of the hidden manna. I will also give him a white stone with a new name written on it, known only to him who receives it. Revelation 2:17

What a strange combination! What does Jesus mean when he promises each believer hidden manna and a white stone with a new name on it? Actually, both pictures refer to him as my Savior.

God's Old Testament people, while wandering in the wilderness for 40 years, had their physical hunger satisfied by the miracle bread God sent them. Manna they called that bread from heaven. For God's New Testament people, there is also manna. Jesus and all that he has done for sinners is the bread that satisfies the soul. To eat this miracle manna means to believe in Jesus as the only Savior. To unbelievers the Savior remains "hidden," because they have no idea of the heavenly nutrition he offers. But for me he truly is the Bread of Life, the only one that can feed my hungry soul.

The white stone with a new name on it is also a picture of the Savior. In the past, jurors at trials used stones for voting. A black stone meant guilty and led to the modern expression of blackballing someone. Dropping a white stone in the box indicated acquittal, finding the defendant not guilty. Jesus is the name on the white stone. Because of his payment for all my sins, the heavenly Judge declares me not guilty. For me his name is the most beautiful in the world. It's the only name that can lift me from earth to heaven. It's the name I have to have.

Blessed Savior, feed me. Assure me of God's "not guilty" verdict as only you can. Amen.

WHAT A STAR!

I will also give him the morning star.
Revelation 2:28

In our town is a church named Morning Star, a title I had never heard before. It made me curious and caused me to dig. I found that expression twice in the book of Revelation. In 22:16 Jesus calls himself "the bright Morning Star." In our verse he promises to give believers "the morning star." Jesus is the Morning Star who promises to give himself along with all his blessings to believers.

What greater blessing can Jesus offer? Like the morning star he shines the brightest in God's heaven. With faith's eyes I see his forgiveness in sin's dark fog. His power in temptation's thick clouds. His assurance in death's deep shadows. Early mariners used the stars of heaven to chart their courses across the seas. I have a Morning Star whose light always shines brightly and whose direction always leads correctly to heaven.

The morning star is one that rules the sky with royal splendor. So does Jesus. He who has won the victory over sin, death, and hell now rules over everything. His name is above every name; to him every knee must bow. When he takes me to heaven, I'll not only see his glorious splendor but even share in it. With all other believers I'll shine like a morning star at his side, not with my own brilliance but with brilliance derived from him, the true Morning Star.

What a name for a church! Better still, what a Savior for me!

Jesus, be my Morning Star and land me safe on heaven's shore. Amen.

WHERE'S THE KEY?

These are the words of him who is holy and true, who holds the key of David. What he opens no one can shut, and what he shuts no one can open. Revelation 3:7

You stand at your backdoor in the rain, both arms filled with grocery bags and can't find the key. "Where's the key?" you ask your wife. "Have you got it?"

When it comes to heaven's door, Scripture leaves no doubt as to who holds the key. It's Jesus. In fact, he is the key. He and he alone opens the door to heaven. On that cross centuries ago, he who is holy and true, he who is the priceless Son of God, suffered and died. He didn't deserve to die; we did. He carried our guilt, not his own. He who had no sin fully paid the penalty for each of our sins. Like a key the Savior opened the door of heaven. And it stands open until he closes it.

Any warning for me in these words? Don't they ask whether I'm only standing before the cross of Christ or kneeling in humble faith beneath it? Whether I only talk about Jesus the Savior or call him my Savior? The door is open for me, but Christ alone knows how long it will stay that way.

Any comfort for me in these words? I don't have to stand around in the rain of life or fear the storms of hell wondering, "Where's the key?" In his grace God has worked faith in my heart and put heaven's key in my hand. May his grace keep Jesus, the key, in the pocket of my faith always.

Lord, thank you for faith's hand that holds
Jesus as my key to heaven. Amen.

Trinity Lutheran Church
1353 FIRST AVENUE S. W.
CEDAR RAPIDS, IOWA

PERMANENT PILLARS

Him who overcomes I will make a pillar in the temple of my God. Never again will he leave it. Revelation 3:12

Like lonely sentinels the freeway pillars stood there. An earthquake had shaken into pieces the road they had supported. And they were all that was left of a once busy highway. What a sad picture!

When Jesus describes believers in heaven as "pillars in the temple of my God," there's nothing sad about his words. It's a glorious picture, a comforting thought. Here on earth believers so often feel like tar-paper shacks. Every wind that comes along seems to rip boards from the walls and lift shingles from the roof. Some days those winds even seem like tornadoes against which believers have little protection. The sins they fall into daily, the temptations they face daily, the struggle with the defects sin has brought into this world whip at them as if there were no safety.

But there is. He who has prepared my salvation promises to protect my soul. He who brings me peace with God will not let the world rob me of it. He who said he will keep me until his eternal day will keep his word. My loving Savior even promises that he will make me into a pillar in heaven. No storm ever reaches God's temple. No tornado will ever twist the pillars that stand there. In his heavenly temple I will be safe forever as a permanent pillar. Now that's something to look forward to! But only for those who by God's grace know his Son Jesus as their Savior.

Lord, keep me safe in faith in Jesus as my only Savior from sin till I stand in your heaven. Amen.

THE ONLY DETERGENT THAT WORKS

And the blood of Jesus, his Son, purifies us from all sin. 1 John 1:7

The stain was still there. Some spaghetti sauce had dripped onto my dress shirt, and I had forgotten to mention it to my wife. "You should have used the stain stick before throwing the shirt into the wash," she reminded me. Many of us know about dirty clothes and how to make them clean. We understand that it takes the right detergent to wash the dirt of daily wear out of our clothes.

In our verse, John writes about the dirt of sin, the grime of daily life that is ground into our souls. He speaks about the mud of sinful birth and sinful life that soils everyone, making us fit only for hell. But then he also points us to the only detergent that can wash sin's stain completely out of our souls. That's the precious blood of Jesus, God's Son. His blood doesn't just brush off sin's outward stain but removes it completely. It doesn't leave an ugly residue but lifts it out totally.

For that blood comes from the veins of him who is not only man but God from all eternity. God who promised forgiveness is faithful. At Calvary's cross we see that he did not merely sweep sin under some carpet but demanded full payment from his Son as our substitute. That Son's suffering and death is the miracle whitener that cleanses even the most corrupt sinner and the most crimson stain. "And sinners who are washed therein Lose ev'ry guilty stain" (CW 112:1).

Lord, thank you that I can say, "Grace and life eternal In that blood I find; Blest be his compassion, Infinitely kind." Amen. (CW 103:2)

THE GIFT ONLY GOD
COULD GIVE

God has given us eternal life, and this life is in his Son. 1 John 5:11

"Give the gift only you can give," says the blood-bank poster. The donation of my blood can help others live a bit longer in this world. God's gift of his Son's blood enables me to live forever.

"God has *given* us eternal life," John writes. Life with God is not something I can earn. It's not payment for my deeds, a prize I deserve. Only one word fits—*gift*. Only one could give this gift—God. He looked down on me, born dead in unbelief, bound inevitably for eternal death in hell's dungeon, and had pity on me. With amazing love he prepared for me a life that never ends.

"This life is *in his Son*," John also writes. Nowhere else can I find life with God but in his Son. Only God's Son could fill the cross, feel hell's pangs, fling open death's grave, and make it count for me. The price for life with God was so steep that only God himself could handle it.

"God has given us *eternal life*," John also reminds me. It's not just something that waits for me in heaven. It's mine already, from the moment God's Spirit brings me to faith. It's not just something that lasts for 10, 20, perhaps 30 years, but forever. And I can enjoy it now. In a world of death, I have life. In a world of dread, I have joy. In a world of doom, I have hope. The gift that only God can give is mine already and will be fully mine in heaven.

Lord, thank you for the life that brings me joy on earth and eternity at your side. Amen.

WHERE'S YOUR HOPE?

In his great mercy he has given us new birth
into a living hope through the resurrection of
Jesus Christ from the dead. 1 Peter 1:3

It's only a small word of four letters, yet what an important role it plays. Unfortunately, for many, *hope* is an ambiguous word, wishful thinking that seldom if ever materializes. But for the Christian, *hope* is a shatterproof word, representing something supremely sure. It's the window through which I can look into God's loving heart and see all his promises fully kept. That's why Peter calls it "a living hope," because based on God's sure promises, it will never let me down.

What's the content of the Christian's hope? All that God promises me in Christ Jesus. His pardon to cover all my sins. His power to help me in the fight against temptations. His comfort to help dry my tears. And especially, his heaven as my home. All this and so much more he promises me.

Where's my assurance that this hope is shatterproof? "The resurrection of Jesus Christ from the dead," Peter reminds me. Jesus' resurrection is the heart of the gospel. Without it I have no spiritual hope. Then my sins still hang like some warped steel beams around my neck. Then my life is only a relentless march to the prison cells of hell. Then my grave is a dark, dank prison that locks me in. Christ's resurrection is proof positive that all God has promised is true. No wonder the New Testament devotes so much space to Christ's resurrection. That's where true hope plants its feet.

Lord, every day take me back to Christ's
resurrection as proof for all your promises. Amen.

WHAT'S YOUR INHERITANCE?

Into an inheritance that can never perish, spoil or fade—kept in heaven for you. 1 Peter 1:4

"We're spending our kids' inheritance now," says a bumper sticker. Unlike past generations, not all parents today are concerned about leaving something for their children. And when they do, often the vagaries of the stock market or the uncertainties of the economy shrink its value.

In sharp contrast, Peter writes of the inheritance God has for his children, "It can never perish, spoil or fade." By using these negative words, Peter highlights the greatness of my inheritance in Christ. Who can rob me of God's full forgiveness for my sins? The devil tries, my conscience accuses, but God points to the cross of his Son. What can spoil the peace I have with God? Storms may rock my boat in life. Tears may dim my faith's sight. But his peace is still there, as sure as the nail prints in the hand that clasps mine. What can devalue the glory of the heaven God has for me? The world may laugh, calling it "pie in the sky by and by," but I have God's assurance that what is waiting for me is far better.

Unlike some earthly parents, my heavenly Father is concerned about an inheritance for me. That's why he sent Jesus to the cross and raised him from the grave. That's why he promises to keep me in faith in Jesus. He wants me to have an inheritance that is truly out of this world.

Lord, raise my eyes to the treasures of heaven, even as I partially enjoy them already here. Amen.

HIS HAND
IS STRONG ENOUGH

Cast all your anxiety on him because he cares for you. 1 Peter 5:7

In New York City's Rockefeller Center stands a statue of the Greek god Atlas, carrying the world on his shoulders. It shows him bending forward, muscles tensed under the tremendous weight. Across the street in St. Patrick's Cathedral stands another statue of a person supporting the world. It's the Christ Child, holding the whole world in the palm of his little hand with no trouble at all.

Each one of us knows something about anxiety. We are sinners. Born with sinful hearts, inherited from sinful parents, we surely must fear the just anger of a holy God. Add to those hearts our many daily sins of thought, word, and deed, and see how the fear of that holy God must increase. As if this weren't enough, we also have the troubles brought into this world when our first parents sinned. Daily we weary in wrestling with the problems that can hit our bodies, the temptations that can assault our souls, the diseases that can finally snuff out our lives.

Who's going to hold us? "Jesus," Peter tells me. And he tells me why. It's because "he cares for [me]." His powerful hands were once stretched out on a cross for me. Those same hands are now stretched around me by One who rose from the grave to show that the debt of sin was paid, death defeated, and heaven opened. Those same hands will be there to carry me when it's time to enter heaven's door. "He cares for you," Peter says. He can hold me in the palm of his hand with no trouble at all.

Hold me by the hand, Lord Jesus, and lead me safely home. Amen.

BOLD BEGGARS

Let us then approach the throne of grace with confidence, so that we may receive mercy and find grace to help us in our time of need.
Hebrews 4:16

Some years ago the mayor of New York City went to war against the beggars in his town. So many of them had become insistent in approaching people that tourists were turned off. "Beggars have no business being bold," he said.

Yet the author of Hebrews urges us to be bold when approaching God's throne. His throne is one of justice, so I would do well to run the other way. Since it is a throne of power, shouldn't I hesitate to approach because his power coupled with his justice could only smash sinners like me in anger? But look, his is also a throne of grace. On it sits the Lord Jesus. The Savior, who loves me, died for me, paid for me, invites me now to come boldly to his throne.

When I come, I find what I need. "Mercy" and "grace" await me there. Both refer to the help I need for my guilt and sin. When I truly understand the penalty for sin, prayers for mercy and grace become my chief concern. With the tax collector, I plead before the Savior's throne, "Be merciful to me, a sinner." With the thief on the cross, I humbly beg, "Remember me." And he will. That's his promise. That's what his mercy and grace are all about. Because the Savior died for me, my Father in heaven never chases me away. Instead, he invites me to be a bold beggar at his throne.

Lord, hear my prayers for Jesus' sake. Grant me forgiveness and peace. Amen.

ON THE ROAD
TO MOUNT ZION

But you have come to Mount Zion, to the
heavenly Jerusalem, the city of the living God.
Hebrews 12:22

If you ever travel in Montana, you have to drive the
Beartooth Highway. One TV commentator describes it with its
beautiful sights and hairpin curves as "the most scenic highway in America."

There's another highway I surely want to travel, the one to
Mount Zion. With this expression the author refers to the
heavenly Jerusalem, not built on an earthly Mount Zion but
in heaven. It's the city of the living God, the one he popu-
lates with all those who believe in the Savior. When the Spirit
brings me to faith in Jesus, he makes me a citizen in this city.
Though on earth I cannot taste fully the blessings of my citizenship, what I have quickens my step on the road to Zion.

Look at the blessings I enjoy on the way. There's pardon for
all my sins. The Lord himself clothes me with the spotless
robe of Christ's righteousness. There's protection on the road.
He who made me a citizen of the heavenly Jerusalem guides
me around the hairpin curves of life. There's the privilege of
prayer, of stepping before him as often as I want. These are
just a foretaste of the blessings waiting for me when I finally
reach the heavenly Mount Zion.

Thank God I have a traveling companion, not just one with
whom to share the sights but one who keeps me on the road.
That's my Savior, Jesus, whose death and resurrection make
him the road to Mount Zion.

Gracious Lord, please, through the gospel, keep
my feet on Jesus, the road home. Amen.

COMPANIONS
ALONG THE WAY

You have come to thousands upon thousands
of angels in joyful assembly, to the church of
the firstborn . . . to God, the judge of all men.
Hebrews 12:22,23

Traveling alone is usually not much fun. With whom do you
plan the sights? plot the way? Who's there to pick you up
when discouraged or spur you on when tired? Thank God for
the traveling companions I have on the way to heaven.
Though I can't see them, countless angels are there. In
heaven they sing the praises of the Lamb who died and
rejoice over each sinner brought to repentance. On earth they
travel with me to care for me on the way and to carry my ransomed soul home at last. What a comfort to know those
angels accompany me with their power.

The church of the firstborn also travels with me. Around me
on the journey are fellow believers. Like the firstborn in Jewish families of old, they have received the greatest inheritance. They, with me, share the best God has to give, the
promise of an eternal home. What comfort to know that I
have them as companions with whom to share the sights and
from whom to receive encouragement.

My best companion by far is God, the judge of all. This judge
not only condemns, but he also acquits. And that he has
already done for me. In heaven's courtroom he has declared
me not guilty because of his Son's payment for all my sins.
When he acquits, his verdict stands. In his grace he has waiting for me the crown of life in heaven. What a promise to
spur me on as I travel the road home.

Great Jehovah, guide me, keep me, accompany
me on the road home to heaven. Amen.

A HIGHWAY PAVED IN RED

You have come . . . to Jesus the mediator of a new covenant, and to the sprinkled blood that speaks a better word than the blood of Abel.
Hebrews 12:23,24

Vacationing on Prince Edward Island in Canada, we traveled roads with a reddish tint to them. Upon inquiring, we learned that the color came from the rocks crushed for the blacktop mix.

Only one highway leads to heaven. And it's one colored completely red with Jesus' precious blood. In the Old Testament, the blood of Abel, when shed by his wicked brother Cain, cried out for vengeance. The blood of Jesus, spilled on the cross, cries out for pardon and peace. God must hear that cry because it comes from the One he sent. His own Son is the mediator of the covenant God made with our first parents in Eden after they had fallen into sin. Jesus went to the cross to put God's promise of salvation into effect. He came as the God-man to pour out his precious blood in payment for sin. There's no other highway to heaven but the one paved red with Jesus' blood.

"Momma," said the little girl after Sunday school, "teacher told us today that God puts people into this world only so that they can get ready for heaven." "Yes, dear," her mother replied, "that's right." "Then why don't we see them getting ready?" the girl asked in all sincerity. A childish question, perhaps, but yet too often true. God help me use my life to get ready for heaven. God lead me to and keep me on the right highway there—the one red with Jesus' precious blood.

Lord, thank you for building the highway to heaven. Please keep me on it safely to heaven. Amen.

THE STORY OF MY LIFE

Christ Jesus came into the world to
save sinners—of whom I am the worst.
1 Timothy 1:15

Biographies will probably not be written about any of us,
other than a few lines in the newspaper obituary column. But
even those lines will leave out the two most important facts
in our lives.

If I were to write the story of my life, wouldn't I start where
Paul did? Wouldn't fact number one be my confession: "I am
the worst of sinners"? Such a confession is not easy to make.
Everything else I like to exaggerate, but sin I like to shrink.
Other peoples' sins I can easily spot, but my own somehow
escape detection. Yet the plain truth remains that I'm a sinner. I don't need a microscope to examine my daily life. Sin's
contamination is clearly visible. My confession is in order: "I
am number one, first in line when it comes to sinners."

Thank God fact number two is "Christ Jesus came into the
world to save sinners." There was only one reason Christ
Jesus left heaven, entered a virgin's womb, and came into
our world of sin and sorrow. Only one reason why he lived
in this world, died in it, and rose again. That was to save
sinners. He came not to judge, but to seek and save the lost.
And he came for me. Because of him God won't write the
word *lost* over my grave, but *saved* by his grace in Christ
Jesus. Come to think of it, what more needs to be said in
the story of my life?

> Lord, let it be said of me that "Chief of
> sinners though I be, Jesus shed his blood
> for me." Amen. (CW 385:1)

LIFE—
TO HAVE CHRIST

For to me, to live is Christ. Philippians 1:21

What's it all about—this thing called life? The 20th-century editor H. L. Mencken answered, "Life is a dead-end street." The 19th-century writer Elbert Hubbard said, "Don't take life too seriously. You will never get out of it alive." What pessimism and hopelessness!

Humanly speaking, Paul might have chimed in with them. He was a prisoner in Rome, with his worldwide missionary work and freedom gone and perhaps soon also his life. How easily he might have asked, "What's this thing called life all about?" Yet what do we read? "For me to live is Christ," he shouts, "and if Christ were taken away from me, there would be nothing left to live for."

Someone wrote, "Christ is not valued at all unless he is valued above all." Isn't that what Paul is trying to tell me? God has given me life so that I might have life's greatest treasure. All the world's stocks and bonds can't bring the peace I have in Jesus. The best house in the subdivision looks like some falling-down shack compared to my Father's house in heaven. When by faith I have Christ, I have it all. When the Savior dwells in my heart, the purpose for my life is fulfilled. God gives me life, long or short, so that by his grace I might know Jesus as my only Savior.

"Dead-end street"? "Never get out of it alive"? Little did they know. "For to me, to live is Christ."

Lord, thank you for bringing the Savior into my heart. Keep him there always. Amen.

LIFE—
TO WORK FOR CHRIST

It has become clear throughout the whole palace guard and to everyone else that I am in chains for Christ. Philippians 1:13

The great apostle could no longer plant new mission congregations and prepare more mission workers. But he could still talk about Jesus. And he did. Every six to eight hours another guard would come to relieve the guard to whom Paul was chained. How many guards did Paul tell about the Savior during his two years in custody at Rome? Satan thought chaining Paul up would curtail his preaching of Christ. Instead, Paul used it as another opportunity to work for Christ.

Not just the pastor has a pulpit from which to preach Christ. So do I. My pulpit is called daily life. Every noon the cross-country Greyhound bus stopped in the same town for a 45-minute lunch break. Forbidden by company policy to single out any restaurant, the bus driver would say, "If anyone wants me, I'll be enjoying a delicious meal at Tony's first-class, spotlessly clean diner directly across the street." And his indirect advertising filled Tony's diner with hungry travelers.

Wherever God has placed me, I can advertise Christ. Sometimes this involves words, witnessing about the only Savior to people I know and people I don't. Always it involves my daily life. By the way I talk and walk, treat my spouse, and train my children, and in a thousand other ways, like Paul, I can work for Christ. My walk is heavenward, but on the way there's work for me to do.

Lord, make me a faithful witness to the Savior so that others may walk with me to heaven. Amen.

LIFE—
TO SUFFER FOR CHRIST

I eagerly . . . hope that I will in no way be ashamed, but will have sufficient courage so that now as always Christ will be exalted in my body, whether by life or by death. Philippians 1:20

To have Christ and to work for Christ—that's what life is all about. Agreed? Of course! But would all nod their heads approvingly if we added that in life believers are called upon to suffer for Christ? Paul would. For two years he had been living with the threat of death at the hands of a Roman executioner. But the great apostle didn't wilt. If death were to come, his eager hope was with the help of the Holy Spirit to face it courageously so that Christ would be exalted.

For us in our country there's no danger of losing our heads because of our faith. Our problem is that we hide our heads because of our faith. When all around us people prattle that truth is what you want to believe, it takes Christian fortitude to preach that only what God's Word says is true. When matters like morals, marriage, and life's meaning flip-flop every other day, it requires strong faith to stand up for what God has said in his unchanging Word. It's not even easy to face the problems in daily life when the devil suggests to me that I'm wasting my time in following Jesus.

"How do you stay so calm?" asked her pastor. The severely tested grandma answered, "When I was a girl, my mother told me that each night she slept well because she rested her head on three pillows—God's grace, God's power, God's wisdom." Those who rely on God's free grace in Christ Jesus, God's power to take care of their lives, and God's wisdom to lead correctly will, along with Paul, have what it takes to suffer for Christ.

Lord, I am weak, but you are strong. Be with me. Amen.

LIFE—
TO DIE IN CHRIST

For to me, to live is Christ and to die is gain.
Philippians 1:21

"Life without Christ is a hopeless end," someone once wrote, "but life with Christ is an endless hope." Paul puts forward the same conclusion in his words, "For to me, to live is Christ and to die is gain." Gain? Who calls death a gain? People call it all kinds of things but not a gain. Only believers like Paul can say "Death is gain because it takes me to be forever with my Lord and Savior. Death is gain because it takes me to that union with Christ that is complete and that nothing can ever again corrode or crack."

When at the church door or elsewhere I'd see couples who were planning to be married, I'd ask them how many days were left before their weddings. Almost invariably they could tell me, to the exact day and with mounting joy. They were waiting for that day to come when they could be together for the rest of their lives.

When God brings Christ into my heart and life, he also brings the desire to be with my loving Savior forever. From that moment on, the countdown begins, not with apprehension but anticipation. "I desire to depart and be with Christ, which is better by far" (Philippians 1:23), wrote the same apostle who in our verse says "to die is gain." Never will I be more fully alive than when God takes me to his heaven. But first I need to know how to get there. There's only one way, through Jesus.

Lord Jesus, in a dying world, fill my heart with the joy of knowing that to die is gain. Amen.

THE FUTILITY
OF THE CONFLICT

Since the children have flesh and blood, he too shared in their humanity so that by his death he might destroy him who holds the power of death—that is, the devil—and free those who all their lives were held in slavery by their fear of death. Hebrews 2:14,15

It was twilight in Washington, DC. Light drizzle was falling. We were standing before the Vietnam Veterans Memorial Wall. As I rubbed my fingers over the names of the two young men from our congregation, I'll admit a sob caught in my throat. They weren't the first or the last to die in conflict. Wars and rumors of war will be with us to the end of time. But it all seems so futile.

The same with our loved ones. Sometimes well past the proverbial 70 years, sometimes far before it, death claims our loved ones. Doctors diagnose, drug companies do endless research, but our dear ones still die. And we cry because we can't do anything about it.

How different with our Lord Jesus! For him death was not defeat. He didn't die because he couldn't live any longer but because he chose to. In fact, that's why he took on our flesh and blood and shared in our humanity. He came to carry our sin, collect its wage of death, and end a corpse on Calvary's cross. Futile, so it seemed to the outward eye that day. Satan seemed to have won again. Hell broke out the champagne for the victory celebration. But you and I know better. That's why I can go out to the cemeteries of life this Memorial Day week without dread.

Jesus, even as I remember loved ones this week, remind me of your victory over death. Amen.

THE NOBILITY
OF THE WARRIOR

Since the children have flesh and blood, he too shared in their humanity so that by his death he might destroy him who holds the power of death—that is, the devil—and free those who all their lives were held in slavery by their fear of death. Hebrews 2:14,15

Ever see the US military cemetery at Normandy, France? We walked up the beachhead assigned to our US Rangers in the invasion and could almost see the blood of our boys washing ashore. In that cemetery are rows of white crosses. So many noble youths cut down like flowers without a chance to bloom. Memorial Day is a time to remember the noble sacrifices behind our freedom.

The same with our loved ones—noble warriors one and all. That and more I would say about parents who gave me life and introduced me to eternal life. Who fought the battle against sin, death, and the devil, and taught me to do the same. Who labored in the Lord's vineyard in the heat of the day and encouraged me to join in. There could never be enough Memorial Days for me to remember what the gracious God has given me through them.

Again how different with our Lord Jesus! Was there ever a warrior like him? He could have God's justice pile ton after ton of sin upon him and remain standing. He could walk into Satan's hell, pick up the tab for those sins, and pay every penny of it. He could even slump in death on the cross and still be the winner. What a noble warrior—the one whom by God's grace I call my Savior!

Thanks, Lord, for those who died for my freedom but, above all, for the freedom you give. Amen.

THE FINALITY
OF THE OUTCOME

Since the children have flesh and blood, he too shared in their humanity so that by his death he might destroy him who holds the power of death—that is, the devil—and free those who all their lives were held in slavery by their fear of death. Hebrews 2:14,15

Will more than firecrackers start lighting up the sky over Red China? Will the Middle East export along with its oil also more of its terrorism? Will the hatred between Arabs and Israelis like expanding shock waves suck the rest of the world in? Who knows? This much we can say for certain. As long as the world stands, conflict will continue, people will battle, and someone will lose.

This much we can also say for certain. Generations come and go. As we lay beloved parents to rest, it hits us that now we belong to the older generation. Someday someone will lay us to rest and hopefully remember where our graves are and plant over us whatever modern cemeteries allow.

Above all, this much we can say with absolute certainty— Jesus *destroyed* death. He took the very thing Satan used to bully us and turned it against Satan. With his payment for every sin, Jesus has bolted hell's door shut and braced heaven's gate wide open. The battle has already been fought, once for all. The victory has already been won, in full. Like some chained dog, Satan now can only use death to bark at us, unless we stray too close to him or too far away from the Prince of Life. Jesus has already won the battle for us. With him beside us, Memorial Day is every day.

Thank you, Jesus, for taking the sting out of death and the victory away from the grave. Amen.

PROMISES! PROMISES! PROMISES!

As for me and my household, we will serve the LORD. Joshua 24:15

Remember the promises we made at our weddings? In this month when many marriages occur, we might do well to review those promises. More so, we might want to look at the promise behind successful and enduring marriages. How has it gone with our promise to serve the Lord?

Unless the Lord in his grace reminds us what he has done for us, we can't even begin to serve him. When sin bends our spirits in marriage, how can we turn to him for relief unless we know him to be the Lord who assures us, "Take heart, . . . your sins are forgiven" (Matthew 9:2)? When sorrow dampens our hearts in marriage, how can we turn to him for comfort unless we know him to be the Lord who says, "In all things [I] work for the good of those who love [me]" (Romans 8:28)? When success fogs our heads in marriage, how can we turn to him for humbling unless we know him to be the Lord who reminds us, "Apart from me you can do nothing" (John 15:5)? And when death ends our marriages, how can we turn to him for confidence unless we know him to be the Lord who promises, "Because I live, you also will live" (John 14:19)? Before we can serve the Lord in our marriages, we need to remember what he has done for us.

The secret to serving the Lord is to let him serve us. When his Word dwells in our homes richly, his pardon in Christ Jesus will cheer our hearts and empower our lives. Joyful service to him will follow. So will remembering and renewing the promises we made to each other on our wedding days.

Savior, we long to walk closer to you. Feed us with your Word so that we can. Amen.

DON'T EVER FORGET
HIS NAME

Therefore God exalted him to the highest place and gave him the name that is above every name, that at the name of Jesus every knee should bow. Philippians 2:9,10

You'd be surprised how many people can't name the four presidents carved into the mountainside at Mount Rushmore in South Dakota. Out of all the presidents, the artist picked these four because of what they had done for our country.

If I had but one name to remember, whose would it be? Paul reminds us. Clearly he says, "Jesus." In fact, he says that Jesus' name is above every name, even the names of those four presidents. Paul even states that every knee should bow to Jesus because of what he has done. What did Jesus do? With *therefore* Paul takes me back to eternity. He shows me God's own Son in love saying yes to the Father's rescue plan for a lost world. Then Paul takes me to Bethlehem to remind me how God's Son was wrapped in my flesh, weighed down with my sins, and sent down into hell's depths to carry out this plan. Because of that Son's work, I can be God's child and live with him forever. How low that eternal Son was willing to go that he might lift me high to his heaven.

The names of those four presidents—George Washington, Thomas Jefferson, Abraham Lincoln, Theodore Roosevelt— great men because of what they did for my country. I may forget their names but dare never forget Jesus' name. His name is above every name. He's my only Savior.

Lord, in your mercy, write my name next to the name of your Son in your book of life. Amen.

MY GIFT CERTIFICATE FROM GOD

Praise be to the God and Father of our Lord Jesus Christ, who has blessed us in the heavenly realms with every spiritual blessing in Christ. Ephesians 1:3

When I retired from synod headquarters, my colleagues gave me a gift certificate. The amount was generous, but I had to add to it to purchase the saw I wanted for my new hobby of woodworking.

What about the gift certificate God offers me? Notice the amount written on it. "Every spiritual blessing in Christ," it says. There's no limit. "Whatever," it says, whatever I need in the way of spiritual blessing. Does this mean that every one of my sins is forgiven? How I need to know! When day after day the fingerprints of sin smudge my life, does he forgive me? When the memory of some past sin that swept me off my feet rattles like some skeleton in the closet of my conscience, does he assure me? When I lay my head down on a pillow at night or on death's pillow, can it be with the peace that only comes from sins forgiven? Yes, that's what God's gift certificate states!

Notice who signed the certificate. It's Christ. He has written the red X of his cross on my gift certificate. At heaven's cash register he put down the amount necessary—his suffering and death—to pay for my spiritual blessings. My certificate from God is complete. I don't have to add to it. My certificate from God has no expiration date. The spiritual blessings it guarantees me last forever. But like that one I received from my colleagues, I need to cash it in.

Lord, give me the hand of faith to receive and use your heavenly gift certificate. Amen.

FULL-FLEDGED CITIZENS

At that time you were . . . foreigners to the
covenants of the promise. . . . But now . . . you
who once were far away have been brought near
through the blood of Christ. Ephesians 2:12,13

Standing in the great hall at Ellis Island in New York City, I
could almost hear the crowds of the past. What hopes drove
them to a new country? What longing for citizenship in a better land?

It wasn't that way with me when it came to entering God's
country. By nature I was a foreigner. The sinful heart I had
inherited from my parents made me a citizen of hell, inden-
tured me to a lifetime in sin's service. I had only a horrible end
awaiting me. And I didn't know any better. When my sins troubled me, I knew not where to turn. When death posed its questions, I had no answers. Emigration to God's kingdom wasn't
even on my mind, but then a gracious God stepped into my life.

When my forefathers came to this country, they needed a sponsor to guarantee financial support for them. The rule was, no
sponsor, no entry. My sponsor for citizenship in God's kingdom
is Christ Jesus. He gave his life, 33 years of perfectly keeping
all of God's laws for me. He gave his life, six hours of unimag-
inable torture on a cross for me. Because of the life he led and
the blood he shed, he is my guarantee to full citizenship in
heaven. This citizenship is mine the moment the Spirit works
faith in Christ in my heart. There's no waiting period, no questions to answer. Just full-fledged citizenship in the most wonderful country of all! And all because of Christ!

Lord, thank you for making me a citizen of
your heaven through faith in Jesus. Amen.

SAVED BY GOD'S GRACE

For it is by grace you have been saved,
through faith—and this not from yourselves, it
is the gift of God—not by works, so that no
one can boast. Ephesians 2:8,9

"How can I make my money grow?" is always a good question
to ask. "How do you get grass stains out of a boy's jeans?"
might bring a few good answers. But what about the question, "How do you get to heaven?" That's not only a good
question to ask but one for which there is only one answer.

Paul sums up that answer with the word *grace*. God's grace is
something completely undeserved, something I in no way
earn or have coming. It is God's free gift. Paul emphasizes
this by writing, "By grace you *have been saved*." It's not
something I do but something done for me by God. And just
so I can't miss it, he adds, "No one can boast." All praise
belongs to God for my salvation.

I cannot speak of God's grace without speaking of Christ.
Jesus is God's grace in person. When I see him bearing my
sins on the cross, I'm looking at God's grace. When I see him
keeping the commandments for me, I see God's grace. God's
gift of salvation is free to me, but it cost him mightily. His
Son's perfect life and innocent death were the price. There's
still more. My faith in the Savior is also a gift of his grace.
Through Word and sacrament his Holy Spirit changes my fist
of unbelief into the hand of faith. Through his gift of faith I
know the answer to life's most important question. I am
saved alone by God's grace in Christ Jesus.

Gracious Lord, humbly I thank you for your gift
of salvation. Help me treasure it always. Amen.

SAVED BY GOD'S GRACE FOR GOOD WORKS

> For it is by grace you have been saved. . . . For we are God's workmanship, created in Christ Jesus to do good works, which God prepared in advance for us to do. Ephesians 2:8,10

Jumping to conclusions is a favorite exercise for many. They hear part of a sentence, observe part of a situation, and rush to a conclusion. Often such jumping leads to falling flat on one's face.

Scripture stresses that we are saved by God's grace in Christ Jesus alone, but some object, "You mean you can do what you want, sin all you please, and you're still saved?" That's not what Paul says. Rather he describes the believer as "God's workmanship, created . . . to do good works." As a believer, I am a unique design of the God of all grace. He who put faith in the Savior into my heart expects me to show it in my daily life. He wants me to follow his Son's example in life, not as a cause for salvation but as a result of it. He wants me, like some child who has received a wonderful Christmas present, to throw my arms around his neck in appreciation for what I've received.

Which motivation is stronger? The "have to" that keeps me looking over my shoulder at someone driving me and that allows me to slack off when I think I can? Or the "want to" that comes from inside of me and keeps me going out of gratitude for what has been received? The answer is obvious. Christians don't do what they want or sin all they please. Gratitude for God's gift of salvation won't let them. Instead, they use their lives to hug the One who has given them heaven.

Lord, thank you for the gift of heaven. Help me use my life to thank you daily. Amen.

THE GREAT EXCHANGE

God made him who had no sin to be sin for us, so that in him we might become the righteousness of God. 2 Corinthians 5:21

"What will you give me in exchange?" is often the question. Getting something for nothing is a concept completely foreign to us. Yet that's what God has done for us in Christ.

He gave us his Son who had no sin. "Holy, blameless, pure" is how the author of Hebrews describes Jesus (7:26). Not once did an unholy thought surge into his mind, an unclean word slip from his lips, an unkind deed surface in his daily life. Never did he have to pray, "Create in me a pure heart, O God" (Psalm 51:10). Always he could stand before his Father as one who had no sin.

But we couldn't. If every sin ever committed in this world were a brick, I wonder how many Empire State Buildings we could erect. If some calculator could automatically make an entry for every sin in just one day of my life, I wonder how high the number would go. How do I even begin to get a glimpse of what Jesus carried for sinners like me when it says, "God made him . . . to be sin for us"?

What do we get in exchange? "The righteousness of God," Paul answers. Instead of sin, I have holiness. Instead of punishment, I have pardon. Instead of hell, I have heaven. This great exchange a loving God has prepared for the world by his Son's work. Thank God I know by faith it's mine.

Lord, thank you for charging my sins to Jesus and crediting his righteousness to me. Amen.

WHO WANTS TO BE A MILLIONAIRE?

I always thank God for you because of his grace given you in Christ Jesus. For in him you have been enriched in every way. 1 Corinthians 1:4,5

Months past, one of the more popular TV shows was entitled "Who Wants to be a Millionaire." Contestants came on the show hoping to win the grand prize of one million dollars. I can still remember the jumping and rejoicing when one contestant hit the jackpot.

I don't want to be a millionaire. I am one! My bank account is nothing to brag about. My dollar and cents value is slight compared to many others. But I am rich, thanks to God's grace. What else would you call someone who has the dollars of Christ's forgiveness to cover all his or her sin? who has the priceless pearl of peace with God through Jesus' blood? who carries in the portfolio of life God's grace to enrich him or her in every way. The gift of the Savior, of the gospel through which I learn of that Savior, of faith in that Savior—all this, Paul says, is due to the grace of God in Jesus Christ.

Why be an undiscerning child who picks the shiny objects when given a choice? I do need the copper pennies of this world for my daily life. And may God always give me a sufficient supply of them. But for heaven I need different currency. Only the priceless blood of God's Son will cover me. Only those who hold Jesus as their Savior in faith's bank account are rich enough to enter. God, make and keep me that kind of millionaire.

Lord, thank you for making me rich in Jesus. Please tighten my grip on heaven's treasures. Amen.

A MILLIONAIRE TO THE END

He [God] will keep you strong to the end, so that you will be blameless on the day of our Lord Jesus Christ. 1 Corinthians 1:8

Earthly riches are so slippery. Needs in life pry them loose from our hands. Falling stock markets reduce their value. Death transfers them to someone else. Almost they seem coated with 3-in-1 oil.

Spiritual millionaires can also lose the riches God has given them. Satan knows what scheme to use to filch the treasure of Christ's forgiveness from our hearts. The treasures, temptations, and trials of this world are capable crowbars in his devilish hands. With them he often succeeds in his breaking and entering attempts into a believer's heart. No wonder the Lord warns me that only those who endure in faith till the end will be saved.

The Lord also has a promise for me. "[I] will keep you strong to the end," he says. He will see to it that we can stand blameless when we step before his throne in heaven. That he would keep a weakling like me in faith till the end can only be credited to his grace. That he will keep Christ's robe of righteousness wrapped around me till my last day is entirely his free gift. He says he will keep me a millionaire in Christ till the end. And I can trust him to do just that because he is my faithful God. One more thing I can do—stay close to my Savior through Word and sacrament. Through these means the Spirit keeps faith's fingers wrapped around heaven's millions.

Lord, don't let me lose heaven's treasures. Strengthen my faith through your Spirit's work. Amen.

COMPLETELY CLEAN

But you were washed, you were sanctified,
you were justified in the name of the Lord
Jesus Christ and by the Spirit of our God.
1 Corinthians 6:11

"Wash this again," my wife said. Helping her with the dishes after a family meal, I had given the broiler pan only a "lick and a promise." Some of the grease from the meat was still sticking to it.

How much like the human heart. New stoves come with sparkling clean broiler pans that don't need washing. But not my heart at birth. It came out of the package of my parents already grimed with sin. That's called original sin because it comes from my origin. Add to that grime sin's daily buildup in my life, and the broiler pan of my life becomes something fit only for the garbage dump of hell. Even if I tried, I wouldn't have a scrubbing pad or dish detergent strong enough to wash it clean.

But God does and did. On Calvary Jesus' blood was strong enough to cut sin's grease and get rid of sin's grime. When God brings me to faith through the washing of Baptism or the working of his Word, he does his scrubbing in my heart. He applies Christ's cleanser directly to me. And not one spot of grime remains. Though I dirty the broiler pan of life with sin daily, I know where to go for washing. It's back to Jesus' blood. When God washes me with the Savior's forgiveness, I am completely clean.

Lord, thank you for cleansing me with Jesus'
blood. Wash me clean again and again. Amen.

BOUGHT AND PAID
FOR BY JESUS

You were bought at a price. 1 Corinthians 6:20

"Bought and paid for." How sweet those words can be. Maybe it was my first car, only a $3,000 clunker, but when I finally made the last payment, it was mine. And I took good care of it.

"Bought at a price," that's what Paul says Jesus has done for me. In the original, the word for "bought" indicates a one-time act. Of course, the apostle is referring to Calvary. That crucifixion scene was a purchase scene. There, once for all, Christ Jesus was the buyer, and what a price he paid! Drops of holy, precious blood; anguished depths of hell; a dark, damp grave were part of the price. But it was price enough, as Easter with its glorious resurrection proved. Christ had paid for all sin and every sinner. Christ has paid for me.

Christ, who bought me, claims me as his very own by bringing me to faith. Look what he does for me. I, who was born God's enemy, am reborn his child. I, who was shot through and through with sin, am a saint in his sight. I, who deserved hell's full punishment as my only future, now have a room reserved for me in heaven. "Bought and paid for by Christ," how sweet those words are!

> Jesus, keep me safe for heaven's highway. For your blood that bought me and for your love that keeps me, many thanks, O Savior. Amen.

THE WONDER OF SALVATION

You see, at just the right time, when we were still powerless, Christ died for the ungodly.
Romans 5:6

"Incredible, beautiful," were our words. The first sight of the Canadian Rockies left us open-mouthed in wonder. But the more we drove through them, the less we wondered, as the beautiful became almost commonplace. So quickly we take things for granted.

That cross on our church altar is there as a reminder of what Jesus has done for me. But it's so smooth and shiny—nothing at all like the crude wood on which the Savior was suspended between heaven and earth. It's so easy to hear "Jesus died to pay for my sins" and not to listen open-mouthed in wonder. Paul reminds me that I dare not. There is no more sublime truth, no greater wonder than that of Christ on the horrible cross, suffering hell's pangs for the ungodly.

Sometimes when I look at myself, I seem smooth and shiny also. I polish the brass buttons on my parade uniform of life and think I can march fitly before God. But that's not what Paul says. "Powerless," he calls me. Like some dead battery in winter's 40 below, I have no power to do or even to think of doing anything worthwhile toward winning heaven. "Ungodly," Paul also describes me. God turns up his nose at my best efforts because I am a sinner in his sight. The more I look at what I once was and at what I now am, the more I'll stand in wonder at what God has done for me.

Please, Lord, help me marvel each time I hear how the Savior died for me. Amen.

WAGE OR GIFT?

For the wages of sin is death, but the gift of
God is eternal life in Christ Jesus our Lord.
Romans 6:23

Wages we expect. When we hire on, an important question is,
What will I be paid? We also know something about gifts. Presents from loved ones or friends delight us. When it comes to
my salvation, which will it be—my wage or God's gift?

Heaven has a pay window. God is the paymaster. Sooner or
later everyone has to step up to that window and receive
what he or she has coming. Strange, though, no one is in a
hurry to draw the check each of us has earned. For on it in
bold letters is written "DEATH." In sin each of us is born.
In sin each of us lives. With all my sins I have to face the
eternal Judge. I don't want the wage, but I can't escape it.
Physical death on earth and eternal death in hell are what
I have coming.

But look at what God offers me instead. "Eternal life," Paul
calls it. God's gift to me is the exact opposite of what my sins
have earned. Instead of death, I receive life. Not just my brief
stay on earth but my forever life in heaven. How can he be
so kind? "In Christ Jesus our Lord," Paul states clearly. God's
free gift can come only through Jesus because he went to the
cross and collected man's wages for sin. On the cross he
received every penny of hell's punishment for the sins of the
world. On the cross he picked up my paycheck for sin so that
I could have God's gift of life.

Lord, by your grace, let it be your gift of life
when I step before heaven's window. Amen.

SAINT AND SINNER

What a wretched man I am! Who will rescue me from this body of death? Thanks be to God— through Jesus Christ our Lord! Romans 7:24,25

"I didn't mean to." How often don't we use these words? We know we shouldn't, we know it's wrong, but we slip into sinful thoughts, words, and actions anyway. How come?

As a Christian, I have two parts. I am a saint because Christ has forgiven my sins and made me God's believing child. I am clean and holy in his sight. But I am also a sinner, because I am still human. I have a sinful heart inside of me, live in a sinful world, and have a devil trying to trip me into sin. As a saint I try to lift up those around me in life; as a sinner I try to push them down. As a believer I try to tell them about Jesus; as a sinner I often turn them off. Every minute of every day, the battle rages between my two parts. And far too often the sinner wins out. Like Paul I cry out, "What a wretched man I am! Who will rescue me from this body of death?"

Thank God, like Paul I also know the answer. Pardon when I fail comes from Jesus Christ. His blood has already paid for my sins. From him also comes the power I need to walk more as his saint. As he builds my muscles of faith through use of his Word, I the saint can more often knock out me the sinner. "Have patience with me. God's not done with me yet," says a bumper sticker. How true! On this earth I need his ongoing help in my life as saint and sinner. In heaven I won't.

Lord, forgive me when my sinful flesh wins.
Strengthen me for my walk as your child. Amen.

MY DEFENSE ATTORNEY

> Who is he that condemns? Christ Jesus, who died—more than that, who was raised to life— is at the right hand of God and is also interceding for us. Romans 8:34

Law and order shows have long been popular on TV. People get caught up in the drama of courtroom scenes. If only they would be even more interested in the scene in our verse!

Paul takes us to heaven's courtroom. God, the judge, is on the bench. Each of us, the sinner, is on trial. Witnesses for the prosecution are the law, death, and Satan. First the law takes the stand. "He's guilty. He's done what I said he shouldn't and didn't do what I said he should. Here are the files, Judge, overflowing with infractions." Next comes death. "Judge, you know what the wage for sin is. You yourself have said the soul that sins should die." Satan hurries to his feet. "Judge," he says, "This sinner belongs in my hell. He's spent much of his life following and listening to me."

The case appears air tight. Hell can be seen opening its jail doors. But then my Defense Attorney approaches the bench. What an attorney he is! Paul describes him as Christ, who died, was raised to life, is at God's right hand, and intercedes for me. My Attorney has already died for me. He rose to show that he had paid enough for me. Now at God's right hand he's busy representing me. And always he's successful. "Case dismissed," the Father has to say when my Savior pleads for me. No earthly courtroom offers such drama. No verdict is more important than this.

> Lord, thank you for Jesus' payment for my sins and for your resulting acquittal of me. Amen.

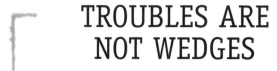

TROUBLES ARE
NOT WEDGES

Who shall separate us from the love of Christ?
Shall trouble or hardship . . . ? No, in all these
things we are more than conquerors through
him who loved us. Romans 8:35,37

"Don't let your troubles become wedges, splitting you loose
from God," says the pastor. "Rather view them as the
golden twine by which God ties you more tightly to himself." Good advice.

Is there anything that can make Christ stop loving me? anything that can cause him to turn away from me and leave me
standing alone? Sometimes I think so. When troubles hit,
first comes my anguished question, "Why me, Lord?" Behind
that question is the bigger one, questioning his love for me.
When trouble's waves keep washing over my boat in life, I can
even jump to the conclusion that his love for me has grown
cold. So quickly the problems in life can turn into wedges.

Paul answers his own question. "No," he states emphatically.
Troubles cannot separate us from the love of Christ. In fact,
because of Christ's amazing love "we are more than conquerors"
in the day of trouble. The Savior's love for me is no hit-or-miss
affair. It's never, "Now I love you; now I don't." It's constant in
all the scenes of life. His cross is the plus sign for my life. It's
the guarantee that his love that laid down his life for my salvation also will lead me in daily life. Like some Kevlar vest, his
love protects me. Though the bullets of trouble may bruise, they
cannot kill me. Because of Christ's great love, I can view the
problems of life as the golden twine by which he ties me closer.

Lord Jesus, keep my eyes on your cross so that
I am more sure of your love in my life. Amen.

GOD'S EPOXY

For I am convinced that neither death nor life
. . . nor anything else in all creation, will be
able to separate us from the love of God that is
in Christ Jesus. Romans 8:38,39

When the powerful glue *epoxy* first hit the market, a catchy
TV commercial helped sell it. It showed a 200-some-pound
football player suspended in his helmet, which was glued by
epoxy to a goalpost.

Epoxy is still going strong. But far stronger is the glue of
which Paul speaks. It's God love for me. His love is so powerful that nothing can ever rip me loose from it. Nothing in
life can do it, regardless how bad. Nothing the future can
bring, regardless how bleak. Not even death, regardless how
foreboding, can separate me from God's love. That love binds
me safely to him for all eternity.

I dare not miss how Paul describes God's powerful love. It's
"in Christ Jesus," he says. When I look at Jesus on the cross,
I see God's love in person. How he must love me to do this
for me! When I hear Jesus on that cross cry out in anguish,
"My God, why have you forsaken me?" I get a deeper insight
into God's love. It even caused him to turn his holy back on
a Son loaded with my sins so that I might stand forever at
his side. When I celebrate Jesus' resurrection, I am assured
that God's steadfast love will raise me. When I look at my
faith to believe all this, I again see his love, which has
worked such trust in my heart.

God, help me ever to turn to his love and trust
it to work in life and death for me. Amen.

JESUS—
LIFE'S RICHEST PRIZE

Then Peter said, "Silver or gold I do not have, but what I have I give you. In the name of Jesus Christ of Nazareth, walk." . . . He jumped to his feet and began to walk. Acts 3:6,8

It was 3:00 P.M., time for the Jews to go to the temple for prayer. Peter and John were among them. As they came to the gate, a pitiable beggar stretched out his hand for a coin. How could anyone refuse this man, who with his withered legs had never taken a step in his life? Imagine the lame man's disappointment when Peter said, "I don't have any silver or gold to give you." But then imagine the man's joy when Peter continued, "But I'll give you what I have. In Jesus' name, walk."

The man had reached for a coin and received a miracle. With the naked eye we can't even see the greatest part of the miracle. We can't see how that man's crippled heart was cleansed of sin and filled with faith. Jesus and his forgiveness, Jesus and his love, Jesus and all his name contains became the beggar's very own to have and to enjoy. No wonder he stayed close to Peter and John. He wasn't about to let loose the ones who had brought him to the Savior—life's richest prize.

When I hold my tin cup up to God, am I looking for the very best he has to offer? The items I need for daily life are only pocket change from God. The real money comes in the form of his forgiveness, peace, and eternal life. He drops such riches into my cup through his Word and sacraments. Through them he says to me again and again, "What I have, I give to you. And it's the best of all."

Lord Jesus, when I have you, I have life's richest prize. Help me remember this. Amen.

JESUS—
LIFE'S NEEDED POWER

The man's feet and ankles became strong. He jumped to his feet and began to walk. Then he went with them into the temple courts, walking and jumping, and praising God. Acts 3:7,8

"In the name of Jesus Christ of Nazareth, walk," Peter had commanded, pulling the lame man to his feet. Now those feet didn't collapse, but they carried him. They even could walk without a lick of training. No wonder he jumped, praising God in the temple. Jesus' power had healed him, body and soul.

Are there times when I need Jesus' power? Perhaps the question better phrased is, "Are there ever any times when I don't need Jesus' power?" Problems with the body, concerns for the family, the particular and peculiar sins that plague me—all these can cripple the feet of faith and lead even to paralysis. How I need his power every step of the way! Sometimes he sends his power in obvious ways, such as when problems are solved and situations cleared up. Other times that power comes in quieter, less recognizable forms, such as not taking my burdens away but strengthening faith's muscles to keep carrying them. Always the power of his love is there to assure me that my greatest burden is gone. My sins can't cripple me because Jesus has removed them.

A businessman had sent a cable to the Rolls-Royce Company to find out the exact horsepower of the engine in his car. From the company that never stated the horsepower of their engines came one word, "Adequate." "More than adequate," is the answer when I ask about Jesus' power.

Lord, thanks for your help in the past. Help me trust your power also in the future. Amen.

JESUS—
LIFE'S FULLEST PURPOSE

Then he went with them into the temple
courts, walking and jumping, and praising
God. Acts 3:8

The lame man when healed didn't make for the nearest exit.
It wasn't a thankful handshake with Peter and then a hurried
good-bye. Instead he went with Peter and John into the temple. He even stood by their sides the next day when the Jewish court investigated the incident. All this already shows a
reaction on his part, one that our verse sums up with the
words, "praising God." We'd like to ask the man, "How long
did you go on praising God in thankful faith?" But that
answer isn't given us. It's enough to know that this healed
man was using his life in thankful praise to God.

Late one night a pastor was called to the hospital. As he walked
down the semi-dark hall back to the intensive care unit, he
almost collided with a man hurrying out. The man took hold of
the pastor's arm and with obvious joy in his face said, "She's
going to make it. She's better, and she's going to make it." Then
the man hurried on. The pastor had never met the man before
and didn't know of whom he was speaking. But that man had
just received good news and had to share it.

Life's fullest purpose is to use it as that healed man did in
praising the Savior. One way I can do this is by sharing the
best news I have—that because of Jesus, people can make it.
They don't have to die but can live forever.

> Lord, as I go about life's daily business, use me
> to tell others about their Savior. Amen.

NO OTHER NAME

Salvation is found in no one else, for there is no other name under heaven given to men by which we must be saved. Acts 4:12

My son-in-law knows the names of the coaches in professional football. He can discuss at length the strengths and weaknesses of each one. But 20 years from now, so what?

How different with Jesus. As long as the world stands, people need to know his name. Even if they forget every other name, they dare not forget his. He is their only Savior. Only his death on the cross pays for all sin. Only his nail-pierced hands fully push open the door of heaven. Salvation can be found in no one else. By him we *must* be saved.

I shouldn't expect the world to be excited when it hears that only the name of Jesus brings salvation. Intellectuals in the classroom and in print, if they speak about salvation at all, seek answers in the supposed goodness of man. Modern Pharisees, inside and outside the church, still point to their own works. In spite of all the failures of past centuries, they still stick doggedly to their errors.

All human efforts are like trying to build a stairway to heaven without steps, when God has already let down a living ladder in his Son, Jesus. God be praised for this Jesus, so like an escalator on which I need simply to stand, holding on with the hand of faith, to be lifted up to everlasting life.

Lord, for me let it be Jesus, Jesus, only Jesus when it comes to my salvation. Amen.

A QUESTION THAT DEMANDS AN ANSWER

Believe in the Lord Jesus, and you will be saved. Acts 16:31

If a fire breaks out in our hotel, we had better know where the nearest exit is. But if someone asks, "Who will win the World Series next year?" we can live without knowing. Some questions demand an answer. But none more so than, "What must I do to be saved?"

A mighty earthquake had just rocked the prison where Paul and Silas were held captive. When the jailer, who hurried from his bed to the scene, saw that the earthquake had also freed his captives, he was aghast. Face-to-face with the divine power behind the earthquake, fearful of what was going to happen to him for losing his charges, he was ready to fall on his sword. "What must I do to be saved?" was his anguished question. And he didn't mean just from the mess he was in on earth but from the sins that condemned him before God's judgment seat.

In answer, Paul held up the cross of Jesus. "Believe in the Lord Jesus, and you will be saved," he assured the trembling sinner. Nothing more is necessary for salvation. That cross is red with Jesus' blood. To that cross he carried all our sins. On that cross he paid for all our sins. To that cross sinners must be directed if they are to be saved. "All our sins on him were laid, all our sins by him were paid," is the only answer to that most important question about salvation. If I know this answer, thank God, for he gave it to me. If I don't know, pray God, he'll show it to me.

Lord, for the Savior who paid for my sins and for the faith to trust in him, I thank you. Amen.

KNOWLEDGE WHEN YOU NEED IT

These are written that you may believe that
Jesus is the Christ, the Son of God, and that
by believing you may have life in his name.
John 20:31

We live in an information age. The modern world of technology places before us so many facts, so much data, that no one can absorb it all. Even if we could, how would we remember it? So today experts talk about "knowledge when you need it." Education's goal is not to teach us everything but to teach us how to find what we need when we need it.

Do I know where to find the most important information of all? Do I even know what that knowledge is? What can be more essential for me than to know that Jesus is the Christ, the Son of God? Of course, I need earthly knowledge. I need to live and make a living, perhaps even make a contribution to the society in which I live. But such life will come all too quickly to an end. Far more important is knowing how to live forever through Jesus. God sent his only Son to earth to pay for my sins, to die my death, to rise from my grave, so that I might stand before him as his living, redeemed child in heaven. That's the life that counts, and it comes only from Jesus.

Where can I find this important information? I surely need it. John reminds me, "These are written," he said. God packed the information about salvation through his Son into his Word so that it would always be there for me. In that Book I have all the knowledge I will ever need.

Lord, teach me to love your sacred Word and to
view my Savior there. Amen.

THE WORLD'S GREATEST BRIDGE

I am the way. . . . No one comes to the Father except through me. John 14:6

This past summer we drove across the mighty Mackinac Bridge, linking the upper and lower peninsulas of Michigan. What a bridge! It took four years, $100 million, and several lives to build this bridge that is five miles long with its approaches. In its construction, 42,000 miles of cable wire were used. It has to be one of the greatest bridges in the world.

But not *the* greatest. That distinction Jesus claims for himself. He spans a gap far wider than five miles, the gap between a holy God and sinful man. Ever since sin entered the world, this gulf has existed, yawning before sinners as something they could not bridge with their own efforts, even if they tried. Only God could be the bridge builder, for only he had the right expertise and material. More than $100 million and miles of cable wire were necessary to erect the bridge between earth and heaven. God used the blood of his own Son. Jesus had to die in order to finish the bridge to heaven.

Earthly bridges have a way of crumbling into the dust. Not this one. Jesus stands till the end of time as the one way to the Father. If you want to, you can charter a boat to ferry you across the Mackinac Straits, or you can drive hundreds of miles around on land. But there's no substitute for God's bridge to heaven. "No one comes to the Father except through me," Jesus said. If I'm to reach the shores of heaven, I must travel Jesus as the way.

Gracious Lord, show me the way to heaven. Keep me in faith in Jesus as the only way. Amen.

LOVE MADE HIM DO IT

But the world must learn that I love the Father
and that I do exactly what my Father has
commanded me. John 14:31

The verse before us is the only one I know of in which Jesus says, "I love the Father." Not until the night of his betrayal, when his dreadful march to the cross began, did Jesus use these words. Jesus always loved his Father, but the march to the cross particularly showed how great his love was.

Imagine the scene in heaven when God said to his Son, "Go and do this work for me. Man has rebelled against me and deserves only that I should destroy him. I love you, my Son, with a divine love as only an eternal Father can love his eternal Son. But I also love all people with an infinite love and cannot endure to see them perish. So, go, my Son, and pay for their sins. The task will not be easy. The burden of sin will not be light. It will even cost your lifeblood."

The Father had commanded. The Son in love obeyed. We know the rest of the story. The pain of the cross and the pangs of hell, the depth of the suffering and the darkness of the grave that Jesus endured in love for his Father. We know even more. We see Jesus raised from the grave by the Father. His resurrection was the Father's loud Easter "Amen" to his Son's Good Friday shout "It is finished." "Well done," his Father said. "Well done because of your love for me and for sinners." All this Jesus did, not just out of love for his Father but also for me.

Lord, help me marvel at the great love
that brought you down to the cross to save
me. Amen.

JESUS—THE WORD

He is dressed in a robe dipped in blood, and
his name is the Word of God. Revelation 19:13

We don't usually think of a word being a person, but it is a
sound in audible form that we use to convey a concept. Yet
doesn't this word fit Jesus? He is *the* Word, God's personal
message to us.

An old Greek proverb states, "A word is the image of the
soul." Just as I use words to show others what's in my heart,
so God showed his heart by sending his Son into this world.
Jesus came to earth to reveal his Father's thoughts to us. To
hear Jesus is to hear God. To look at Jesus is to look into
God's heart. That's why Jesus says in John 14:9, "Anyone who
has seen me has seen the Father."

What does Jesus, the Word, show me about his Father's
heart? Something that I really need to know. My Father's
heart overflows with love for me. Instead of flinging me
aside in my sins as I deserved, he sent his Son to earth to
tell me about his love. And he did not send Jesus only to
speak but also to act. Jesus dipped his robe of life into his
own blood on Calvary's cross. His suffering for my sins displays a Father's heart that would do anything to save me.
Jesus is God's love in capital letters.

I can't see the living Word in person today. But I can turn to
the written Word. In it I see Jesus, and in him, my Father's
heart of love.

Lord, teach me to love your sacred Word and to
view my Savior there. Amen.

JESUS—
FRIEND OF SINNERS

This man welcomes sinners and eats with them. Luke 15:2

It was meant to cut down, to criticize, to condemn—that name, Friend of sinners. But it fits. If ever there is a friend of sinners, it is Jesus. When he walked on earth, Jesus took time to seek out, talk with, reach for sinners. He even sat down at the dinner table with them.

He didn't just eat and drink with them. He died for them. Sin is sin in God's eyes. No sin is greater than another. Though some sins are more heinous in our eyes because of their consequences on others, each sin weighs the same on God's scale. And each sin deserves the same punishment. Sin cuts the sinner off from God, calls down his righteous anger, and condemns the sinner to an eternal hell. Jesus came to pay for all sins of every sinner. He came for those mildly dusted with sin, if ever there could be such a sinner. He came for those thickly coated with sin's dirt. And thank God, he also came for me!

"This is our spiritual hospital. It has room for every sinner," says a sign in the entry of one of our churches. "How appropriate," I thought. Regardless of my sins, Jesus is my Friend. When I push before him my wheelbarrow of life, loaded to overflowing with daily sins, he has the forgiveness I need waiting for me. As the hymn writer put it, "Plenteous grace with you is found, grace to cover all my sins." I want to sit down with such a friend every day.

Jesus, when I call you "Friend of sinners,"
it's with gratitude and praise for being my
Friend. Amen.

JESUS—SERVANT

For even the Son of Man did not come to be served, but to serve, and to give his life as a ransom for many. Mark 10:45

Of what do you think when you hear the word "servant"? In my mind flashes a movie scene, set in England of old. The banquet table is elaborately laid with nobility seated properly before it. Behind them hover obsequious servants, towels over their arms, ready to take care of their master's every whim.

When Jesus calls himself "servant", he has something far greater in mind. He came not to pour wine, serve the main course, and remove the dishes. He came to give his life as a ransom for many. Sin held everyone in bondage and demanded a ransom only God could give. No one or nothing else could cover sin's cost, collect death's wage, and cancel Satan's hold. God had to become man, hang on the cross, suffer hell's punishment, and in this way, ransom sinful mankind. He is *the* Servant.

He's still serving today. At the baptismal font he sent his Spirit to put the sign of his cross on my heart to show that he had redeemed me. Through his Word as I use it, he offers me the wholesome food of his forgiveness. At his Communion Table, he gives me his most precious body and blood with the bread and wine to assure me that his forgiveness is real and that my sins are gone. Never does he tire of serving me in these wonderful ways. Hopefully I'll never grow bored with his service. Jesus, my Servant, converts me into true nobility, a child in the family of the heavenly King.

Please, Lord, serve me all my days so that I can sit at your banquet table in heaven. Amen.

JESUS—WISDOM

You are in Christ Jesus, who has become for us wisdom from God—that is, our righteousness, holiness and redemption. 1 Corinthians 1:30

"I may not know much, but I know what I need to know," said an elderly widower. He hadn't finished high school. He hadn't made a name for himself in the world. He was one of those members who blended anonymously into the church bench. But he knew Jesus and in Jesus had the wisdom he needed.

I may fill my shelves with volumes, take course after course, earn professional degrees, and yet lack wisdom. I may be able to solve the world's hardest equations, conduct the most intensive research, deal with mankind's most complex issues, and yet not have the knowledge I really need. All such wisdom, as high as I can pile it, can be useful. But it cannot answer life's most important question, "How can I get to heaven?"

Beginning to understand why the apostle calls Jesus "wisdom from God"? Jesus is my "redemption." He bought me back from sin's bondage. He is my "righteousness." His payment for my sin and his perfect keeping of God's commandments enable me to stand unafraid before the heavenly judge. He is my "holiness." When God looks at me, he no longer sees a hated sinner but his dear child.

When God's grace leads me to Jesus, I'm truly wise. Then I know what I need to know.

Teach me, Lord, to know my Savior Jesus. Keep teaching me till I reach heaven's shores. Amen.

JESUS—THE BRIDEGROOM

The bride belongs to the bridegroom. John 3:29

Can there be a happier occasion than a wedding? The bridegroom, dressed in his best, waits at the altar for his beloved bride. The bride, in all her beauty, makes her way down the aisle to his arm. Together they stand rejoicing before the Lord.

What a picture of Jesus! Also what a difference. The heavenly Bridegroom dresses not himself but the bride. He went to great pains to prepare the wedding dress she wears. If we look closely, we see that it's a beautiful white—with red threads. If we look closely, we see that the hand with which he clasps his bride has wounds on it. This Bridegroom poured out his lifeblood in payment for his bride. He went to the cross to claim her as his very own. In his love he changed her from an unbeliever into a believer, from an ugly sinner into his beautiful bride. In his love he now waits at heaven's door to claim her for the life that never ends. How he loves his bride, unworthy as she is!

And the bride? When I try to grasp my Bridegroom's love, I'm like a child trying to grab hold of the whole world with two little arms. When I listen to his words of love for me, nothing else sounds so sweet. When I look forward to spending my life with him, nothing else is as important. When I anticipate being his totally and forever in heaven, my joy can only increase.

Lord, thank you that I can say, "I am yours and you are mine." Never let the wonder of your saving love cease to amaze me. Amen.

UNCHAINED

He brought them out of darkness and the
deepest gloom and broke away their chains.
Psalm 107:14

How huge each link looked. We were touring the harbor at
the Norfolk Naval Station in Virginia. As we strolled by a US
destroyer, I couldn't help but notice its heavy anchor chain.

Sin is like an anchor chain. Each sin is a heavy link in the
chain. One link is already enough to anchor me, not to some
watery bottom, but to a never-ending hell. Day after day I
keep sinning, adding new links to my chain. Often I don't
even feel the weight of my sins. I think I can walk upright
before God and fool myself into thinking that sin's links are
made of paper instead of heavy steel. Or I sink into despair
as sin's chain chafes the neck of my soul and wearies the
shoulders of my life. What am I ever going to do? What kind
of bolt cutter or acetylene torch can I use to cut through the
links and cast off sin's heavy chain? I need to know!

The psalmist answers. Jesus has already cut me clear from my
chains of sin. God sent him into this world to free me from
guilt's despair and hell's darkness. On the cross he said of
sin's payment, "It is finished," and the heavy chain of sin
with all its links sank to the bottom of the sea. From the
grave he rose to show that I'm free from death, the ultimate
punishment for sin. Unchained—that's what I am! Naval ves-
sels still have anchor chains. But my chain of sin is gone.

Thank you, Jesus, for freeing me from sin's
heavy weight and for heaven's glory. Amen.

WHAT IF GOD COUNTED?

If you, O LORD, kept a record of sins, O Lord, who could stand? But with you there is forgiveness; therefore you are feared.
Psalm 130:3,4

"Every time you grumble, I'll put a nickel of your allowance into this bowl," said his mother. In two days his week's allowance was gone, and Jimmy realized how often he complained.

What if God did something like this with my sins? What if each day he kept track one by one of my filthy thoughts, biting words, and unkind actions? What would I have left? More than losing a weekly allowance, I would be without a blessed eternity with him in heaven. Unfortunately, like Jimmy I often meander through life not realizing how often I sin each day. If I could see a bowl overflowing with my wrongs, I would have to cry out with the psalmist, "How can I stand before you, O Lord? I'm lost!" Where would he find a bowl big enough to hold all my sins?

But the psalmist goes on with words I need to hear. "With you there is forgiveness," he said. God sent his own Son to empty the bowl of my sins. Jesus took the whole mess to Calvary's cross, suffered hell's penalty for each one of them, and restored my allowance of eternal life. As a result, I can "fear" my gracious God, not shrinking back in abject fear from him, but giving him the praise he deserves for what his love has done for me. Thank God, he credits Jesus' payment to me instead of recording my sins against me.

Thank you, Lord, for wiping my record clean through Jesus' payment for all my sins. Amen.

WHAT HAPPENS
TO OUR SINS?

[You] hurl all our iniquities into the depths of
the sea. Micah 7:19

On the way home from church Timmy was unusually quiet.
"What are you thinking about?" his dad asked. "I was just
wondering," Tim answered, "when God forgives us, where do
our sins go?"

Good question. Haven't you ever asked it? At times we wonder about the sins of the past, especially those that like some
tornado swooped down on us and left us with wreckage. Every
so often the memories of them come back to haunt us. Does
God forgive—can God forgive that "special" sin? Or what
about those run-of-the-mill sins, those pet sins that are so
ingrained into the fabric of my life that I don't always recognize what they are? Does God forgive—can God forgive when
I come back again and again with the same old stuff?

"They're all gone," Micah tells me. "God has hurled them into
the depths of the sea." Jesus came to wrap all those sins into
one gigantic ball, load it on the barge of his love, and dump it
into the deepest part of the ocean. What a picture! God has
paid for my sins with the blood of his Son. He's put them
totally out of his sight as if they never happened.

Where do my sins go? Into the depths of the sea, where God
no longer sees them and where he places the sign "No fishing allowed," so that I leave them alone too.

> Lord, please remind me daily how you have
> totally removed my sins through Jesus'
> blood. Amen.

FREEDOM IS NOT FREE

If the Son sets you free, you will be free indeed. John 8:36

"Miss Liberty" she's called—that statue with fingernails as large as dinner plates and who's 151 feet tall from her sandals to her torch. But it's not her size that impresses, it's the message inscribed on her pedestal, "Give me your tired, your poor, your huddled masses yearning to be breathe free." The Statue of Liberty still stands in New York harbor, and we are still free. But our freedom was not without a price. Thousands gave their lives in four major conflicts in the 20th century alone so that Miss Liberty might stand tall and we can breathe free.

"The cross of Calvary" it's called, those timbers set up on that skull-shaped hill. The wood's long gone, but not the liberty secured there. On that cross God's Son secured a freedom far more precious than any other in the world. That cross speaks of freedom from sin's curse and Satan's slavery. No more accusing pangs of a guilt-pierced conscience. No more frantic scrambling to secure salvation with our own futile works. No more chilling fear of death's cold chamber. The Son has set us free.

This freedom also had a price. Nearly 2,000 years ago, the God-man hung on that cross enduring the worst that both earth and hell could dispense. But he secured liberty in full with his complete payment for all sinners of all time. Now he offers that precious liberty to me without price. It's mine free of cost. I'm free to live for God and with God, on earth and in eternity.

Blessed Savior, help me appreciate the precious liberty you've earned for me. Amen.

ALWAYS REJOICING?

Restore to me the joy of your salvation.
Psalm 51:12

Remember the "smiley" symbol? That round, yellow face with two dots for eyes and a mouth always curved upward in a smile? People stuck them on notes and wore them on lapels to encourage others to be happy. But it doesn't work that way. People were still unhappy and grumpy.

Only one kind of person can live happily all the time. That's the believer in Christ. No, a Christian's life is not always filled with sunshine. He or she doesn't always walk on a super smooth highway. In fact, often believers have more problems than unbelievers. In his wisdom, God knows that all sunshine and no rain is not conducive for growing the flower of faith.

So how can believers rejoice all the time? How can they smile in the midst of tears and be happy even when they hurt? Doesn't the psalmist remind me? He points me to God's salvation. When I have complete relief from life's greatest hurt in the form of forgiveness for my sins, I have a joy that no outward circumstances can strip from me. When I have the Savior, as the pearl of great price, I am ecstatically rich even if my earthly treasures slip away. When I have heaven as my destination, I can keep on smiling even though the potholes of life jar my very existence. I don't need a "smiley" symbol pasted on me. By God's grace I have Jesus as my Savior and in him a never-failing source of joy.

Lord, restore to me the joy of your salvation so that each day I rejoice in Jesus. Amen.

SLEEP WELL

I will lie down and sleep in peace, for
you alone, O Lord, make me dwell in safety.
Psalm 4:8

"Sleep well," my mother would say as we went up the stairs
at bedtime. Sometimes she would also add humorously, "Don't
let the bedbugs bite." The psalmist says the same, though he
leaves the bedbugs out.

Sometimes sleep doesn't come easily. Life's problems clutter
my mind and keep sleep at bay. Life's worries weigh heavily
and don't punch the time clock when my head hits the pillow at night. Often only little things, yet they loom like
giants before me. And what about my sins of the day? How
can I pretend they didn't happen? How can I go to sleep as
if they were of no account? If I am at all concerned about
standing before God in heaven, I have plenty to keep me
awake in dread.

Want to sleep well? There is a way. It's bound with the grace
of God. He not only promises to send his angels to watch
over me throughout the night. He assures me that he has
made me his own for all eternity. Through his Son's payment for sin and his Spirit's gift of faith, he has made me
his dear child. He says to me, "Sleep well," and makes it
possible. As his redeemed, restored, forgiven child, I can lie
down and sleep in peace because he alone makes me dwell
in safety. And that safety covers me every night, including
my final night.

Lord, for your peace through Jesus, I thank
you. Help me sleep well because of it. Amen.

SOMETHING TO SING ABOUT

Sing to the Lord a new song, for he has done marvelous things; his right hand and his holy arm have worked salvation for him. Psalm 98:1

"I learned a new song in Sunday school," said little Laura.

"Sing it for me," encouraged Grandpa.

And she did. With joy she sang, "I'm as happy as can be. Jesus takes good care of me."

Nothing can beat the enthusiasm with which a child sings. How sweet the praise from a child's heart must sound in Jesus' ears! And nothing can top the reason why Laura was singing. It was because of Jesus. "Jesus loves me," she had been taught. The love of her Savior was real to her. It brought her peace and forgiveness, something a child's heart also can appreciate. And Jesus' love assured her that he would take care of her.

What I need is a heart like that little girl's—a childlike heart. Sometimes I forget what Jesus has already done for me. I subconsciously rub away at my sins as if I had to eliminate their spots. I worriedly peer ahead at heaven's door as if I had to pry it open with my own deeds. Instead of singing, I mope around. I need a reminder of the marvelous things my gracious God has already done for me—how his right hand and holy arm have worked salvation for me in his Son, Jesus. A new song—that's what I need and that's what will come when I kneel beneath the cross of my Savior. Then also I'll be able to sing in life's other areas. He who has taken care of my sins will take care of me.

Lord, teach me to sing with joy because of your salvation. Amen.

FROM NOBODY TO SOMEBODY

Once you were not a people, but now you are the people of God; once you had not received mercy, but now you have received mercy. 1 Peter 2:10

The Sunday newspaper highlighted it as a success story. Once on drugs and a high school truant, the man had gone on to college to become a scientist for the National Aeronautics and Space Administration in Houston. Because of a caring teacher, he went from a nobody to a somebody.

The success story of the believer is far more striking. Sinners don't belong to God and have nothing to do with his family. In fact, as a sinner I was an enemy of God. I was high on the drug of sin, a truant who could only rebel against the Lord. Rather than wrap his arms around me, God as a holy judge could only raise his fist in punishment at me. And there was nothing I could do to change the scenario. As one of Satan's slaves because of my sin, I was doomed to an eternal hell.

Then God's mercy entered the picture. "Mercy" reveals God's heart feeling for me in my need and his arms rolling up divine sleeves to meet my need. Mercy shows my caring Father sending his own Son, Jesus, to rescue me. Mercy led his Son to a horrible cross, a hideous penalty, a heavenly cure. It paid for my sin with Jesus' blood. It opened my unbelieving heart by the sanctifying work of the Spirit. God's mercy in Christ Jesus has changed me from a nobody to a somebody, a person he has included in his beautiful label *"My* people."

Lord, thank you for your rich mercy in Christ Jesus that really made me something. Amen.

HIS BRAND'S ON ME

I have redeemed you; I have summoned you by name; you are mine. Isaiah 43:1

On the wall of the western museum was a collection of branding irons. Each rancher had his distinctive brand to mark cattle as his very own. "They belong to me," each brand said clearly.

The Lord has a distinctive brand too for those who belong to him. When he says "I have redeemed you," he's pointing to the cross of Jesus. I was a maverick who didn't belong to God. With sins' strands, Satan had me tied hand and foot. When the time for the eternal roundup came, the devil would want to lock me forever inside his corral of hell. But the God of all mercy stepped in. He sent his Son to buy sinners back from Satan. Not so and so many dollars per head but the precious blood of his only Son was the ransom paid. And this price was sufficient for all sinners of all times.

When God says "I have summoned you by name," he speaks of even more grace. Not only did he pay for me with his Son's blood, he also brings me into his herd. Through Baptism he brands me, putting the sign of his Son's cross on my heart. Through his Word and Holy Communion he works to refresh that cross by strengthening my faith. My God is a rancher who is able to keep me and all whom he has made his own through faith safe for the glorious roundup on the Last Day.

"You are mine," the God of all grace says. That's why I can say with joy, "His brand's on me."

Lord, thank you for making me your own through faith in Jesus. Keep your brand on me. Amen.

HE CARRIED THE LOAD

We all, like sheep, have gone astray, each of us has turned to his own way; and the LORD has laid on him the iniquity of us all. Isaiah 53:6

"Here, Dad, let me carry it for you," said my strapping six-foot-three son. I had come home with the back end of the car loaded down with lumber for a project. As I scratched my head wondering how to get it unloaded, my son stepped in.

What a load I piled up for God's Son to carry! When Isaiah writes "Each of us has turned to his own way," he's not being complimentary. Those words are chilled with judgment. My way was not God's way. It was not the road leading to, but away from, him. Like some stupid sheep, I drifted off, sometimes negligently, often willingly, to paths overgrown with sin's briar bushes. Foolishly I didn't even stop to think of what I was doing and what punishment I was earning. In self-deception I kept right on, meandering down my own sinful way, as if life had no end and sin no reckoning.

But then God sent his Son to carry the load for me. Not six-foot-three but all powerful and all loving, Jesus said, "Move over and let me take your place." His shoulders were broad enough to carry sin's weight. His blood was precious enough to pay sin's penalty. His resurrection was proof enough my guilt was gone. No more scratching of my head in despair when I look at the heavy timber of my sins. Jesus has unloaded them forever.

Lord, thank you that I, a wandering sheep, can say, "The Savior died for me." Amen.

JESUS' GIFT OF HEALTH

Praise the LORD, . . . who forgives all your sins
and heals all your diseases. Psalm 103:3

Dr. Gordon Alles was a chemist who helped develop insulin as
a treatment for diabetes. Today many still benefit from his
research. Did you know, though, that Dr. Alles himself died
of diabetes in 1963? He didn't even know he was sick.

There is no greater spiritual illness than sin. But many do not
know they have it. The Pharisee thanked God that he wasn't
like other people—robbers, evildoers, adulterers (Luke 18:11).
He was mortally sick with sinful pride and didn't even recognize the symptoms. The rich young ruler thought he was good
enough to merit heaven but couldn't think of parting with his
possessions (Luke 18:18). He had influenza brought on by the
sin of loving goods more than God. And my disease? Do I know
how sick I am? How terminally ill with the sickness of sin?
Unless I do, I'll feel little need for the healing a gracious God
provides in Jesus.

What a caring physician the Lord is! He doesn't just diagnose
my sins, using the X rays and MRIs of his law to tell me how
sick I am. Instead, he wrote out and filled the prescription
for my healing. He sent his Son for sinners like me. Because
Jesus died for my sins, he took them with him into the grave
and left them there. He is the medicine my dying soul must
have. And, unless they refuse him, this divine physician
never loses a patient.

Lord, every day remind me of my sins so that I
reach for the healing of your forgiveness. Amen.

NOT ONE CENT

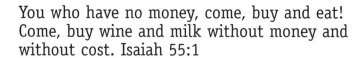

You who have no money, come, buy and eat!
Come, buy wine and milk without money and
without cost. Isaiah 55:1

"Free this week—a jar of mayonnaise," said the grocery ad in
the newspaper. At the bottom in fine print were the words
"with a $20 purchase." What appeared to be free really wasn't.

When the Lord invites me, "Come, buy wine and milk without money and without cost," there's no fine print in his
offer. He really means it. And he's not talking about groceries
for my body. He's referring to the milk of his grace and the
wine of his love. He's offering the forgiveness for sin that my
hungry soul needs. I have no money with which to purchase
pardon from a holy God. I don't have even one cent in my
pocket with which to walk into his heavenly supermarket.
Left to myself my soul would limp through life horribly hungry and end up emaciated in hell.

Does this mean no money—no forgiveness for me? That's not
what the Lord said. When he says "without cost," he means for
me, not for him. My forgiveness cost God plenty. He paid not
with a check with six or seven digits on it but with the precious blood of Jesus for the food my soul needs. Now he offers
pardon and peace free to sinners like me. Never do the shelves
in his heavenly grocery run out of stock. But I need to know
the address of his store. It's called "God's Word," the only supermarket where hungry sinners can find his free food.

Lord, feed me with the free forgiveness bought
by Jesus' blood and offered in your Word. Amen.

REPELLENT FOR SIN

I have hidden your word in my heart that I might not sin against you. Psalm 119:11

"Where's the mosquito repellent?" I asked my wife as I hurried into the house. I had been working in the bushes out in the yard, and the mosquitoes had almost carried me away.

Sin is far worse than a mosquito bite. Its poison makes my soul itch for more than a little while. When sin stings me, the results can last forever. I walk through life, if I am a thinking person, scratching away at sin's horrible itch on my soul, and I dread the end of life because with it comes the never-ending torments of hell.

My wife pulled the "no itch" stick off the shelf, and its ointment soothed the bites a bit. But not completely. The red blotches were still there the next day. How different with the "no itch" stick that God offers. Jesus' payment for sin does more than just alleviate the bite. It takes it away completely. His blood doesn't just soothe the blotches. It removes them as if they were never there.

Then my wife handed me the repellent. Covered by it, I could go back to my work. So also with God's Word. When I spray a liberal amount of God's Word on my soul, sin can't bite quite as much. I do, however, need to apply God's Word regularly if I want protection. That's why the psalmist wrote, "I have hidden your word in my heart that I might not sin against you."

Lord, cover me with Jesus' pardon when sin bites and with his power when sin buzzes near. Amen.

A HOME THAT IS PERMANENT

Now we know that if the earthly tent we live in is destroyed, we have a building from God, an eternal house in heaven, not built by human hands. 2 Corinthians 5:1

When our children were young, we toured many of the national parks. We could set our six-person tent up at night and take it down in the morning, hopefully not in the rain. But we were always glad to get back home to our permanent house with its hot showers and comfortable beds.

The apostle compares our existence in this world to tenting. The world in which we live won't be here forever. Neither will the bodies in which we walk through it. Far too many people value their earthly existences as permanent. They dig a basement, pour concrete walls, erect as beautiful a structure as possible as if they were going to be here forever. When the time comes, as it always does, for the tent stakes of this life to be pulled up, they turn frantic. What they thought permanent was only temporary. And they have no home to go to but hell.

Waiting for me is an eternal house in heaven. God himself has built it, and that truth makes it certain. So does the material he used in the building. The blood of his beloved Son, his perfect payment for all my sins, and his complete keeping of all God's commandments are the concrete and lumber for my eternal home. That house will stand forever. In it I will find joys beyond measure and pleasures forevermore. How good it will feel when I am finally home!

Lord, raise my eyes to your permanent heaven and keep me in faith on the way home. Amen.

GOD'S OWN DYNAMITE

It is the power of God for the salvation of everyone who believes. Romans 1:16

Remember the name Alfred Nobel? He's the man after whom the Nobel Peace Prize is named. Years ago this Swedish inventor discovered dynamite. But he didn't know what to call it. So Nobel used the Greek word for power and named this powerful explosive dynamite.

The apostle used the same word for the gospel. *Gospel* means "good news." In fact, it is the "best news." What can be better news than John 3:16 "God so loved the world that he gave his one and only Son, that whoever believes in him shall not perish but have eternal life"? God's gospel takes me back to eternity to show me a love that planned my rescue even before man was made. God's gospel takes me down to Bethlehem, up to Calvary, and out to the Easter tomb to show me a love that went the ultimate distance for me. God's gospel takes me up to heaven to show me a love that has an eternal home waiting for me. Good news—indeed, the best news I can ever hear.

Not only does the gospel tell me this good news. The gospel also is God's power to bring me to faith. The gospel is both God's message and God's means. My gracious God uses it like some stick of dynamite to blast open my stony heart of unbelief, convert that heart into a home for my Savior, and keep my heart in faith in his Son as my only Savior. Alfred Nobel gave the world the explosive power of dynamite. The Lord gave me, the sinner, something far more powerful in his gospel.

Lord, help me treasure and use the power of your gospel as your message and means. Amen.

CHRIST'S CROSS = GOD'S LOVE = MY SALVATION

May I never boast except in the cross of our
Lord Jesus Christ. Galatians 6:14.

Ever notice how often the Bible connects God's love with the
cross? John 3:16 speaks of a God who so loved that he gave
his one and only Son, a giving that led to the cross. Another
well-known 3:16 says it too, "This is how we know what love
is: Jesus Christ laid down his life for us" (1 John).

What kind of love is this? A love that seeks to repay family
or gain favor from friends I can understand. But a love that
gives the ultimate for enemies, a love that repays hatred and
hostility with pardon and peace, how can I describe it? What
can I do but marvel at it?

Why did God connect his love with Christ's cross? The Bible
answers that important question too. It was for my salvation.
Salvation is what I need as a lost sinner. Salvation is what God
came to earth to bring me. For my salvation he was crucified,
died, and was buried. With his precious blood and innocent
death he paid for all sins, from the first one in Eden's Garden
to the last one in the last second when the world ends. "Finished," the cross says of sin's payment. "Open," it says of
heaven's door. "Built," it says of the highway to heaven, laid
and paved with his atoning blood. All this Jesus has done for
me with the cross on which his Father's love held him.

Christ's cross = God's love = my salvation. So simple and so
awesome! So worthy of my praise!

Lord, keep your cross my trust and joy till
in heaven I can praise you fully for your
love. Amen.

DON'T PUT GOD OFF

I tell you, now is the time of God's favor, now is the day of salvation. 2 Corinthians 6:2

"Special Sale This Wednesday, 8:00 A.M.–11:00 A.M." said the department store ad. It even offered an additional 15 percent discount for seniors. I needed a present for my wife but didn't roll into the parking lot till 11:30 A.M. Guess what? The sale was over, and I missed out.

How patient God is! He gives me life as the time in which to take advantage of the bargain of his forgiveness and salvation. He doesn't just discount what he has to offer; he offers it free. He wants me to know my sins are washed away by Jesus' blood. He wants me to enjoy the peace that comes from being his child because of Jesus. He wants me to look forward to heaven's shores where I can see Jesus. Every day that I open my eyes is a time of his favor—his grace—another day he grants me so that I might seek his salvation.

But God's patience has a limit. How many more days does he have for me? How much more time for me to learn of my Savior? He who gives life also measures life. When he says that it's time, my life will end and with it my opportunity to seek his salvation. If I've dallied along or not even left the garage of life, I'll miss out on the best bargain in the world. I'll have to face eternity without the Savior Jesus and with no one to blame but myself.

> Lord, don't leave me to myself or else I will only waste the opportunity you have given me. Open my heart to the news of your Savior. Give me the hand of faith to hold him as my treasure. Amen.

WHAT TO DO WITH SIN

If we confess our sins, he is faithful and just and will forgive us our sins and purify us from all unrighteousness. 1 John 1:9

That's the number one question, isn't it? What to do with my sin? Should I, like so many others, ignore them, pretending that they don't count? Should I, like the modernist, excuse them by pointing to surroundings and social customs? Should I, like the Pharisee, think that everybody's sins are greater than mine? Or should I confess them? To confess sin means to admit it, to see sin as God sees it, to face sin's enormity squarely, and feel its guilt deeply. It means to beg before my heavenly Father, "God be merciful to me, a sinner."

When I confess my sins, I can be sure of cleansing through Jesus' blood. That blood does more than brush off sin's outward stain; it washes out that stain completely. That blood comes from the veins of him who is not only man but God from all eternity—the faithful God who promised forgiveness. At Calvary's cross I see how faithful he is to his promises. That God, who cleanses from all unrighteousness, is also just. At Calvary's cross I see that he didn't merely sweep sin under some carpet but demanded full payment from his Son as my substitute. Jesus' suffering and death is the only answer for my sins.

What to do with sin? It's important to ask that question. It's more important to know the answer.

Lord, thank you for showing me Jesus as the answer for my sins. Amen.

GOD'S TRAFFIC SIGN

Your word is a lamp to my feet and a light for my path. Psalm 119:105

Some years ago our country adapted standardized traffic signs. Now wherever we travel, we find the same signs directing our way. We even have to learn them to pass the driver's test.

In his Word, God has given me traffic signs for his highway to heaven. The on-ramp sign is clearly marked and safely carries me to heaven's freeway. That on-ramp sign, just like the free-way, has two initials on it—JC for interstate Jesus Christ. And it truly is a free way. There are no tollbooths. Every square inch of heaven's highway has been paid for by Jesus' death. There are no stop signs, no detour markers, just one straight road leading to the Father's house above. If I get lost, it's not the roadway's fault. It's because I thought I knew better and turned off to some secondary road that was only a dead end.

God has also given traffic signs in his Word for my travel on this earth. The lane-ending sign means watch out. If I keep on driving down the lane of sin, I'll end up in the ditch. The speed-reduction sign warns me not to press on in my sins because there is danger ahead. The flashing sign means a dangerous intersection is ahead when I allow what I want to cross what God wants. If I ignore these signs, it's at my own peril. Or should I say, at eternal danger for my soul? Like those traffic signs I once memorized, I need God's Word with its signs for my road in life and my travel to heaven.

Lord, let me learn your Word so that I have safe travel. Amen.

THE FATHER'S WAITING

While he was still a long way off, his father **saw him** and was filled with compassion for him; he ran to his son, threw his arms around him and kissed him. Luke 15:20

For so long the father had been waiting for his son's return. Day after day he scanned the horizon, yearning for that familiar figure to come down the road. And then one day it came true. None but a loving father's eye could have recognized in that scruffy wreck the son who had left home so confidently earlier. The father ran as fast as his legs could carry him to embrace his son. When the son began to stammer about his sins, the father cut his confession short. He saw the change of heart in his son's eyes. Best of all, the father received his son back, not as a servant but as a son in full standing. The best suit of clothes, the finest shoes, the signet ring were given him as sign of that sonship. A sumptuous banquet was prepared with the son as the guest of honor. All because the son who was as good as dead to the father was now alive and safely back home.

The parable of the prodigal son is really a story about the waiting father. I know who the prodigal is. It is I who so foolishly and so often have left the Father's house. What I need to know is about the heavenly Father. Does he write me out of his will or long for my return home? Will he slam the door of heaven in my face or open his arms to me? Will he treat me like some slave or take me back as a son or daughter? Here's the answer! Because of another Son, named Jesus, who left his Father's house on the task of salvation and returned with it completed, my Father will be waiting for me.

Father, thank you for still waiting for me **although I often** wander from home. Amen.

NO STRING
ON GOD'S FINGER

I will forgive their wickedness and will
remember their sins no more. Jeremiah 31:34

"Should I tie a string on your finger?" my mother teased my
dad. On his way to the mill with a load of feed to be ground
for the cattle, my mother wanted him to stop at the store for
some sewing supplies. From past experience, she didn't quite
trust him to remember.

God has no trouble remembering my sins. He sees and knows
them all. Even the ones I'm not aware of as I bumble through
the day. Even the ones I try to hide from other people's eyes
as my sinful heart does its churning. Not a single one of my
sins escapes him. Every one of them earns his punishment
that comes in the form of his displeasure on earth and eternal death in hell.

So how come there aren't any strings on God's fingers when it
comes to my sins? How come he says he remembers them no
more? It can't be that they slip out of his mind or slowly fade
from his remembrance. The answer is far more blessed than
that. It's because he forgives my wickedness. In his love, God
sent his beloved Son to take care of my sins. His Son took each
one of my sins to the cross of pain and the suffering of hell to
pay for them. Now the Father remembers them no more. His justice has been satisfied by his Son's payment. His Son's holiness
counts for me. Gone from my loving Father's fingers is the
remembrance of my sins, untied by my Savior Jesus.

Lord, turn me in humble repentance for my
many sins to the cross of your Son. Let me
see his love removing my sins from your
remembrance. Amen.

WHAT'S MY ANSWER?

"But what about you?" he [Jesus] asked. "Who do you say I am?" Peter answered, "You are the Christ." Mark 8:29

It's not that people don't know about Jesus. Rather, they don't really know who he is. Just as when the Savior walked on earth, so many give wrong answers to his question, "Who do you say I am?"

"You're my supply sergeant," some answer. "You're the one whom I ask when I need this or that in life." Unfortunately many popular preachers reinforce this error with their shallow teaching. Is that all Jesus means to me? Just some "genie in a bottle" who answers when I call? What about the Jesus who warns me not to gain the world and lose my own soul? who talks about taking up his cross and losing my life to save it?

"You're my example," others answer. "You show me how to live so that I can have a positive life. You give me the inner zest and self-esteem I need to be successful." Again, far too many religions put the trump on this error. Is that all Jesus means to me? Someone whose philosophy I can fit into my life instead of fitting my life into his? Someone who helps me go where I want to go?

Jesus still asks his question. He still waits for my reply. Who do I say he is?

> God, help me answer with Peter, "You are the Christ. You are God himself come into the flesh. Your blood paid for sin and your resurrection guarantees heaven. You are my Savior." Amen.

THE SAVIOR'S TREASURE HUNT

And when she finds it, she calls her friends and neighbors together and says, "Rejoice with me; I have found my lost coin." Luke 15:9

In the past each president took the china bought for his table along when leaving office. Collecting pieces from each president's set for a China Room display in the White House was no easy task. Some of the china had been lost; some sold to collectors. Only with great effort was the collection completed.

The woman in our parable shows similar diligence. She's not rich. She has only ten pieces of silver, each worth about a day's wage at that time. One day in her house she drops one of them. Quickly she lights a lamp and looks over the floor. Then she gets down on her knees and runs her fingers over every crack till she finds her coin. At that moment her spirits soar, and she hastens to tell her neighbors.

What a faint picture of how diligently Jesus searches for souls. His love propels him on the greatest treasure hunt this world has ever seen. This hunt reached its height on Calvary's wondrous cross. So precious did Jesus consider each sinner that he was willing to pay the maximum price for each one—his own blood! Now his love sends him out every day to search for lost sinners through his Word.

Presidential china and lost coins can be replaced. Not so with my immortal soul. How can I ever thank Jesus for the diligent love with which he "found me—wondrous thought!—Found me when I sought him not" (CW 385:2)?

Thank you, Jesus, and please keep me safe in your hand. Amen.

ALL YOU HAVE TO DO

For God so loved the world that he gave his one
and only Son, that whoever believes in him
shall not perish but have eternal life. John 3:16

When the Betty Crocker Company first came out with cake
mixes, all the cook had to do was add water. But the mixes
didn't sell well. Market research revealed that people wanted
to be involved in producing the cake. So the company
changed the recipe and required the customer to add an egg
to the mix too. Then the product took off like wildfire.

Satan's most effective weapon is whispering in the sinner's
ear, "You need to do something for your salvation." "It's too
easy," Satan says when the sinner hears that all he has to do
is believe in God's Son as his Savior. And sinners concur. They
want to produce the whole cake of salvation from scratch,
using the ingredients of their own works. Or they want at
least to add an egg or two of their own efforts to the mix.
Salvation that requires no work whatsoever on their part just
doesn't appeal. Of course, Satan forgets to mention that the
cake of salvation the sinner tries to bake can only turn out
to be a flop, one that will give stomachaches when sins trouble and when death draws near.

There is something sinners need to do. "Believe," God said.
"Trust my one and only Son as your Savior. Look to his cross
and see salvation complete. Look at his empty tomb and see
sin forgiven. Throw yourself completely on Jesus' blood and
righteousness and eternal life is yours." All I have to do is
believe. And even my faith is a gift of God's grace.

Lord, for the gift of faith in Jesus, I thank you.
For its continuance, I trust you. Amen.

GOD'S SPIRIT
DOES THE IMPOSSIBLE

No one can say, "Jesus is Lord, " except by the Holy Spirit. 1 Corinthians 12:3

"Don't ask him to do what he can't," my wife said. Our little boy was crying loudly, his feelings deeply hurt. "Stop that this instant," I demanded, only to have his sobs increase. Then my wife picked him up in her arms and soothed his tears.

When God tells me to believe in Jesus as my Savior, he's asking the impossible of me. How can I give myself a heart transplant, exchanging one that's dead in unbelief with one that beats in faith? How can I effect the about-face from being an enemy of God to one who loves him? How can I pry open the clenched fist of unbelief so that it becomes the hand of faith into which God can pour all the blessings of Christ's salvation? I can't! That's spiritually impossible for me!

Only God can. That's the special work of his Holy Spirit. He uses the Word not only to tell me about Jesus but to create faith in me. With the powerful jackhammer of the gospel, the Spirit pulverizes my rocky heart. With the loving power of Baptism, he plants faith in my heart. With the continued touch of the gospel, he causes that faith to grow. Leave the Spirit out of the picture, and I'm back where I started, sobbing in unbelief. Add him to the picture through regular use of Word and sacrament, and he keeps doing the impossible for me. "I believe in Jesus as my only Savior," I can say. But only because the Spirit works that faith in me.

Lord, thank you for the gift of faith.
Strengthen my faith through regular use
of your Word. Amen.

HOW'S IT GOING TO END?

Just as man is destined to die once, and after that to face judgment, so Christ was sacrificed once to take away the sins of many people.
Hebrews 9:27,28

Halfway through a good book, I wonder, "How's it going to end?" Sometimes I even flip to the last chapter to find out ahead of time. But what about my life? What's the last chapter like?

One thing I know—I'm destined to die. Death is a sure event I cannot avoid. And death is serious because judgment follows. At death's moment, God's verdict is pronounced. My soul goes either to heaven or to hell, to be followed on the Last Day by my body. I don't need to flip to the last chapter to be reminded of this sobering fact. It's with me rather frequently.

One more thing I need to know. That's how to stand in God's judgment when my end comes. The author tells me plainly. He says through Christ. And he tells me why. It's because "Christ was sacrificed once to take away the sins of many people." God's Son didn't just die on the cross. He was "sacrificed." He was there as the Lamb of God to take away the sins of the world. His sacrifice was a onetime effort with nothing more needed or necessary. His blood has paid for all sin. His sacrifice covers "the sins of many people"—of all people. I know death is inevitable. How much more I need to know that Christ was sacrificed for me. Then I can be sure of how God's judgment is going to end.

Lord, cover me with Jesus' payment for my sins so that I can stand bold before you. Amen.

STOP THE FUNERAL!

When the Lord saw her, his heart went out
to her and he said, "Don't cry." . . . He said,
"Young man, I say to you, get up!" . . . and
Jesus gave him back to his mother. Luke 7:13-15

Headlights on, special flags on car tops, funeral processions make their ways to cemeteries. Nobody stops them. Dead is dead, and the grave is waiting.

Only once does Scripture record that Jesus visited the city called Nain. He went to stop a funeral. A widow was carrying her only son to the grave. Who would still her sorrow as a mother? Who would provide for her in the days ahead? Who could give her an answer for the fear that a funeral always brings—the haunting concern about sin, for which death is the wage?

Jesus did more than stop a funeral that day. He made it unnecessary. With a heart of compassion and a voice of power, Jesus brought that son out of the casket back into his mother's life. Should I expect the Lord of life and death to do the same for me? Or should I look for more from him? Hasn't he promised that those who die believing in him still live in heaven and that on the Last Day their bodies, once laid to rest in graves, will also live in heaven? Isn't the eternal life that Jesus offers far superior to what he restored when he stopped the young man's funeral procession at Nain?

"Here, Daddy, fix it," said the little girl whose helium balloon with a single *boom* had fallen to her feet. Who's going to fix my life punctured by death? Only Jesus can, he has already suffered death to pay for my sins.

Lord of life and death, help me to believe.
Amen.

ALIVE OR DEAD?

God has given us eternal life, and this life is in his Son. He who has the Son has life; he who does not have the Son of God does not have life. 1 John 5:11,12

All people in this world fit into two categories. Either they are alive or they are dead. This doesn't mean that they are either still breathing or already under the sod. This truth is deeper. It refers to the only life that counts and where to find it.

What's the only life that counts? John says, "God has given us eternal life." The Creator did not make me just to have my heart beat so and so many times per minute for so and so many years. He intended that I live forever. He didn't fashion my frame just to exist on earth through the different stages of life but to end up in eternal life. Without that eternal life, I'm dead in his eyes. I may walk and talk, marry and give life to others, work and play, but I have no real life. I'm dead in unbelief and doomed to a hell that Scripture so fittingly labels as eternal death.

Where do I get eternal life? John answers, "God has given [it]." Eternal life is an undeserved gift from God's gracious hand, offered me only in his Son, Jesus. God sent his eternal Son to earth to die that I might live. With Christ's payment for sin, death has lost its sting. When God brings me to faith in Jesus, I have life already in this world and in all its fullness in heaven. But only through Christ. It's as impossible for me to have life without Christ as it is to have Christ without having life.

Thank you, Lord, for placing me into the category of those who are truly alive. Amen.

ONE SIZE FITS ALL

He is the atoning sacrifice for our sins, and not only for ours but also for the sins of the whole world. 1 John 2:2

For my birthday my granddaughter gave me a cute cap. The front said "I love my grandpa," with a heart in place of the word *love*. But the cap didn't fit. The adjustable band was supposed to make it fit anyone. Either my head was too big or the band was cut too short.

The cross of Jesus fits every sinner. The love he showed on the cross covers everyone. His suffering in the depths of hell paid for every sin. He died on that cross in the place of every sinner, from the first Adam in the garden to the last Adam when the world ends. And when Jesus rose on the third day, he showed his payment for sin was sufficient to cover the whole world. "The atoning sacrifice," John described him, a sacrifice that is sufficient to cover. "Not only for ours but also for the sins of the whole world," John added. There can be no doubt. Jesus' cross fits all.

It fits me. The Savior was tailor-made for me. My sins may be like so many others—my guilt just as serious as theirs. But the difference is, they're my sins and that's my guilt. I need to know whether Jesus paid for *my* sins. I need the peace that comes only from knowing God as a loving Father instead of a righteous Judge. I want to be able to step before him with confidence when my last breath comes. "Not just for the sins of the whole world but yours too," Jesus' cross assures me.

Savior, raise my eyes to your cross. Remind me that your sacrifice covers every sinner. Amen.

DO YOU KNOW WHY SHE WAS CRYING?

She began to wet his feet with her tears. . . .
Jesus said to her, "Your sins are forgiven. . . .
Your faith has saved you; go in peace."
Luke 7:38,48,50

"Now why are you crying?" I'll ask my wife as we sit in our recliners watching TV. Almost without looking I know when her tears will come as some poignant scene plays out on the screen.

Why was that woman in our verses crying? When we hurt people we love, sorrow and tears often come. That woman's life was riddled with sins. How many and what kind, we can only guess. At her Savior's feet she cried because she realized that every one of them was ultimately something done to him. Repentance brought the tears with which she wet Jesus' feet.

So did gratitude. She was crying not only because of what her sins had done to Jesus but also because of what Jesus had done to her sins. From her Savior she heard it again. "Your sins are forgiven," he assured her. They're gone no matter what they were. "Your faith has saved you," he continued. It's my gift to you so that you can lay hold on me. "Go in peace," he concluded—wonderful peace that only the forgiven sinner can appreciate.

When I know what my sins have done to Jesus and what Jesus has done to my sins, tears will come to my heart if not also my eyes.

Lord, tears are in order when I see how my sins have hurt you and how your love has forgiven me. Amen.

WHAT A DIAMOND!

The Son of Man came to seek and to save what was lost. Luke 19:10

Waiting to pick up my repaired watch in the jewelry store, I browsed the display cases. So many diamonds, so many rings, and so many necklaces. But some of them caught my eye more than others did.

Like some jewelry store, Scripture is filled with precious gems. And like the diamonds in that store, some of its gems catch our eyes more than others do. Such are Jesus' words in our verse. What gems they are, sparkling with God's love and promising wealth to anyone who wears that love.

The word *lost* doesn't sparkle. It promises me nothing but tells me everything. It reminds me that I came into this world from my mother's womb a lost sinner. The heart I inherited from sinful parents already doomed me to a horrible hell. The life that my heart led me to was no better. Though I could fool myself sometimes and my fellowman more often, even my best deeds were shot through and through with sin. *Lost*—the word fits. And there was no escape for me.

In sharp contrast, how the Savior shines! He came to seek and to save lost sinners like me. He lived among sinners, spoke to sinners, suffered at the hands of sinners, hung between two sinners, and died for sinners. That's what he had to do in order to rescue me. That's what his divine love moved him to do for a sinner like me. How rich I am because of Jesus!

Lord, thank you that I can say, "Jesus has lived and died for me." Amen.

GRACE TO COVER ALL MY SINS

As he began the settlement, a man who owed him ten thousand talents was brought to him. . . . The servant's master took pity on him, canceled the debt and let him go. Matthew 18:24,27

"Impossible," we say. How could the master forgive that servant such a huge debt, equivalent to $10 million in those days? Today we'd have to talk in terms of trillions. Yet the master wiped out the debt completely, not because the destitute debtor deserved it but because the master had pity on him.

Impossible? Isn't that what God does for me? He looks at the tonnage of sin that bends the shoulders of my soul. He looks at my abilities and sees nothing that can help me get rid of that horrible weight. So he lifts those sins off me and puts them on the One who can carry them. "The Lord has laid on him the iniquity of us all," Isaiah 53:6 reminds me. That "him" is Jesus, the sinless Son of God. On him God heaped the sins of the world and through him hurled them forever into the depths of the sea. With my sins paid by Jesus' blood, I can stand debt free before God.

The English pastor who authored the hymn "Rock of Ages" estimated that by the time a person reached the age of 20, he had sinned 630 million times. By the age of 50, he supposed the count had gone up to a billion and a half sins. I don't know how good that pastor's math was. I do know how numerous my sins are. And I don't even know half of them. But thank God I also know that Jesus bore them all when God laid on him the iniquity of us all.

"I lay my sins on Jesus, The spotless Lamb of God; He bears them all and frees us From the accursed load" (CW 372:1). Yes, thank God for Jesus. Amen.

IS *SIN* A DIRTY WORD?

I said, "I will confess my transgressions to the
LORD"—and you forgave the guilt of my sin.
Psalm 32:5

Last Sunday, sick with the flu, I missed worship. Bundled up
in my chair, I turned on the TV. Flicking from one religious
program to another, I noticed something seriously missing.
Those TV preachers said little about "sin." I think I know
why—because *sin* is a dirty word in so many people's minds.
They don't like to talk about sin. They much rather prefer
words like *shortcomings* and expressions *like alternate
lifestyles*. The word *sin* is just too harsh for people who like
to think that they aren't really so bad after all.

One of my seminary professors told us, "Preach the law as if
there were no gospel and the gospel as if there were no law."
King David in our verse would agree. When the finger of
God's clear commandments pressed hard on the infected
spots of David's sins, the king cried "Ouch!" When God sent
the prophet to hold the mirror of the law before David's sin-
smirched soul, the king hung his head. Otherwise, he went
about life as if his sins of coveting, adultery, and murder
were just mistakes or an alternate lifestyle. And when David
felt the guilt of his sin, he then could also appreciate the
fullness of God's forgiveness. Simply, the prophet told him,
"God has put away your sin," and great was the joy that
gospel message brought him.

Lord, show me my sins with your
commandments. Then show me your
forgiveness through the good news
about your Son, my Savior. Amen.

THE WAY GOD FEELS ABOUT IT

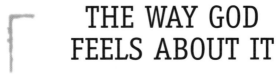

But God demonstrates his own love for us in this: While we were still sinners, Christ died for us. Romans 5:8

"If that's the way you feel about it, forget it," said the wife. Trying to patch her marriage back together with a husband who had cheated on her, she asked whether he would ever do it again. When he responded, "I don't know," she withdrew her offer. How could she go back to someone who plainly didn't appreciate the love she was trying to show him?

Could I complain if God treated me the same way? If, having received his forgiveness for my past unfaithfulness to him, I cheated on him again time after time? If God were like us human beings, he would say, "Forget it." But God doesn't think and feel the way I do. His love doesn't depend on what I do. He doesn't show goodness only to those who are good. That would make his love and concern as imperfect as mine.

The sweet story of the gospel is simply this—Christ died for me and all people while we were still sinners. God's eternal Son came to earth to give his life as a ransom for me while I was nothing but a disobedient, dirty, damned sinner. His grace that brings me salvation in Christ is entirely onesided. It is totally undeserved by me, a working of his divine love. That's the way God feels about it. And I'm glad he does.

Lord, please don't forget about me, but
remember me in your love for Jesus' sake. Amen.

THESE NAMES
NEVER FADE

Rejoice that your names are written in heaven.
Luke 10:20

Pompey's Pillar National Monument in Montana contains the only physical evidence of the Lewis and Clark expedition through the area. In 1806 Captain William Clark carved his name on this huge sandstone formation. See-through glass now protects it from the ravages of time.

God also has recorded some names. It's as if God keeps a family record in heaven, something like our forefathers did in their family Bibles. It's as if he writes down in his book the names of all his children, grandchildren, and great grandchildren. Of course, he doesn't really have such a list on paper or in some computer. He doesn't have to. He knows every believer by name. He has each of their names written not on sandstone but in his memory, where time's passing can't erode them.

How did my name get recorded in God's book? If I had my say, my name would still be on Satan's register with an eternal room number in hell assigned to me. But God in his grace recorded my name in heaven. He had to love me so much that he was ready to send his Son to a cross for me. His Son had to leave behind his heavenly throne and endure hell's suffering to pay for my sins. His Spirit had to call me by the gospel, enlighten me with his gifts, sanctify and keep me in the true faith. Looking at Clark's signature on that sandstone cliff, I had to marvel at his stamina and courage. Looking at my name written in heaven, I have to marvel even more at God's grace and love.

Lord, fill my heart with gratitude and joy for writing my name in your book of life. Amen.

HIS FOOTPRINTS ARE SO BIG

Christ suffered for you, leaving you an
example, that you should follow in his steps.
1 Peter 2:21

Twelve inches of snow had fallen, blocking the highways and
closing schools. Mark and his dad had the day off and were
in the front yard making tracks in the snow. For a while Mark
tried to match his little steps to his dad's ahead of him, only
to exclaim, "You're footprints are too big."

I don't have to match Christ's footsteps when it comes to my
salvation. They are just too big and deep for anyone to do
that. And it is not necessary. When Peter wrote "Christ suffered for you," he was referring to a done deal. Christ took
that deep step down from heaven, that giant step up to the
cross, that horrible step into hell's suffering, and that victorious step out of the grave. He took steps that only God
could, and because he did, my salvation is complete. I don't
even have to walk to heaven; the Savior will carry me.

Jesus, however, does want me to walk like him on this earth.
Peter mentions just one area, that of suffering. Silently the
Savior suffered the shame unbelievers heaped on him without retaliating. When people poke fun at my faith—when living the Christian life seems like walking in foot-high snow
drifts—I need to keep my Savior's footprints ahead of me. I
know I can't travel as far and as fast as he did. But if my footprints just go in the same direction as his, that's good enough
for me.

Savior, on my way to the heaven you've
prepared for me, help me walk more like
you. Amen.

MORE PERMANENT THAN THE MOUNTAINS

"Though the mountains be shaken and the hills be removed, yet my unfailing love for you will not be shaken nor my covenant of peace be removed," says the LORD. Isaiah 54:10

Mountains are among the most permanent things we know on earth. A massive white peak in Alaska has been measured as over 20,000 feet high. Named Mount McKinley by us and Denali by the natives, this highest mountain north of the Andes was there long before any explorers found it and we named it. And it will be there long after we are gone.

Even if an earthquake could level Mount McKinley to the ground, God's love would still remain. It's an "unfailing" love that nothing can destroy. It's a love that shines most brightly on another mountain—the one called Calvary. On that hill God's own Son climbed the steepest mountain in this world. He took the massive load of the world's sins, carried it all the miles into hell's furor, and victoriously planted the flag of salvation in Joseph's garden. Because he did, I, the sinner, now have peace with God. He is my Father, and I am his child. Heaven is my home, and there he will take me. His love, unshakable in this world and stretching to the next, assures me.

On our two trips to Alaska, we tried to see Mount McKinley, but the season was too late and the clouds too thick. Thank God the view of Mount Calvary and God's unfailing love is always clear.

Lord, take me to Calvary's holy mountain to be assured of your unfailing love. Amen.

HIS PROMISE HOLDS

If we are faithless, he will remain faithful, for he cannot disown himself. 2 Timothy 2:13

What to do? I had put the check into my shirt pocket and forgotten all about it. My wife found it after she had washed the shirt. The paper was pasted together and the writing blurred. But the signature was still legible. At the bank the teller called the one who wrote the check and I got my money. His signature was all that counted. It was his promise to make good.

I have some wonderful promises from God. At Calvary, when his Son bled for sins, God promised that counted for me too. At my baptism, when God wrote my name as a believer in his book of life, he promised that I would be his child. At the Lord's Supper when he comes to me with the very body and blood used to pay for sins on Calvary, he promises that I can go in peace. On the day I close my eyes for the final time, he promises he will send his angels to carry me home to heaven. His check for my salvation is good. He signed it with his love.

I foolishly may forget about that check. Perhaps I stuff it into the pocket of the shirt of life as I busy myself with other things I consider more important. Perhaps I even throw his check into the wastebasket thinking I have little use for it. But God doesn't void his check. Instead, wanting me to repent and return, he reaches for me. When his grace brings me back, he doesn't have to write out a new check for me. His promise of my forgiveness is still good. After all, he signed it.

Lord, forgive me for my unfaithfulness.
Comfort me with your faithful promise of
salvation. Amen.

I DON'T KNOW WHAT GOD SEES IN ME

He has clothed me with garments of salvation
and arrayed me in a robe of righteousness.
Isaiah 61:10

"I don't know what she sees in him," sniffed the mother about the man her daughter was dating. He looked more than a little rough around the edges and had little going for him, at least on the surface.

Must God not say the same about me? Why should God even be interested in me? What does he see when he looks at me? Do I appear to be a fitting candidate for his family? Do I appear to be a worthy bride for his Son, Jesus the Bridegroom? Worse than some Cinderella, I'm covered with the soot of my own sins. I'm wearing the tattered rags of my sinful works. Why should he even take a second glance at me? In fact, a holy God would have to tell me, "Out of my sight forever."

And yet, thank God, I know what he sees in me. I'm dressed for a heavenly wedding celebration in the wedding clothes his Son has sewn for me. Jesus wove the fabric himself on the loom of the cross. He stitched it with the red threads of his own blood. He sized it to cover every one of my twisted thoughts, my wicked words, my devious deeds. Then he even dressed me in it. By bringing me to faith in the Savior, he clothed me with his forgiveness—made me sparkle with his holiness. "Come," this gracious God now invites me, "come, enjoy the marriage feast in heaven." When God looks at me, he sees a bride for his Son, dressed for a wedding in his Son's righteousness.

Jesus, thank you for making your blood and
righteousness my beauty and my glorious
dress. Amen.

WHAT A SPREAD!

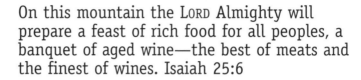

On this mountain the LORD Almighty will prepare a feast of rich food for all peoples, a banquet of aged wine—the best of meats and the finest of wines. Isaiah 25:6

The meal was terrific. Members had invited us along to the ritziest hotel in town for Sunday brunch. As we surveyed the numerous tables laden with rich food, we didn't know where to start.

What a spread the Lord has prepared! Isaiah describes it as a feast where the rarest wine is uncorked and the finest meat carved. God's banquet table groans under the weight of the best of foods. And I'm invited. I don't know why. Those members took me to brunch because I was their pastor. God seats me at his table, not because of what I am, but what he is. He's a God of love. At no time does his love shine more brightly than when it invites undeserving sinners to his table of salvation.

Out on Calvary his love shone just as brightly as when it prepared the rich food for his banquet table. Love put his Son on that cross in my place. Love had his Son die in payment for my sins. Love raised his Son from the grave to show my sins were gone. Now love spreads the table with rich food for my soul, the forgiveness of sins, life, and salvation it needs.

God invites me to Sunday brunch to be fed richly through the Word I hear in church and through his Holy Supper. And daily he invites me to pick up a fork and dig into his Word.

Lord, feed me with your Word till in heaven my soul no longer needs your forgiveness. Amen.

DISASTER IN THE DARKNESS

In him was life, and that life was the light of men. The light shines in the darkness, but the darkness has not understood it. John 1:4,5

One morning sudden fog blanketed a section of the freeway near us. Before minutes had passed, over 60 vehicles had smashed into one another with a number of fatalities. One driver commented, "I couldn't see anything. All I heard was the crunch of metal smashing into metal."

Scripture frequently uses the picture of darkness to describe a world lost in unbelief. Man doesn't think he's driving in the fog. He thinks the sun is bright in his heavens and the road is safe. He even thinks he can make his own light. But the more he tries to light up his way to heaven with the kind of person he tries to be and the kind of things he tries to do, the denser sin's darkness becomes. He steps on the gas, not even realizing he's heading for the horrible crash scene in hell.

The fog of unbelief will be here till the world ends. But I don't have to drive in it. There's light for me. John calls it the light of life and reminds me it's found only in Jesus. Jesus came into this world to be the light of salvation for sinners lost in sin's darkness. He came to be the light of eternal life for sinners already spiritually dead and doomed to hell's eternal death. When Jesus comes, the fog lifts and I can see all the way to heaven. Let me not forget, though, that Jesus brings his light through his Word. Only his Word reveals him as the light that dispels sin's disastrous darkness.

Lord Jesus, light my heart and the way to heaven with the light of your gospel. Amen.

MAKE ME A CHILD

I tell you the truth, anyone who will not receive the kingdom of God like a little child will never enter it. Mark 10:15

She looked back with a frown on her face. Then she commented to her husband, and he glared too. The little one in the stroller, unhappy with his confinement and hungry for his lunch, was crying up a storm. And the noise was a bothersome distraction for those two middle-aged shoppers.

People today have little time for children. At best they're viewed as obligations that need to be cared for. At worst, as obstacles on the road of life. Have such people forgotten what they once were and who took care of them? Now look at the Savior. On the day Jesus spoke the words of our verse, he was extremely busy. But he took time to cradle the little ones on his lap and cover them with his blessing. He even used those little ones to teach his disciples a lesson about faith.

"You'll never enter the kingdom of God unless you become like a little child," he said. He didn't mean babies are born sinless. He didn't mean that they come into this world with hearts that believe in the Savior. The exact opposite is true. He meant that I need childlike faith. Like an infant, I'm to take God at his Word—to trust what he says. With simple faith I'm to answer, "If you say so, Dad," when my heavenly Father points to the cross of Jesus and tells me it covers all my sins.

Make me more like a child, Lord, for only you can. Remove my doubts and fill me with simple faith in your precious promises. Amen.

BETTER THAN MAPLE SYRUP

From the fullness of his grace we have all
received one blessing after another. John 1:16

Every Christmas one of our members gave us a gallon of pure
maple syrup. If you've ever tasted the real thing, you know
how the artificial ones don't even come close. When my wife
made pancakes, it was a treat to pour the genuine syrup over
them in abundance.

In our verse, John reminds us that we've received God's grace
in abundant measure. The word *grace* takes us into the cham-
bers of God's heart. It shows us a love that is totally undeserved. A love that wouldn't let the sinner perish in hell as he
deserved but had planned salvation for him. A love that shines
most brightly in the person of Jesus Christ. When we see God
in the Bethlehem manger, on the Calvary cross, out of the
Easter tomb, we are looking at the fullness of God's grace.

And God's grace, unlike our gallon of maple syrup, never runs
dry regardless of how much I use it. And use it I do! When I
sin, his grace lifts my eyes to Calvary's holy mountain to
assure me that Jesus has paid for me. When I weary under
life's temptations, his grace points me to a powerful Savior
who knows how to strengthen me. When I worry about death,
his grace reminds me of the risen Savior, who has defeated
this last monster for me. When I stand in heaven someday,
his grace will be the main theme of my praise. How good life
tastes when it's covered with his grace in Christ!

Lord, cover me with your grace in Christ richly
every day. Amen.

GOD WANTS EVERYONE

He is patient with you, not wanting anyone
to perish, but everyone to come to repentance.
2 Peter 3:9

At a family reunion, the younger ones and those who think
they are still young get into a spirited softball game. When
choosing up sides before the game, there's always the problem of who's going to take the younger or less athletically
gifted persons for their team.

Is that how God functions? Does he look at us when it comes
to picking players for his team of believers? If he does, whom
would he choose? We're all so disabled by sin that we're no
good whatsoever. We're all so deserving of hell that God
wouldn't even waste a first glance at us.

Now look in contrast at how God actually functions. "He is
patient with you," Peter said. Not only is he patient, he is
gracious. Instead of sending us to be on Satan's losing team
in hell, he sent his Son from heaven to take care of our sins.
He's prepared the uniform of salvation. It's his Son's payment
for every sin and perfect obedience of every commandment.

God wants every single sinner on his team. He sent his Son
to pay for every single sinner. He gives life to every single
sinner as the time to learn of the Savior and be readied for
heaven. Those who reject Jesus do so at their own peril.
Those who are clothed with him rejoice in God's grace.

Lord, thank you for bringing Jesus' salvation to
me. Amen.

TOMORROW CHRISTIANS

I tell you, now is the time of God's favor, now
is the day of salvation. 2 Corinthians 6:2

Do you know any "tomorrow Christians"? They're people who
answer, "Tomorrow, when I have more time, I'll get interested
in religion." "Tomorrow, when I'm older, I'll start thinking
about preparing for death." "Tomorrow, when my sin no
longer pleases me, I'll think about quitting it."

How many tomorrows am I sure of? How do I know whether
I'll even make it through today? Somehow I fool myself into
thinking I'm in control of the length of my life. Even when I
notice the wide variety of ages in the obituaries, I still con
myself into thinking that won't happen to me.

"Now," Paul said, "is the time of God's favor, now is the day
of salvation." Like some precious gift from his hand, today
stands before me. Today is the time a gracious God gives me
to learn of the salvation he has prepared in his Son Jesus. Not
that Jesus' forgiveness has as an expiration date on it, but
my life does. And that expiration date may be today.

Sounds urgent, doesn't it? Perhaps a better question than
"Do I know any tomorrow Christians?" is "Am I a tomorrow
Christian?" Don't lose out on God's grace in Christ. Don't wait
till tomorrow. Today is the time of God's favor. Tomorrow is
the judgment.

Lord, through your Word, keep me close to the
Savior every day. Amen.

A MILLION TIMES BETTER

Father, I want those you have given me to
be with me where I am, and to see my glory.
John 17:24

How do you describe heaven? How do you make its joy concrete? "Think about something that really made you happy," I'd tell the kids in confirmation class. "Now multiply that joy by a million," I'd go on. Even if I could do just that, I'd still have only a glimpse of heaven's joy.

Jesus gives me more than a hint about heaven's perfect joy. He says that heaven is being where he is. To see the Savior's face, to stand fully in the sunshine of his love, to share his home forever will be part of heaven's joy. Here I so often glance away from his face, put the umbrella of doubt up against the sunshine of his love, and sometimes even wonder if there is such a place as his eternal home.

Jesus also says that in heaven I will see his glory. All of his divine glory, power, wisdom, and honor will radiate from him. Especially will he shine with glory as my Savior. In this life, though, I marvel at the love that brought him down to be my Savior. I can't grasp its richness totally. In heaven I'll not only fully understand what he has done for me, but I'll give my Savior the glory he deserves.

A million times better—that's right. But note for whom—those whom the Father has given Jesus by bringing them to faith in their only Savior.

Lord, make and keep me your own so that I can
be with Jesus in heaven and see his glory. Amen.

MADE ON FRIDAY

Who [Christ] loved me and gave himself for
me. Galatians 2:20

"Don't buy a vehicle made on Friday or Monday," someone said.
He was suggesting that autoworkers' concentration might not
be as good when the weekend was approaching or just over.

I don't know about autoworkers, but I do know about Jesus
Christ. He died for sinners like me on a Friday. And there was
nothing incomplete or imperfect about his work of salvation.
He said of sin's payment, "It is finished." His suffering covered
every sin totally because he is the Son of God. His blood was
divine blood with power to compensate for all sin of all time.
Like some foreman in quality control signing off on a vehicle,
the Father raised his Son on Easter Sunday. Salvation was done,
complete, perfect. That's why we've labeled it "Good Friday."

"Made on a Friday" doesn't mean much until it becomes
"Made on a Friday for me." I need to do more than know
about Jesus' death and resurrection. I need to believe that he
loved me and gave himself for me. I need the God of all grace
to send his Holy Spirit to work on me. The Spirit, through the
powerful message of what Jesus did on that first Good Friday,
must work in my heart. He must root out the unbelief in my
heart, replace it with faith in the Savior, and remake every
day into a Good Friday for me. Then I can look at Jesus' salvation and say, "Made on Friday for me!"

Lord, draw me to your cross and its payment
for all my sins. Let that cross be my joy in life
and death. Amen.

CHRIST LIFTED SIN'S WEIGHT

Christ redeemed us from the curse of the law by becoming a curse for us, for it is written: "Cursed is everyone who is hung on a tree." Galatians 3:13

Exactly 472.5 pounds. That's the weight Hossein Rezazadeh lifted at the 2000 Olympic Games in Sydney, Australia. Whether the record still stands, I don't know. But I do know of a weight lifting feat that no one will ever top.

Sin was crushing the whole human race. Just my sins alone were ton after ton. Add in the total of all sinners since the world began, and how out of sight the total soars. How could the world get rid of sin's crushing load? Who would lift its killing weight? Man in his folly has tried. He flexes his muscles, makes a grab at his load of sin, and tries lifting it with his own works. But nothing happens. He only makes matters worse as even his best efforts are filthy in the sight of a holy God.

What man cannot do, God did. Jesus came to lift sin's curse from us forever. His shoulders looked no bigger than ours, but because he is the God-man, they could carry sin's weight. His blood looked no redder than ours, but because he is both divine and human, it was precious enough to pay for all sin's guilt. His death was just as real as ours, but because he is God's Son, it counted for each sinner. Now all who believe in him as their only Savior can breathe again. Not just 472.5 pounds, but all of sin's crushing weight has been lifted off their souls.

Lord, thank you for lifting sin off me so that I can breathe in peace. Amen.

FAIL-PROOF INVESTMENTS

Store up for yourselves treasures in heaven, where moth and rust do not destroy, and where thieves do not break in and steal.
Matthew 6:20

How are your investments doing? Did you lose quite a bit in the downturn during the first years of this new century when the stock market went into a tizzy? Have you done any shuffling of accounts?

Earthly treasures will always be subject to change. If the stock market doesn't keep us guessing, something else will. The moth and rust of Jesus' day may take on newer forms, but thieves will always be thieves. And all earthly investments will face their ups and downs.

Jesus offers a lasting treasure. His forgiveness for sin knows no ups or downs. It's always there in full force for me when I come in repentance to his cross. His peace for my soul is not subject to cancellation when I sully my life with my usual sins and stew about whether God will still accept me. His insurance policy, cosigned at Jesus' resurrection, maintains its benefit of life in heaven for me whenever my death comes.

When my earthly investments take a tumble, I'll still live somehow. But I cannot live without the fail-proof treasures God has given me in Christ.

Lord, thank you for making me rich in Christ.
Help me treasure the Savior. Amen.

DIVINE PROTECTION AGAINST SIN'S ULTRAVIOLET RAYS

The LORD is your shade at your right hand; the sun will not harm you by day. Psalm 121:5,6

Medical science has shown the close link between exposure to the sun's ultraviolet rays and the incidence of skin cancer. Yesterday's sun worshipers with their bronze tans are today's skin cancer victims. Many people are far more careful today about intense exposure to the sun.

I can stay out of the sun or cover my exposed skin with a suitable sunblock lotion. Against sin's deadly rays, however, I cannot protect myself. Standing in its burning heat, I can only wait for sin's cancer to claim me. I have no sunblock lotion, nothing of my own to use in protecting myself.

Did I read what the psalmist wrote? "The Lord is your shade," he assures me. The loving Lord spreads himself like an impenetrable umbrella over my soul. He doesn't just deflect sin's rays. He caused them to strike his Son in my place. On the cross Jesus endured the intense heat of punishment for the world's sins. Like gigantic burning rays they seared his soul in the fires of hell. But he emerged victorious. No longer can sin's cancer claim me. Through Jesus I am safe.

In his Word the Savior-God offers himself as my umbrella. I surely don't want to leave him parked unused in the closet of life.

Lord, hide me under the shadow of your loving, protecting arm for Jesus' sake. Amen.

MY HERO

Let us fix our eyes on Jesus, the author and perfecter of our faith. Hebrews 12:2

Do you have any heroes? Joe DiMaggio, the famous "Yankee Clipper," was one of mine. I wanted to play baseball the way he did. Years later I can still remember seeing him in the crowd as I made my way through the Chicago airport. I think I stood there with my mouth wide open.

Standing tall above any hero is Jesus. "The author and perfecter of our faith," the inspired author describes him. Jesus is both the object and the cause of my faith. He gives me both something to believe and the faith to do so. No one else could do what he did. Only Jesus could step under God's commandments and make his perfect keeping of them count for me. Only Jesus could fill the cross and free me from sin. Only Jesus could empty his grave and give me a preview of what will happen to mine. Only Jesus with the power of his Word could bring me to faith in him as my Savior. Only Jesus through that Word can keep my faith going till I reach his side in heaven. He's the author and perfecter of my faith, my hero in the highest sense of the word.

I didn't get a chance to meet Joe DiMaggio that day in O'Hare Airport. But I guess I can live with that. I can't, however, get to heaven without meeting, listening to, and keeping my eyes fixed on Jesus. That opportunity I have daily when I turn to the pages of his Word.

Lord, teach me to love your sacred Word and to view my Savior there. Amen.

HEAVEN'S NARROW DOOR

Make every effort to enter through the narrow door, because many, I tell you, will try to enter and will not be able to. Luke 13:24

The zoo offered free camel rides. To qualify you had to fit through a door no more than four feet high and two feet wide. This kept the bigger children and adults from climbing up on the camel.

There is a door to heaven. Jesus said so. He ought to know because he's the carpenter who, with his payment for sin, built it. In fact, he is the door. In John 10:9 he said, "I am the gate; whoever enters through me will be saved." With *whoever* Jesus indicates that he is the door that opens heaven for all people. Yet at the same time he describes this door as being narrow. How come?

Because I can only enter heaven through him. Puffed up with my own worthiness, I can't make it through. Carrying my sins makes me too wide. Sinners who try are like the Three Stooges in the old comedies. Trying to get through a doorway, they turn this way and that with their pieces of lumber but always end up sideways.

Is that narrow door a warning for me? It's time to ask again: "Just what does Jesus mean to me? Is he really my only door to heaven? Do I show that he is by my efforts to draw closer to him through his Word? Is that narrow door a comfort for me?" When sin swamps me again in another week of life, what assurance to know heaven is still open because of Jesus!

Jesus, keep me safe in faith in you as heaven's only door. Amen.

August *22*

FILL UP
WITH THE RIGHT STUFF

Why spend money on what is not bread, and
your labor on what does not satisfy? Listen,
listen to me, and eat what is good, and your soul
will delight in the richest of fare. Isaiah 55:2

The manager in the rental-car-return garage was fuming. A
customer ahead of me had returned a car after putting in the
wrong kind of fuel. When the workers wanted to move the
car, it stuttered and stalled.

Isaiah was speaking of the same mistake. People spend their
money and their lives filling up with the wrong stuff. They
chase power, possessions, and pleasures of this world as if they
were high-octane fuel. Or they pull up to the pump of their
own efforts, thinking they can run to heaven on their own
works. Yet when their tanks are filled, they only stutter and
stall. Such human fuel can't cut it. It doesn't satisfy the need.

"Listen to me," God says. How can I do that? Through his
Word. That Word is like a fuel pump dispensing what I need.
In his Word, God offers super premium fuel. The news that he
has paid for my sins in Christ, the assurance that he wants
me to be his child, and the promise that he will take me to
live with him in heaven are like high-test fuel that powers up
my engine of life. As I read his Word or listen to it in worship, God's at work, filling my soul with the right stuff. Can
anything be more important in my life or for eternity than
regular stops at God's station?

Your Word inspires my heart within; Your Word
grants healing from my sin. Your Word has
pow'r to guide and bless; Your Word brings
peace and happiness. Amen. (CW 282:2)*

*©1993 tr. Mark A. Jeske. Used by permission.

GOD'S WORD NEVER FADES

All men are like grass, and all their glory is like the flowers of the field; the grass withers and the flowers fall, but the word of the Lord stands forever. 1 Peter 1:24,25

At our wedding, my wife carried a bouquet of yellow roses. When she gave birth to our first child, I brought her a dozen yellow roses. They went home with her from the hospital, but it wasn't too many days before we threw them out. Their petals had fallen; their beauty had faded.

Human beings are like those roses. We come into the world, bloom for a while in one field or another, and then fade. Though some fool themselves into thinking they will live forever, the fading comes. Though others arrogantly act as if their blossoms will shine without end, they also wither and fall. We've learned this lesson. We live with it, even if we may not like it.

God's Word never fades, Isaiah reminds us. How could it? It's the Word of the eternal God. When he threatens that unbelievers will end up in hell, he means it. Sooner will the fires of hell stop burning than this threat not come true. When he promises that believers in the Savior Jesus will live forever with him in heaven, he means it. Sooner will heaven and earth pass away than this promise not be fulfilled. In fact this world and all in it will indeed pass away. But just as he promised, the Lord will gather all believers in heaven. God's Word never fades.

Lord, all around me are things that wither and fall. Fill my heart with the beautiful promises of your eternal Word. Amen.

MY INHERITANCE

Surely I have a delightful inheritance.
Psalm 16:6

"All this is mine," said the wealthy landowner. The pastor had come to visit and was getting a tour of the man's holdings. Proudly the farmer pointed to the buildings, the acres, and the herds. Everything as far as the eye could see was his. The pastor quietly asked, "Is Jesus yours?"

Good question. Is Jesus mine? Can I say with the psalmist, "Surely I have a delightful inheritance"? Nothing in this world can top the treasures God offers me in the Savior. When the dollars and cents of this world are lined up against the precious blood of Jesus that paid for my sins, how short they seem. When the buildings and holdings of this life are placed on the scales, how light they weigh in contrast to the pardon and peace Christ brings me with the heavenly Father. When the acreage of life's holdings are exposed to eternity's evaluation, how much like dust in the wind they seem compared to the eternal home in heaven waiting for me. "Delightful," the psalmist calls the inheritance God has prepared for me in Christ Jesus, the Savior.

The question still remains, "Is Jesus mine?" That little word *mine* is so important. What good is an inheritance if my name isn't on it? Or what good is an inheritance if I don't claim it? Thank God if he's opened the hand of faith for me to claim the riches Jesus has prepared for me. Pray God that he keep my hand of faith wrapped around such a delightful inheritance.

Lord, thank you for your gift of Jesus and all he brings. Keep me in faith in him always. Amen.

A LIVING ROCK

The LORD lives! Praise be to my Rock! Exalted be God my Savior! Psalm 18:46

Sounds like a contradiction to me. How can a rock live? I've picked my share of rocks from the fields to know that rocks don't live. They just lie there in the way or are piled up in some fencerow.

David knew rocks much better than I do. In the wilderness he huddled behind them to find protection from the burning rays of the sun and the stinging sand driven by the storm. But he couldn't carry those rocks with him. How different with the Lord! He's a living rock that's with me wherever life takes me. One that holds his mighty hands over me regardless how severe the storm. One that shades me from the burning rays of temptation and trouble. Praise be to my Living Rock!

David also knew that rocks form a good foundation. Sand constantly shifts, mud constantly settles, but rocks stand firm. You can build on them, and what you build will stand. How much like the Lord. He's a living rock, a reliable foundation for my life. When the winds of change blow in life and when the present is foggy and the future even more so, I need rock on which to plant my feet.

I especially need him when it comes to my salvation. "God my Savior," the psalmist calls God. "Rock of Ages," I sing of Jesus. He's the reliable rock on which faith's feet stand securely. He's the only Rock of Salvation that keeps me safe into eternity. Praise be to my Living Rock!

Eternal Rock of Ages, my only Savior, please plant my feet even more firmly on you. Amen.

NO SUBSTITUTION ALLOWED

If righteousness could be gained through the law, Christ died for nothing! Galatians 2:21

Yesterday's newspaper reported that a cheese firm was fined for using vegetable oil instead of cream in its products. The company pretended their cheese spread was the real thing, but it wasn't.

Our country's Food and Drug Administration is on the lookout for such switches. Often people's taste buds also notice the difference. Too bad the same isn't true when it comes to salvation. One of Satan's most effective attacks against Christianity is deceiving people into thinking they can substitute for Christ's work of salvation. When people look to their own efforts to satisfy their hunger for heaven, Satan has them in his grasp and heads for hell.

Jesus said of sin's payment on the cross, "It is finished." The sinner mistakenly says, "I must add something with my own works." Jesus says to the penitent sinner, "Go in peace." The sinner foolishly insists, "How can I have peace when I don't know whether my works have done enough to save me?" Jesus says to the dying believer, "Today you'll be with me in paradise." The sinner anxiously worries, "Are my efforts sufficient to help hold open heaven's door?"

Begin to understand why Paul insists, "If I try to substitute my own works fully or in part for Christ's completed work of salvation, Christ died for nothing."

Please, Lord, preserve me from such fatal, false thinking. Cement my faith on Jesus' work alone. Amen.

GOD'S UNBREAKABLE RECORD

But I will not take my love from him, nor will
I ever betray my faithfulness. Psalm 89:33

On September 21, 1998, a remarkable record came to an end.
After 16 years and 2,632 consecutive games, Cal Ripken Jr.
wasn't in the lineup for the Baltimore Orioles baseball team.

In this world, all human streaks have an end. But God promises me, "I'll never stop loving you." How I need those
words! When I look at myself, I have to wonder how God can
keep on loving me. Even though I know him as my Savior, I
still walk like some drunken sinner, weaving this way and
that from his will. Even though I know how precious his
Word is, I still put it often on the back shelf in my life. Even
though I know that I'm only a stranger here, I still try to
put down my roots in this ball of mud as if I'm never going
to leave. My batting average so often is less than .100, my
strikeout total astronomical. Yet God keeps me in the lineup
on his heavenly team.

How can God do it? David answers, "Because he cannot betray
his faithfulness." God promised that Jesus has paid for all my
sins. His faithfulness makes him keep that promise when I
kneel in repentance before him. He promised that he would
never leave me nor forsake me till I stand with him in
heaven. His faithfulness compels him to do just that for those
whom Jesus has made his dear children and heirs of his eternal heaven. God's streak of faithfulness keeps going forever.

Lord, thank you for your divine love in Jesus
that never comes to an end. Amen.

SIN'S BLEMISH REMOVED

You forgave the iniquity of your people and covered all their sins. Psalm 85:2

The artist was to paint a portrait of Alexander the Great, famous king of Macedonia and conqueror of the world. But there was one problem. From a wound received in battle, the king had a visible scar on one cheek. Should the artist risk the king's displeasure by painting the scar or make the painting less than lifelike by leaving it out? The solution? He asked Alexander to pose on his throne with his hand raised in thoughtful reflection, covering the scar.

Each of my sins is like some hideous scar on my soul. It makes me ugly in the sight of a holy God. Not only does God dislike what I look like, but he also has to banish me from his presence forever in that horrible place called hell. No eternal portrait for me, just a never-ending place in hell's prison.

But a gracious God came up with a solution. He asked his Son to take care of sin's horrible scars. On the cross of Calvary, Jesus gave his all in payment for all sin. He didn't just hide them with his hand. He did radical surgery on them. Moreover, this Surgeon comes to me individually through his Word and offers his forgiveness to me. He even works faith in me so I can call him my Savior. Now my soul can stand scarless before the holy judge. Not one hint of sin's ugly scars remains. My portrait is ready to hang on heaven's walls.

Lord, thank you for removing my sins through Jesus' work. Cover me with his forgiveness so I can stand in beauty before you. Amen.

JESUS TOOK THE CHARGE

He himself bore our sins in his body on the
tree. . . . By his wounds you have been healed.
1 Peter 2:24

When our church's roof was redone, the contractor discovered
that the lightning rods hadn't been properly installed. The
rods stood there with heavy wire running down, but they
were not attached to anything on the lawn below. How could
the ground absorb a lightning strike if the charge never
reached it?

The lightning of God's just anger over sin had to strike. That's
what his justice means. If his anger were to hit sinners,
they'd be fried to a crisp in the fires of hell. So God in his
love provided a lightning rod system for us. He deflected the
punishment for sin from us to Jesus.

There was no question whether or not Jesus could absorb the
horrible charge. On the cross he hung as the God-man come
into our flesh to pay for our sins. He had to be man in order to
be able to die. He had to be God in order that his death might
pay for all sins. Already in the mystery of his being, we see
God's marvelous love. That God should become man and hang
with his own body on the tree is beyond our comprehension.
So is the love that brought him to earth and to that cross.

How foolish for unbelievers to think they can ground God's
lightning strikes for sin! How blessed are those who are connected by faith's wire to Jesus!

Lord, keep me hooked up to Jesus so that I can
stand safely in heaven before you. Amen.

HAMMER AND FIRE

"Is not my word like fire," declares the LORD, "and like a hammer that breaks a rock in pieces?" Jeremiah 23:29

What do you do with a hammer? It depends. You can use it to tear down or to build up. When a wall needs replacement, first you hammer away at the old. When it's knocked down, you pound into place the new. It's the same with fire. You can use it to destroy debris or to ignite a jet engine.

Ever think of God's Word as being a hammer or fire? Like some hammer it pounds away the sin-hardened heart. Nothing but the force of God's gospel can make a dent in an unbeliever's heart. Only its mighty blows can tear down the unbelief that rules in the sinful heart inherited from our parents. Like some fire God's gospel reduces to ashes the self-righteousness that packs the human heart. Only the gospel's purifying flames get rid of the human instinct to earn one's own salvation.

Like some hammer the gospel then builds up. It fills my heart with faith in Jesus. It pounds into place the beautiful structure of salvation through Jesus' payment for sins. Like some fire it ignites the engine of faith within me. It heats me up with the conviction that Jesus paid for my sins, that God loves me, that heaven is my home. Only those on whom God's Word has done its work like a hammer and fire know what we're talking about. They also know that you don't leave God's Word like some tool unused on the workbench of life. You reach for this hammer and fire regularly.

Lord, keep using your Word as a hammer and fire on me. Amen.

THE WORLD'S MOST IMPORTANT DISCOVERY

See what God has done! Numbers 23:23

On May 24, 1844, the inventor Samuel Morse sent a message by telegraph from Baltimore to Washington. His message contained only four words: "What hath God wrought!" (KJV). That successful demonstration sold his invention, and news-gathering agencies turned to its use. In our day of satellite television and cellular phones, we have to go to a museum to learn about Morse's invention.

There is no replacement for the telegraph God uses to transmit his message to us. Just as to the generations before and after us, God speaks to us through his Word. The methods used to carry his Word may change. Through television and radio, the computer, recordings of all kinds, the printed page, and the witness of people, we receive God's message. In the future, who knows what means might pop up? And we'll thank God even as we try to harness those means to get his Word out.

But the message will still be the same. It'll still be, "See what God has done." It'll point at the sinner with the chilling reminder of God's law—what man has done can only doom him. Then it'll point to God with the saving revelation of God's gospel—what Jesus has done is more than enough to save the sinner. "See what God has done in his amazing love to save the sinner. See what God has done in his enduring love to ready that sinner for heaven." For that timeless message there can never be a replacement.

Lord, through your Word let me hear you telling me what you have done to save me. Amen.

MORE THAN "I'M SORRY"

Repent and believe the good news! Mark 1:15

"I'm sorry," Tom said as his dad had told him to after the argument with his sister. But as soon as Dad was out of sight, Tom stuck his tongue out at her. Was he really sorry?

Repentance is not just mouthing the words "I'm sorry." Sometimes those words mean "I'm sorry that I got caught." "I'm sorry that I'm being punished." "I'll be more careful next time so that I get away with it." Or they can mean "I truly feel bad that I hurt you and I won't do it again."

The repentance to which Jesus calls me is far more than a superficial feeling. The word Jesus uses means a change of heart. As with the cheating tax collector Zacchaeus, repentance means admitting my sins, recognizing what hurt to my fellowman and Jesus I have caused with them, making amends for those sins, and then fighting against them.

See the connection between repentance and salvation? Only those who truly repent of their sins will find in the gospel the good news they need. To those who don't feel their sins, repentance is only a term, not a treasure. To those who don't realize how serious sin is, its weight is measured only in pounds, not tons. To those who shrug aside sin's punishment in hell, Jesus' blood is only picture language, not cleansing power. Before I can enjoy Jesus' forgiveness, I need his call to repentance.

> Lord, change my heart by bringing me to
> repentance so I might treasure your
> forgiveness. Amen.

A LOVE THAT KNOWS NO ENDING

I have loved you with an everlasting love; I have drawn you with loving-kindness.
Jeremiah 31:3

On the back of her photo she had written: "Dearest Tom, I love you with all my heart. I will love you forever." But under her signature was this PS: "If we ever break up, I want this picture back."

How unlike the amazing love of our God! His love doesn't change with the wind or passing emotion. God's love is permanent and so is what he in his love has done for me. When he says, "[I] so loved the world that [I] gave [my] one and only Son, that whoever believes in him shall not perish but have eternal life" (John 3:16), that's as true today as it was when his words were recorded more than 2,000 years ago. When his apostle writes, "He [God] loved us and sent his Son as an atoning sacrifice for our sins" (1 John 4:10), that stands for me just as for those who first read John's words.

His unchanging love leads God to action. "I have drawn you with loving-kindness," he reminds me. When his love reached for me at my baptism, it wasn't to hold me only for a while. When he announces his love to me through his Word, it's not just for today. When he feeds my hungry soul with Christ's forgiveness in the Lord's Supper, it's to draw me even closer. "Loving-kindness" pictures his unbreakable love. I may foolishly let go of that wondrous love. That's my fault, not God's. He waits faithfully for me to return so that he can wrap his ever-loving arms around me.

Lord, assure me of your unchanging love. Let me see that love in Jesus my Savior. Amen.

LABOR? FOR WHAT?

God said to him, "You fool! This very night your life will be demanded from you." Luke 12:20

In this month when our nation observes Labor Day, it's time to ask the question, For what am I laboring? Is it for how much I can get or how much I can keep?

Jesus calls the man in the parable a "fool," not because of his laboring but because all he could talk about was "I" and "mine." All that the man could think about was how much he could get. The same temptation is there for us. We eat vitamin-enriched foods, ride in air-conditioned cars, watch TV programs beamed across the miles, lose our anxieties by taking pills, die without pain because of modern drugs, and are laid to rest in parklike cemeteries. All this we have and most of it is good. But what good is my life if it revolves only around these things?

"Laid up for many years," the rich man said of his goods. But God said, "This very night your life will be demanded from you." With his goods that man couldn't prolong his life a single second, pay God for a single sin, or buy one square inch of heaven. He asked the wrong question, one about getting instead of keeping. What about me? To be rich toward God means to treasure the pardon he has prepared for me in Christ, to use my earthly treasures for the spreading of his Word, to look forward to my rich inheritance with him in heaven. Labor? For what? The question is simple, deceptively so. The answer is serious, eternally so.

God, give me the right answer in the Savior Jesus Christ. Amen.

HAPPINESS IS
BEING POOR IN SPIRIT

Blessed are the poor in spirit, for theirs is the kingdom of heaven. Matthew 5:3

Happiness is . . . How would you finish that sentence? Happiness is having a million dollars? being successful? being able to do what you want? In his Sermon on the Mount, Jesus gives some unexpected answers. Reading them, we must remember that he's speaking to believers, not the rank and file. Also he's reminding them not how to be saved but how the saved are to live.

"Blessed are the poor," Jesus says, using a word that described the down-and-out, the penniless, helpless, hopeless beggar. No, he's not urging me to get rid of all I have if I want his blessing. He says, "The poor in spirit." He's speaking of people like the tax collector in the temple who had nothing to point to except his sins. Standing a spiritual pauper before God, he begged, "God, have mercy on me, a sinner." Poor-in-spirit believers confess their utter sinfulness, count all their efforts as worthless ashes, and commit themselves completely to the Savior's love.

"Theirs is the kingdom of heaven," Jesus reminds us. They hold in faith's hand citizenship papers for heaven. God counts them in his heavenly census. They enjoy all the riches of God's kingdom—pardon for sins, peace with God, promise of eternal life. In the world's eyes they are poor, but in God's kingdom they are rich. Their God in his grace through the Savior has made them rich. That's why they are happy.

Lord, grant me the happiness that only believers in Jesus can have. Amen.

HAPPINESS IS MOURNING

Blessed are those who mourn, for they will be comforted. Matthew 5:4

"Blessed are those who mourn," Jesus continues in his Sermon on the Mount. With *mourn* he refers to a grief that grips the heart. What is it that grips my heart the hardest as a believer and makes it grieve the most? Must I not answer, "My sin"? The Christians who are truly Christian mourn deeply over their sins. They don't just go through the motions of confessing them but pour out their hearts before their God. When I see the true nature of my sin, the guilt it lays on me, the damnation it earns me, I mourn in genuine sorrow.

The evil that sin brings into the world causes me to mourn too. At the graves of loved ones, in the midst of life's troubles, under the cross I carry as Christ's follower, tears flood my heart, if not my eyes. My journey through this vale of tears is no picnic. Often I have to reach for the tissue box.

Mourn I will, but not forever. Jesus assures me, "Blessed are those who mourn, for they will be comforted." The Savior has what it takes to dry my tears. Do I mourn over my sin? He says that I should be of good cheer, because my sins are forgiven. Do I mourn because life is squeezing me with all its problems? He says, "In all things God works for the good of those who love him" (Romans 8:28). Does death put its scare into me? He says, "Whoever lives and believes in me will never die" (John 11:26). From Jesus comes comfort here on earth and perfection in heaven at his side. That's why I have happiness.

Lord, dry my tears with the assurance that your love provides all I need for body and soul. Amen.

HAPPINESS IS
BEING MEEK

Blessed are the meek, for they will inherit the earth. Matthew 5:5

"Blessed are the meek," Jesus says. But people would rather say: "Blessed are the strong. Blessed are those who go after what they want. Blessed are the ones who stick up for their rights."

Meek Christians live humbly before their God. They submit their lives to God's will and humbly follow his Word. For them the question "What does God want?" comes before "What would I like?" Toward the neighbor too they exhibit a meek spirit. When hurt, the meek don't hit back. When taken advantage of, they don't scheme how to get even. When disagreement arises, they don't insist on their rights. They leave such injustices to the hand of a just God. How can I do otherwise as a believer? When I truly realize how poor I am in God's eyes and how much sin I have to mourn, how can I puff out my chest before God or lord it over my neighbor who's in the same fix as I am?

"Blessed are the meek," Jesus says, "for they will inherit the earth." It just doesn't seem to work that way. Only those who fight hardest and longest seem to get anywhere. Then I need to remember what my Savior says. He always speaks the truth. He promises the meek peace and plenty. He reminds me that his children are content with whatever he gives them. Appreciating the treasures Jesus has given my soul, I'm happy with whatever of the earth's store he showers on my life.

Lord, keep my eyes on heaven's riches so that I live in true meekness. Amen.

HAPPINESS IS HUNGERING AND THIRSTING FOR RIGHTEOUSNESS

Blessed are those who hunger and thirst for righteousness, for they will be filled. Matthew 5:6

When's the last time any of us felt true hunger pangs or thirst's burning sensation? Patients fresh from surgery or people marooned for days in a snowstorm can describe real hunger and thirst.

So can the believer. Jesus says, "Blessed are those who hunger and thirst for righteousness." As God's child I'm to be constantly hungry, ever thirsty for the holiness God has prepared for sinners in the Savior. My eyes of faith can never look enough on the Lamb of God who takes away the sins of the world—mine included. My ears can never hear too often of how in Jesus, though my sins are scarlet, they shall be as white as snow. My lips can never sing too frequently, "Plenteous grace with you is found, grace to cover all my sins." Someone described a little boy as an appetite with skin stretched around it. Good description for God's children. Their ever-present desire for God's Word with its satisfying food of Christ's righteousness stays till in heaven they hunger and thirst no more.

As God's child, filled with his forgiveness, I hunger also for a life of righteousness. God has made me his child. Now he asks me to live as his child. With Christ's strength, I'm to walk in newness of life, showing forth the praises of the One who has made me righteous. When the world views me, they are to see a satisfied customer, one who has true happiness because of God's grace.

Lord, make me ever hungry and thirsty for your Word with its message of salvation. Amen.

HAPPINESS IS
BEING MERCIFUL

Blessed are the merciful, for they will be
shown mercy. Matthew 5:7

True mercy begins in the heart and leads to action. It involves
both heart and hand. Want an example? How about our Lord?
He didn't just say of the world speeding to hell: "That's too
bad. I cry for you." His mercy kicked into high gear. He sent
his Son to rescue sinners from hell. In daily life he also shows
abundant mercy. He doesn't just say "I feel sorry for those
foolish people," and then let us blow our world to ribbons, let
our worries drive us out of our minds, and our illnesses run
unchecked. His mercy acts. Every day in every phase of life it
takes care of us.

In this world true mercy is rarer than the proverbial four leaf
clover. What passes for mercy is often just selfishness, helping
out of a sense of duty or with the expectation of receiving help
in return. Only God's children can exhibit mercy of both heart
and hand. Only hearts that have experienced God's mercy in
forgiving sin and providing daily care can flow with mercy
toward others in need. The more God causes me to feel his
mercy the more I can be a "good Samaritan" to others.

"Blessed are the merciful, for they will be shown mercy,"
Jesus says. He knew how difficult showing mercy could be in
this world. So he encourages me with his promise to show me
mercy in every need. What a Lord I have! First he makes me
merciful by bringing me to faith, then he promises me more
mercy when I try to be like him toward those in need. In his
promise I have happiness.

Lord, scrub the selfishness out of my heart by
showering your mercy upon me. Amen.

HAPPINESS IS BEING PURE IN HEART

Blessed are the pure in heart, for they will see God. Matthew 5:8

During Jesus' days on earth, people thought the heart was the seat of life. We still talk that way today. So I understand that Jesus is referring to every part of me—to my thoughts, words, and deeds. "Pure" leaves no doubt as to how Jesus wants me to be. He, the holy Lord, demands holiness from me. He wants a life that has no bugs on the windshield, no dirt on the wheels, just total sinlessness. Isn't he asking the impossible? By myself I can't clean a single sin from life's windshield or stop even one sin from smearing it more. What I can't do, Jesus came to do. He died on the cross to cleanse my heart from all sin and present it spotless before my God.

Now he wants my pure heart to show in my life. "Be pure," he says referring to all my thoughts, words, and deeds. Here on earth I'll never reach that ideal. My life will still be tainted by daily sin. But I'm not to stand still. Like riding a bicycle up some hill, if I'm not pedaling forward, I'll be rolling backward. I need the strength for forward motion that comes from Jesus through his Word.

Again he offers a promise to encourage me. "They will see God," he says of the pure in heart. In heaven I'll see God in all his fullness. Here on earth I view him in his Word. There his love, care, and ways are outlined for me. The more I see his loving face in his Word, the more power I'll have to keep pumping the bicycle of holiness up the hill of my life. And even to find happiness in doing so.

Lord, create a new heart within me that knows the Savior and loves to follow his ways. Amen.

HAPPINESS IS
SHARING HIS PEACE

Blessed are the peacemakers, for they will be called sons of God. Matthew 5:9

I simply cannot be a peacemaker without being a peace possessor. So Jesus reminds me by referring to "sons of God." God is the true peacemaker. He sent his Son as the Prince of Peace to restore the family relationship with him that sin had ruptured. True peace can be found only in that Savior. In Romans 5:1 Paul writes, "Since we have been justified through faith, we have peace with God through our Lord Jesus Christ." The peace that surpasses all understanding is mine through his Son who prepared it and his Word that brings it to me.

The closer the Spirit draws me through the Word to the Prince of Peace, the more I'll become a peacemaker like him. I'll try to seek peace as he did, even sacrificing to have it. I'll let nothing stand in the way of peace, even giving my best to win it as he did on Calvary's cross. Not only will I be called "God's child," I'll look more like him in my peacemaking contacts with my fellowman.

Happiness will follow. Jesus says so. "Blessed are the peacemakers," he promises, "the spouses, parents, and children who don't insist on having their own way or the last word. Blessed are the Christians in the community who work together with neighbors and respect other people's opinions. Blessed are the believers in the congregation who avoid gossiping and griping, who in all things work to keep peace." God already acknowledges them as his children, and so will their fellow Christians.

Lord, fill me with your peace so that I can live more at peace with those around me. Amen.

HAPPINESS IS BEING PERSECUTED FOR HIM

Blessed are those who are persecuted because of righteousness, for theirs is the kingdom of heaven. Matthew 5:10

How far removed I can be at times from this beatitude! How little I care for and how much I'll do to avoid being persecuted for following Jesus! I'll go places, laugh at jokes, do things I shouldn't so that the world around me won't pick on me. How often I'm hesitant to stand up for Jesus, much less suffer for him! I'll steal away into the shadows of silence instead of speaking up for what his Word says. I'll even pull back when he asks some service or offering from me, lest I be inconvenienced.

Jesus doesn't talk about my taking up a pillow and following him. He mentions a cross. Jesus doesn't promise that the road of discipleship will be without a bump or danger from competing traffic. He describes my life as a race that requires every ounce of my endurance and every minute of faith's concentration. I hate to ask the question, but could it be that I haven't found the world to be such a severe enemy because I've been too much of a friend with the world?

Again Jesus states a promise to encourage me. "Theirs is the kingdom of heaven," he says. Not that my bravery in the face of enemy fire earns me heaven. It shows that I have heaven. It plainly tells the world in whose army I'm fighting. And it states clearly my conviction that Jesus will take me to heaven, where I can praise him for having counted me worthy to suffer shame for his name.

Lord, help me find happiness in standing up for Jesus and his Word in this hostile world. Amen.

THE FARE'S BEEN PAID

God presented him [Jesus] as a sacrifice of
atonement, through faith in his blood.
Romans 3:25

Heading back to our room one night, we boarded the city bus
in Mainz, Germany, through the rear door. At once the bus
driver shouted at us and didn't quiet down until I presented
to him the day's pass our son had purchased for us. The driver
was right—you have to pay to ride.

It's the same principle with the road to heaven. Someone has
to pay for the ticket. Only this time it was the eternal Son of
God. God is a holy God who can't just wink at sin as if it were
of no account. He can't just sweep my many transgressions
under the rug as if they don't matter. Scripture says very
clearly, "The wages of sin is death" (Romans 6:23). The price
required was extremely high. Again the Bible says emphatically, "Without the shedding of blood there is no forgiveness"
(Hebrews 9:22). The fare for heaven's bus was not cheap. It
cost God the best he had—his own Son. Jesus paid my fare
to heaven with his holy, precious blood.

How do I get a ticket on that wonderful bus? "Through faith in
his blood," Paul reminds me. Just as my son paid for that bus
ticket in Mainz, so God's Son paid the price and gave me the
ticket to heaven. The faith God's Spirit works in me through the
gospel hangs on to Jesus and shows him confidently when anyone challenges me. I'm on my way home, thanks to God's grace
in Christ Jesus.

Lord, thank you for sin's payment. Help me
hold on to the free ticket to heaven you gave
me. Amen.

NO ONE TURNED AWAY

Whoever comes to me I will never drive away.
John 6:37

"What's she doing here?" whispered a member to her neighbor in the church bench. In another aisle a lady, who everyone knew had a shady reputation, had just taken a seat.

Was that member correct? Little did the critic know that the pastor had encouraged the sinner to come. Earlier in the week she had sat in his study, sobbing out her repentance, seeking forgiveness for what she knew was so wrong. "Your sins are forgiven," the pastor had assured her. "Come to worship next Sunday," he encouraged her, "and hear even more of that forgiveness."

In this world, though we claim not to, we set up pecking orders. Somewhat a sinner, more so a sinner, and very much a sinner are the categories into which we sort people. And unfortunately we do the same when Christ welcomes a sinner. Have we forgotten what the Savior himself said? He won't drive away any sinner who comes to him in repentance. He has no sin-o-meter that weighs one sin more heavily than another, no list of the 10 or 20 worst sinners. Just full forgiveness for everyone.

Come to think of it—I'm no better than that woman in the church bench. I'm glad Jesus doesn't say "What are you doing here?" when I come seeking his forgiveness.

Lord, remind me that chief of sinners though I
be, you shed your blood for me. Amen.

HIS HEART WAS MADE UP

> As the time approached for him to be taken
> up to heaven, Jesus resolutely set out for
> Jerusalem. Luke 9:51

When my dad got a certain look on his face, we knew his mind was made up. Nothing we could do or say or ask would change it. He was going through with what he had decided.

"Jesus resolutely set out for Jerusalem," our verse says. Nothing could stop him from what lay ahead. He knew what awaited him in Jerusalem and out on Calvary. He even told his disciples about it several times in advance. The rejection by his countrymen and the betrayal by his friend, hurry-up trials before the Jewish court and the Roman judge, the crown of thorns and the awful whip, the crude cross and the flesh-splitting nails, the sun-drained darkness of Calvary and the soul-draining depths of hell's punishment—all this Jesus knew about. Yet he resolutely set out for Jerusalem.

"Why did Jesus die on the cross?" five-year-old Colter's mom asked as they talked about his Sunday school lesson. After a moment's silence, Colter answered, "Because he couldn't get off." In a sense that little boy was right. Jesus had more than enough power to turn his journey to Jerusalem into something far different than an ending on the cross. But his love wouldn't let him. His love for sinners brought him to that cross and kept him on it. There his love poured the lifeblood from his sacred veins for sinners like me. His heart was made up. And that's why he went to Jerusalem.

> Lord, fix my eyes of faith resolutely on Jesus'
> cross as the only salvation for sinners. Amen.

TEACHER OF THE WORLD

The people were amazed at his teaching, because he taught them as one who had authority. Mark 1:22

"Congratulations, Mrs. So-and-So, teacher of the year," said the sign on the brick wall of the middle school. Students had nominated her, the panel had selected her, and she received recognition.

They weren't handing out awards that day in the synagogue at Capernaum, but they did recognize Jesus as a good teacher. They sat there amazed, with mouths wide open. Makes one wish that Mark had recorded Jesus' sermon. But he didn't. He does, however, tell us why the people were so awestruck by Jesus' teaching. It was because "he taught them as one who had authority."

Later this teacher from heaven told them, "He who sent me is reliable, and what I have heard from him I tell the world" (John 8:26). Don't these words hint at what he taught in the synagogue? Jesus is God's one and only Son, sent by the Father's love, to die for sin so that none need perish but have eternal life. The message of such love could only bring amazement for those who heard it.

In his Word, Jesus speaks to me. The Bible is Jesus' voice. In it he teaches me the same beautiful truth—that because of his redemption, I have eternal life in heaven. That message of divine love still brings astonishment to the ears of the sinner. What a teacher of the world Jesus is!

Lord, open my ears to hear the news of salvation and my heart to rejoice because of it. Amen.

MY GO-BETWEEN

For there is one God and one mediator between God and men, the man Christ Jesus, who gave himself as a ransom for all men. 1 Timothy 2:5

My ice-covered snowball broke the neighbor's window. Of course she came over to tell my mother. When I finally showed my face, Mom scolded me and said Dad would deal with me when he came home from work. Anxious, I asked my mom with her caring heart to help me with my dad.

Not some snowball, but my many sins have shattered my relationship with the holy God. Even just one sin is enough to put me on his punishment list. A holy God has to demand payment for every sin. How can I stand before him when it's time for me to come home? Believers are not just anxious but terrified. I dread that day coming. I need a mediator who will speak to the Father for me.

Jesus is that go-between. He not only speaks for me before the Father but does so effectively. The Father listens to him because Jesus has already paid for the gigantic snowball of sin I roll in life. That's why God came to earth. He became man to give himself as a ransom for all people. As the God-man, his blood was precious and his death powerful enough to cover a whole world's sins. When the Redeemer mediates between the holy Father and me, the sinner, I'm safe. "Forgiven," the Father will say, "still my redeemed, restored child because of the blood of my Son." With Jesus as my go-between, I approach the holy God confidently and call him Father.

Jesus, when I sin, remind me of your forgiveness and plead for me before our Father. Amen.

AN ANCHOR THAT HOLDS

We have this hope as an anchor for the soul,
firm and secure. Hebrews 6:19

All at once Mark's kite was gone. The wind had carried it high
into the sky where it fluttered so beautifully. But Mark had
been distracted and let go of the string. Off the kite sailed
into the woods.

Like that kite, my hope for salvation needs a string or as our
verse pictures it, an anchor. An anchor is only as good as the
ground into which it sinks its flukes. Water surely won't work,
neither will sand for long. To hold the boat securely, the anchor
needs to be imbedded in the right ground. Do I ask what the
anchor might be for my hope of salvation? There is only one
anchor—Jesus. "Salvation is found in no one else, for there is
no other name under heaven given to men by which we must
be saved," Scripture asserts (Acts 4:12). "I am the way and the
truth and the life. No one comes to the Father except through
me," the Savior himself said (John 14:6).

These verses stretch the picture to show that Jesus is both
the anchor and the ground for my soul. Like some anchor
whose strong flukes cannot be twisted out of shape, so I have
in Christ an absolutely strong and reliable hope. Like some
anchor that holds only when fixed in the right ground, so I
have my hope anchored in the right spot—the one who is my
only Savior. Mark let go of the string and lost his kite. God,
help me hold onto Jesus with faith's fingers.

> Lord, help me believe that my hope for
> salvation can be built on nothing less than
> Jesus' blood and righteousness. Amen.

THE MAGNET
OF THE CROSS

But I, when I am lifted up from the earth, will draw all men to myself. John 12:32

In our mission congregation in Canada, back in the 1960s, we had people from a variety of lands. Because of more lenient immigration rules, they had come from Estonia, Germany, Scotland, Poland, Greece, and Finland to carve out a new life for themselves in a new land. It was an international congregation, but in one respect the members were alike. Christ's cross had drawn them.

Just as the Savior said, all people would be affected by his being "lifted up from the earth." With this expression Jesus was referring to his crucifixion when he would hang above Calvary's ground. His cross would be a magnet having an effect on all people. Either they will kneel beneath it in faith in the Savior or turn from it in damning unbelief. Salvation through Jesus' death and resurrection either attracts or repels sinners.

The woman at the well in Samaria, the Roman centurion whose servant was ill, the Greeks who came looking for Jesus, and the believers of Our Saviour's Lutheran Church of Sault Ste. Marie, Ontario, are examples of those whom Jesus' love drew to his cross. What an international church the God of all grace is building for his heaven! With his blood shed on the cross, Jesus has "purchased men . . . from every tribe and language and people and nation" (Revelation 5:9). He has also paid for me and wants his cross to draw me to him as my only Savior.

Lord, may the gospel message of salvation draw and keep me ever close to the Savior. Amen.

SAFE IN GOD'S ARMS

God is our refuge. Psalm 46:1

The husband hurried to the hospital emergency room. His wife, injured in an accident on the freeway, had been brought in by ambulance. When he reached her bedside, she started crying. Wrapping his arms around her, he comforted her. And her tears slowed.

How unprotected people must feel who don't know about God's almighty arms! How afraid are those who don't trust his arms to hold them safely! When their sins crash into them like some speeding car, where do they turn? When life's uncertainties spook like foreboding ghosts before them, what's their refuge? When their last day draws near with its summons to stand before the judge, what's their hiding place?

Thank God for my Father's arms. Because of Jesus' payment for sins, those arms are there for me. Because of the Spirit's gift of faith, I trust those arms. When Satan comes stalking me like some roaring lion seeking to sink his teeth into my soul, I find strength in God's protecting arms. When sin has done its daily damage to my soul, I find forgiveness each night in God's loving arms. When life's storm clouds gather over me, I find safe shelter in God's almighty arms.

> Other refuge have I none; Hangs my helpless soul on thee. Leave, ah, leave me not alone; Still support and comfort me. All my trust on thee is stayed; All my help from thee I bring. Cover my defenseless head With the shadow of thy wing. Amen. (CW 357:2)

I AM WEAK, BUT HE IS STRONG

God is our . . . strength. Psalm 46:1

Sometimes I don't feel weak. I flex my physical and spiritual muscles like some beefed-up weight lifter and think that I can heft any amount. That's how the world entices me to feel. It looks at what it has already accomplished and thinks the sky's the limit. The spanning of the seas, the soaring into space, the splitting of the atom are already in the history book as part of what man has done. Ahead lies who knows what, but man is sure he's up to it. And the world's false optimism is contagious.

But how soon my muscles turn into flab. Illness pushes me on the ropes, and I throw in the towel. A loved one has problems my muscles can't lift, and I turn away in frustration. The years speed by, and my vaunted strength degenerates into debilitating weakness. Worst of all, if I am a thinking person, I worry about sin, that little word with the big consequences. Deep down I know that all is not well between God and me. Deep down I realize when my end comes, I must give an accounting to him. Speak about weakness—here's an area where I have no strength or muscles at all.

"They are weak, but he is strong," declares an old spiritual. God is the strength of my life. He helps me climb the steepest mountain, ford the deepest river, cross the widest desert in life. God is the rock of my salvation. He has canceled sin's curse, closed hell's door, cracked open forever heaven's door through his Son's payment on Calvary's cross. In him I find the strength I need.

Lord, fill me with your strength. Especially lead me to trust your Son for my salvation. Amen.

NO NEED
FOR A CELL PHONE

God is . . . an ever-present help in trouble.
Psalm 46:1

Several years ago we purchased a cell phone especially for my wife to use when traveling. If an emergency should arise, all she had to do was dial 911 and help would soon be on the way.

As a believer I don't need a cell phone to call God to my side. He's there all the time. "An ever-present help in trouble" is how the psalmist describes him. My greatest trouble is sin. It's at the root of all the world's problems. Sin is the soil in which the troubles of man grow—all his pains, temptations, even death. Every day the dandelions of sin shoot up in my heart, threatening to choke out all else. Daily I must confess that I sin much and deserve nothing but punishment.

So what do I do? Pick up the cell phone and call 911? Man can't help me, but God did. He sent his Son to pay sin's penalty and destroy sin's curse. On the cross he provided the only help that works, his Son's blood in payment for all my sins and as power against sin's temptations. Through his Word he stands at my side with that forgiveness. It's there as real as his Son's cross that prepared it and his Word that offers it. His Word is my "cell phone." When I use it, there's no waiting for my Savior's help. "Trouble with you people is that you think you're better than the rest of us," said an unbeliever. "No, not better," answered a Christian, "just better off." How true with God as my ever-present Savior!

Be near me, Lord Jesus, to help me with my
sins and bless me with your forgiveness. Amen.

A HIGH PRICE FOR A PRECIOUS GIFT

No man can redeem the life of another or give to God a ransom for him—the ransom for a life is costly. Psalm 49:7,8

What's life worth? "Nothing," some say as they snuff it out inside the womb or outside in the world. "About ten dollars," the scientist calculates as he analyzes the chemicals in the human body. "Precious," God answers as he looks at what he has given. And his answer is the one that counts.

Life is a gift that only God can give. Every moment of our lives is his gift to us. Just as with other gifts from God, life has a purpose. In fact, its purpose makes life a most precious gift. It's the time a loving God grants each individual to learn of the Savior Jesus and be readied for heaven through him. Because of this purpose, God carefully protects life, commanding others to keep their sinful hands off the time of grace he gives each person.

Life's value is most apparent when I look at the price God has paid for it. Not often will someone give his life for another. Such sacrifice may prolong life on earth but cannot save it for heaven. Human blood has no value to lift sinners to heaven. Only the blood of God's own Son could pay the ransom required to restore sinful man to his Creator. That God should send his Son to pay the ultimate price of his atoning death plainly indicates what value God has attached to people. What am I worth? Nothing as a sinner, but I'm precious in God's sight because of his love and Jesus' blood.

Lord, thank you for life. Even more, thank you for Jesus through whom I have eternal life. Amen.

⌐ HIS GUIDANCE LEADS

Yet I am always with you; you hold me by my right hand. Psalm 73:23

Is there a more appealing sight? The little child gets up on wobbly legs and tries its first hesitant steps. All because a parent's strong hands are holding and guiding.

Did I hear the psalmist? "I am always with [God]," he said, "[God will always] hold me by my right hand." Or to put it another way, "God is always with me." Note well how this close and constant connection of the believer with God comes about. It's not I who reaches for God's right hand but God who comes down from heaven to me. Left to myself, I the sinner want nothing to do with God. The sinner couldn't care less about God's guidance. Till God reaches down, stretching his hand of grace all the way from heaven to work faith in my heart. Then and only then can I say to God, "I am always with you."

Notice what the psalmist said will follow when God holds me by the right hand? "You guide me with your counsel," he wrote. "God leads me in the way I should go. Most of all do I need that blessed guidance when it comes to my sin. Painfully I must admit that my thoughts, words, and deeds daily stray across the centerline on life's highway. Sin's ruts in my daily life are so deep that my tires run in them almost automatically. Sometimes sudden sin sends me spinning out of control. But when God holds me by the right hand, I am washed whiter than snow by Jesus' blood and recharged with his power for new life.

Jesus, still lead on Till our rest is won.
Heav'nly Leader, still direct us; Still support,
console, protect us Till we safely stand In our
fatherland. Amen. (CW 422:4)

┌HIS GOODNESS ASSURES

Whom have I in heaven but you? And earth has nothing I desire besides you. My flesh and my heart may fail, but God is the strength of my heart and my portion forever. Psalm 73:25,26

Do I hear the psalmist? He says that nothing in heaven or earth could come close in value to his Lord. The Lord was his highest treasure, his only treasure, his lasting treasure. And nothing could rob him of that treasure, not even death when his heart and flesh would fail him. The Lord was the strength of his heart, the rock, and the sure stronghold on which his heart put its trust. The Lord was his portion forever, an inheritance that would not end with this world but reach its fullest value in heaven. Luther caught the psalmist's meaning when he wrote, "If only I have the Lord, I care nothing for heaven and earth."

Last summer we revisited Old Faithful geyser in Yellowstone Park. Near it was a digital clock that predicted how many minutes were left before the next eruption. We browsed the shops, but kept a close eye on our watch. When a few minutes were left, we hurried out to see the big event. But the workers in the park paid no attention. While we oohed and aahed and clicked our cameras, those workers didn't even look up. Old Faithful had grown way too familiar to them.

Nowhere is God's goodness more visible than in the Savior Jesus. Let me never take the forgiveness he offers me as something commonplace. It's new and rich for me every day. It's the one treasure I must have in this world and in the next.

Lord, thank you for your goodness. Amen.

HIS GLORY AWAITS

You hold me by my right hand. . . . And afterward you will take me into glory.
Psalm 73:23,24

Recently I read the definitions of life that a college newspaper printed. "Life is a joke that isn't funny," one student commented. Another said, "Life is a jail sentence for the crime of being born." How sad! Even worse, how tragic! Those who are not held by God's right hand wander aimlessly through life and head helplessly toward hell.

Only the believer in Christ can say, "Afterward you will take me into glory." Those on whose hearts God in his grace has impressed his Son's filled cross and emptied tomb know about the heaven that awaits them. They know that, because of the sin-carrying, sin-conquering Son of God, heaven is theirs when life's little day ebbs so swiftly to its close. For them death is not the end-it-all for their lives but the entrance into most glorious lives with their Lord in heaven.

I'll admit that I have questions about that glory. What will it be like to leave behind all the tears and troubles of this life? What will it be like to stand next to Jesus and share in his glory? There are many things God hasn't told me about the glory of heaven. But what I need to know he has revealed plainly, prominently, plentifully. Only Jesus with his perfect payment for my sin can take me there. Only when he holds me by the right hand can I be sure of the glory that awaits me.

Lord, through your Word, hold me by my right hand and never let go of me. Amen.

NO COLLECTION AGENCY AFTER US

He forgave us all our sins, having canceled
the written code, with its regulations, that
was against us and that stood opposed to us;
he took it away, nailing it to the cross.
Colossians 2:13,14

Before we left to serve for four months in a Montana congregation, I called the cable company to put their connection on
hold. Imagine my surprise when three months later I received a
letter from their collection agency telling me to pay up or else.

God's commandments are like that collection agency. They tell
me that I owe God for what I have or haven't done. The plain
word for this debt is *sin*. How can I get a holy God, to whom I
owe so much, off my back? I can't! When I try to scratch
together the works in my life as payment for my sins, God labels
them for what they really are—counterfeit. When I try to tear
up the dunning letters from his commandments, they only keep
coming stronger and stronger. "Pay up or else," they demand.
And I'm afraid that for me, the sinner, the "or else" means hell.

Sin's debt is real. So is the forgiveness God has prepared in
Jesus. On Calvary, Jesus took my sins and nailed them to his
cross. They hung there with him. They hung there on him.
Because he was God's own Son, he could take care of them.
With the crimson ink of his precious blood, he wrote across
my debt of sin, "Paid in full." For the believer, instead of dun-
ning letters from a collection agency, comes a love letter from
God that says, "I have forgiven all your sins."

Lord, thank you for paying my debt with Jesus'
blood. Fill me with the joy of his salvation. Amen.

FROM POVERTY
TO RICHES

For you know the grace of our Lord Jesus
Christ, that though he was rich, yet for your
sakes he became poor, so that you through his
poverty might become rich. 2 Corinthians 8:9

The world is full of stories of people striking it rich. Perhaps
they invented some software or made the right investments
in the market. Once in a while, we also read of people losing
it all. Through some quirk of fate or fault of their own, they
end up in bankruptcy court.

Jesus lost all his wealth. No, that's not accurate. Jesus gave
up all his riches. He could have come with the richest gold
crown on his head, the most expensive jewels on his fingers.
He could have paraded around in glory such as only heaven
knows and the world has never seen. Instead, he exchanged
his gold crown for one of thorns, his throne of glory for a
cross of suffering. He even gave up his holiness and saddled
himself with my sins. Why such poverty? Our verse tells us,
"For your sakes he became poor." He made himself poor
because of his love for me, the sinner.

Look what I gain from his poverty. No longer do I face hell,
where I'll have to suffer for every sin—not just pennies on
the dollar but full punishment forever. Instead, I wear the
diamond ring of Jesus' pardon on faith's finger. Instead, I
look forward to a crown of glory at Jesus' side in heaven. I've
struck it rich. No, change that to read—God has made me
rich by making his Son poor for me.

> We are rich, for he was poor; Is not this a
> wonder? Therefore praise God evermore Here on
> earth and yonder. Amen. (CW 64:3)

FIX IT, LORD

A broken and contrite heart, O God, you will not despise. Psalm 51:17

Playing with his toy horses, my grandson became a bit rough and broke the leg off his favorite one. "Fix it, Grandpa," he pleaded, placing the pieces in my lap. But I couldn't. The glue wouldn't hold.

"Fix it, Lord," the psalmist David also pleaded. But he had more in mind than a broken toy horse. His heart was in pieces, shattered because of his sins. God's law had shown David how serious his sins were and what he deserved because of them. Heavy with sorrow over his sin, David begged the Lord to pick up the pieces and put his broken heart back together again.

David knew the Lord could fix his heart. Confidently he pleaded, "A broken and contrite heart, O God, you will not despise." He knew what God's grace was going to do with sin-shattered hearts. In his psalms, David sang about the Savior who would bring healing at the price of his own blood. God's pardon in Christ glues broken hearts back together and makes them better than new.

Where do I find this glue? God knows I need it. And God has amply provided it for me. In his Word he points me to his Son's cross where payment for all my sins was won. Through his Word he works faith in my contrite heart so that I know Jesus' blood paid for each of my sins. "I can fix it," my heavenly Father tells me when I bring my broken heart to him.

Lord, my heart is heavy because of my many sins. Heal me with the pardon of your Son. Amen.

REALLY THICK FROSTING

And my God will meet all your needs
according to his glorious riches in Christ
Jesus. Philippians 4:19

Money was tight when I was growing up. We didn't get cake
very often. But on our birthdays Mom would make our
favorite and smear the top with really thick frosting.

The thick frosting is a little picture of what God does for his
own. Visiting members in the hospital either before surgery
or after bad news, I would often quote Paul's words. As believers we have a God who promises to meet all our needs. Paul
doesn't say that God will meet our needs just on our birthdays or now and then. He doesn't hint that perhaps God will
hold back or scrimp, telling me I've had my share or to wait
till it's birthday time next year. He wrote, "My God will meet
all your needs."

For assurance he points to the glorious riches God has already
given us in Christ Jesus. Through his Son, Jesus, God has paid
for all my sins. When I come dragging my heels because I'm
ashamed of how often I have fallen, he doesn't hesitate to
assure me of rich forgiveness. When I trundle my weekly
wheelbarrow of iniquity to him on Sunday morning, he
always says to me, "I have been merciful to you and have
given my only Son to be the atoning sacrifice for your sins."
In Jesus, my Father spreads the thick frosting of his forgiveness on me. How can he do anything else but help me with
all my other needs?

Lord, cover me with Christ's rich forgiveness
and come to help me with all my needs. Amen.

DONE BY ME
OR FOR ME?

Come, you who are blessed by my Father; take
your inheritance, the kingdom prepared for you
since the creation of the world. Matthew 25:34

Faith is invisible. No one can look into another's heart to see
whether faith is there. And yet faith is very visible. On the
Last Day, Jesus will point to faith visible in the lives of
believers. He will reference the works they did as outward
indication of the invisible faith in their hearts. Unfortunately, some still misunderstand that salvation is something
done for us, not by us.

In his preview of the Last Day, note what Jesus calls believers. They are "blessed by my Father." They stand in heaven,
not because of what they have earned but for what the Father
has given them. In their hands is the salvation prepared by
Jesus. Even the faith that holds this salvation is not their
own working but a gift from God's Holy Spirit.

Note that Jesus also uses the word *inheritance*. An inheritance is a gift from the donor not some wage earned by my
efforts. So the kingdom of heaven is God's free gift, graciously willed to me because of what his Son has done. To
make it even clearer, Jesus calls it the kingdom prepared *for*
you, not *by* you. God has done all the work—planning my
salvation in eternity, preparing it on Calvary, and planting
faith in me to receive salvation through the power of the
gospel. Would I want it any other way? What can be more
secure than a heaven guaranteed by the efforts of my gracious God?

Lord, when I stand in glory at your side, all my
praise shall be that you did it all for me. Amen.

LIFE'S GREATEST TREASURE— WHAT IS IT?

The kingdom of heaven is like treasure hidden in a field. When a man found it, he hid it again, and then in his joy went and sold all he had and bought that field. Matthew 13:44

In Jesus' day, people had only the fields in which to hide their valuables. In the dark of night or at the approach of an enemy, they would bury their treasures under the sod. A treasure might stay there for years if something happened to the owner. Then one day a farmer working in the field would feel a tug on his plow, and the treasure would lie exposed. What a find! There it is. It's his and he's rich.

Of what treasure is Jesus speaking in his parable? He means himself. He means the rubies of forgiveness for all my sins, made red by his own blood. He means the gold pieces of his peace for my soul, restored to fellowship with my Maker. He means the diamonds of eternal life, glittering in heaven for me. Christ and all he is, all he offers, all he has, are the treasures he wants me to have.

Several years ago, more than a million people trooped to the Museum of Science and Industry in Chicago to view an exhibit of artifacts from the *Titanic*. Much of their interest was for the lifestyle that vessel represented. The experts tell us that 11 millionaires with a combined wealth of nearly $200 million went down with that ship. What do you think those 11 would have said that day about life's greatest treasure?

What do I say? Hopefully, it's Jesus, Jesus, only Jesus.

God, make it so for me. Amen.

LIFE'S GREATEST TREASURE— WHERE DO I FIND IT?

The kingdom of heaven is like treasure hidden
in a field. When a man found it, he hid it
again, and then in his joy went and sold all he
had and bought that field. Matthew 13:44

People are still looking for the treasure supposedly buried somewhere in Arizona's Superstition Mountains. Every so often some con man takes people for a bundle because he claims to have a map showing where the gold is hidden.

Where do I find Jesus, the supreme treasure? What's the map that leads me to the gold of his pardon and peace? In the parable the man found his treasure right before him in the soil beneath his plow. The wise men from the East found their treasure in the house at Bethlehem. The aged Simeon found it in the temple. The woman of Samaria found it at Jacob's well. Mary of Bethany found it at Jesus' feet. The dying malefactor found it at the center cross. You and I have found it in our parents' homes, at baptismal fonts, in church benches, and at communion rails. All these instances have one thing in common, the blessed gospel message of God.

God's Word is the map he has given me to find life's real treasures. That's why God gave the Scriptures, "to make [us] wise for salvation through faith in Christ Jesus" (2 Timothy 3:15). In his Word, God speaks to me. And his main message is about his Son, my only Savior. Where to find life's real treasure? There's no other place but in the Word.

Lord, help me use the road map of your Word
to know and treasure Jesus all my days. Amen.

LIFE'S GREATEST TREASURE— WHAT DOES IT COST ME?

The kingdom of heaven is like treasure hidden in a field. When a man found it, he hid it again, and then in his joy went and sold all he had and bought that field. Matthew 13:44

The treasure in the field cost the finder nothing. Someone else had paid for it. Yet it cost him everything. He sold his all in order to buy the field so he might have the treasure for himself.

So it is with the treasure of my salvation. Forgiveness for my sins, peace with God, heaven for my future is free for the taking. But only because someone else has already paid for it, a price far beyond my means. My salvation cost Christ everything. Its cost brought him from heaven to take my hideous sins to the cross, to take them into hell for total payment, to take them away forever that he might take me to his heaven. Only God himself could afford the redemptive price for my soul. Now he hands his treasure of salvation freely to me. Christ has covered the cost.

And yet that free treasure costs me everything. When Christ gave his treasure to the disciples, we read, "[They] left everything and followed him" (Luke 5:11). When Paul received this treasure, he declared, "I consider everything a loss compared to the surpassing greatness of knowing Christ Jesus my Lord" (Philippians 3:8). The Savior in my heart means the Savior in my life. New values, attitudes, and actions are mine in life, not because they are forced on me or pressured out of me but because I treasure what God has given me in Jesus more than anything else in the world.

Lord, let my response to your gift of salvation be, "Lord, I give my life and all to you." Amen.

A TRUE BARGAIN

Come to me, all you who are weary and burdened, and I will give you rest.
Matthew 11:28

Bargains are not always bargains. The words "Have I got a bargain for you" not only entice us but also make us wary. We've learned by experience that you only get what you pay for.

In contrast, listen to Jesus' bargain. "Rest" he calls it. He offers removal of sin's guilt, release from its punishment, restraint of its temptations. Often the Savior uses the word *peace* as a synonym for this rest. With sins forgiven the believer can live at peace in the eye of the hurricane called life.

"I will give you rest," Jesus says. His offer hinges on that word *I*. The "I" who offers me forgiveness is the One who forged it on the anvil of his cross. There the hammer of sin's punishment pounded him mercilessly. But when Good Friday's darkness was over, the sunshine of God's forgiveness shone brightly. And I get what Jesus paid for. That's why it's such a bargain. My salvation truly is free for me, a gift of God's grace.

Someone estimated that in the course of a 40-year ministry a preacher speaks from the pulpit a total of about 8,280,000 words or about 270,000 words per year. But none of the preacher's sentences are more comforting than these 16 words: "Come to me, all you who are weary and burdened, and I will give you rest." The Savior himself spoke them. The bargain is real!

Lord, through the Word offer me your bargain
of salvation all the days of my life. Amen.

HE'S THE REAL THING

When John heard in prison what Christ was doing, he sent his disciples to ask him, "Are you the one who was to come, or should we expect someone else?" Matthew 11:2,3

"It's the real thing," said an old Coca-Cola commercial, setting its cola above others. What soft drink may slake my thirst is hardly a vital issue. What salvation can satisfy my soul is!

John the Baptist asked Jesus, "Are you the real thing?" Whether John, in Herod's prison, himself had doubts or whether he was pointing his disciples more to Jesus, we aren't told. More important is how Jesus answered. "Your God will come . . . to save you," Isaiah had written. "Then will the eyes of the blind be opened and the ears of the deaf unstopped" (35:4,5). Isaiah had also written of the coming Savior, "The LORD has anointed me to preach good news to the poor" (61:1). Wasn't that exactly what Jesus was doing? He had to be the real thing, the promised Savior who had finally come.

John's serious question is not strange in our 21st-century world. So many don't even bother to ask about Jesus because they couldn't care less about him. Others, including some within the church, ask the question and then don't accept Jesus' answers about himself and his work. He said, "Scripture cannot be broken." They say, "The Bible is a fallible book containing human errors." He said, "I am the Son of God." They say, "Jesus is only an ideal man." He said, "I am the Savior whose blood covers all your sins." They say, "Jesus is an excellent example who teaches man how to live right." What's my answer to John's question? Eternity depends on it.

God, grant that I reply, "You are the Savior promised by God's love, my only Savior to take me to heaven." Amen.

PRECIOUS IN GOD'S SIGHT

Keep me as the apple of your eye. Psalm 17:8

Is any part of my body more precious than my eyes? With them I watch the evening news, gaze at my loved ones, marvel at the grandeur of God's creation. Consider also how the Creator protects my eyes. He surrounds them with a strong fortress of bone and curtains them with eyelids, eyelashes, and eyebrows. I too try to take good care of my eyes, wanting them to last into old age.

In our verse David claims to be as precious in God's sight as the most important part of the eye, the "apple" or "pupil" as it's called today. How could David be so bold? Had he forgotten what he really was? No, he wrote also of himself, "I was sinful . . . from the time my mother conceived me" (Psalm 51:5). He lamented also of his life, "Against you, you only, have I sinned and done what is evil in your sight" (Psalm 51:4). Apple of God's eye? More likely the object of God's just anger.

Yet David compares himself, if God had a body, to the choicest part. So precious had God made him. And David knew how God did this. It was through the coming Savior who would cleanse him from all sin. That Savior made David into a ruby, an emerald, a diamond, a pearl to shine in God's heavenly crown. Because of Jesus, David could turn to God and pray confidently and forcefully, "Keep me as the apple of your eye." When by faith I can pray the same way, it's only because the Savior has made me precious in God's sight.

> Lord, even more than you protect my eyes,
> assure me you'll protect my soul. Amen.

PROTECTED BY HIS WINGS

Hide me in the shadow of your wings.
Psalm 17:8

"Hide me in the shadow of your wings," David prayed, using a beautiful picture. Every spring for some years a mother robin returned to the nest she had built securely between the wall and the pipe bringing the electrical service to our house. There she sat with her wings completely covering her little brood. But then one spring the neighbor's cat spied the nest, climbed up the pipe, killed the mother, and ate her little ones. So much for safety in the shadow of that mother's wings.

How different with our all-loving, all-knowing, almighty God! Over his own he spreads nail-pierced hands. Those hands speak of his love, a love so great that he's already rescued me from sin and hell. Such hands surely can keep me safe as I make my journey from earth to heaven. When temptations spot my nest, the Savior is my very present help. When sin fouls my nest, the Savior comes with his cleansing blood. When sorrow shinnies up the pipe, his love makes all things work for my good. When death is ready to pounce, Jesus keeps me safe through the valley of the shadows.

What would I call the baby bird that tries to crawl out of its mother's nest and away from its mother's care? The same that I'd call a person who strays from God's Word through which the Spirit creates and continues faith in Jesus. The Word is the nest God has built in which I must sit to be shaded by my Savior's ever-loving arms.

Lord, keep me in your Word and under the shadow of your wings. Amen.

A THREEFOLD PRAYER FOR SUCCESS

May God be gracious to us and bless us and make his face shine upon us. Psalm 67:1

Last week I browsed in the bookstore while my wife shopped in the mall. Computers for dummies and investment strategies for the semi-skilled were just a few of the how-to books lining the shelves.

The psalmist has a how-to prayer for a successful life. He starts with a prayer for God's grace. I can master the computer and know how to invest but without God's grace have nothing. Where God's grace isn't present, his anger is. Where he's not welcomed as Father, he comes as judge. Successful living means praying: "For Jesus' sake forgive my sins. Be my Father and keep me your child."

"May God bless us," the psalmist continues. From God's gracious hand comes all I need for peaceful existence on this earth. I can only receive as he gives. And I can only ask. In answer to my prayers, my Father in his own measure will grant what I need for both body and soul. In his own wise ways he'll "watch over [my] coming and going both now and forevermore" (Psalm 121:8).

"May God make his face shine upon us," the psalmist concludes. I can't make my way successfully in life without God's love shining on me. I need each day lit up with his forgiveness when I fall into sin, his strength when I fight temptation, his life when I face death. Daily I need his Word where his face shines on me. Here's a how-to prayer that I had better take off the shelf and use. It works.

Lord, be gracious to me and bless me and make your face shine upon me for Jesus' sake. Amen.

FOR WHAT WOULD I ASK?

"What do you want me to do for you?" Jesus asked him. The blind man said, "Rabbi, I want to see." "Go," said Jesus, "your faith has healed you." Immediately he received his sight and followed Jesus along the road. Mark 10:51,52

The genie offered three wishes to the three men marooned on a desert island. "I wish I were back home," the first said, and he was gone. "I wish I were at the World Series game," asked the second, and again it was so. "How I miss those two guys," said the third. "I wish they were back."

Jesus' offer is far more factual and important. When he asks "What do you want me to do for you?" how would I respond? The blind beggar that day asked for sight. His plea, "Lord, Son of David, have mercy on me," reveals just for what kind of sight he was asking. The blind man wanted not only his eyes to see but also his heart. He appealed to Jesus as the promised Savior who was to come from David's line. On the Savior's mercy he threw himself, recognizing he had no merit of his own. And he asked in faith. Jesus said so as he healed the beggar. That faith showed in the way the beggar walked with Jesus along the road on the way to Jerusalem and the cross.

Ah, Jesus, how I appreciate your offer. I have so much I need from you, such a long shopping list I could bring. But first and foremost I need the sight you gave that blind man's heart. Give my heart the same 20/20 spiritual vision. Every day lift my faith up to you, Lamb of Calvary, Savior divine.

Dear Jesus, hear me for your mercy's sake when I ask for spiritual sight. Amen.

SO MANY BROTHERS

Both the one who makes men holy and those who are made holy are of the same family. So Jesus is not ashamed to call them brothers.
Hebrews 2:11

I had three sisters but no brothers. Many a time I wished I did. We could have played ball together, stuck up for each other, been pals for life. But brothers were not in God's plan for me.

Yet I have more brothers than I can even imagine. Our verse reminds me that all those whom a gracious God has made holy are my brothers. More important, our verse reveals how God makes sinners holy. It's through the redemptive work of his holy Son, Jesus. That was God's great plan, devised by his love already in eternity. His sinless Son would come to earth to be my brother. The eternal Son of God would become a little pinpoint of life in the womb of a virgin, be born just as I was, walk this earth and taste its pain. Best of all, he would do this for me. He was conceived and born, crucified and died, to pay for my sins. What a brother I have in Jesus! Through his saving work, how many more brothers I have! All those whom God brings to faith in the Savior are numbered with me in God's heavenly family.

When Jesus calls me "brother," I'm happy. I have a big brother who sticks up for me like no one else can. He promises to be my pal—not just for this life but forever. Here on earth he also surrounds me with others related through faith to me. In their company I have joy on the road to heaven.

Jesus, Savior, thank you for becoming my brother. Keep me in faith as your brother. Amen.

LOVE AND FEAR CAN'T BE ROOMMATES

God is love. Whoever lives in love lives in
God, and God in him. . . . There is no fear
in love. But perfect love drives out fear.
1 John 4:16,18

"God is love," John wrote. More than a description of God,
this phrase is an all-inclusive name for him. Luther once
wrote, "If we should desire to paint a picture . . . to represent God, it would have to be a picture of pure love, to bring
out the fact that the divine nature is, as it were, a furnace
aglow with love that fills heaven and earth."

From God's actions I can learn more about this God of love. "Do
you love me?" a child might ask his parent and in response
receive a big hug. "Do you love me?" I ask God and in response
am pointed to Calvary's cross. There his love stretched out nail-
pierced hands in the warmest and widest hug my world will
ever receive. Now through the gospel he reaches down into my
heart and brings me to faith so that I can share with Jesus that
living intimate union with him, the God of love.

When God's love goes with me, there's no room for fear. With
fear John refers to the terror that comes from knowing my sins
have displeased a holy God and deserve hell's punishment.
When God's love enters the heart, more and more such slavish
fear is thrown out and boldness in the day of judgment enters
in. As a believer I know my case has already been settled at Calvary and the verdict is favorable. God is love. Those people
whose hearts he fills with love have no room left for fear.

God of love, through your Word fill my heart
with Jesus so fear dwells there no more. Amen.

MUCH MORE
THAN A GREETING

Grace and peace to you from God our Father
and from the Lord Jesus Christ. Romans 1:7

"How are you?" we'll ask when we meet on the street. "Have a good one," we'll say as we move on. More often than not, such words are just greetings rather than words from the heart.

The apostle Paul begins each of his letters with our verse or a variation of it. *Grace* was a common greeting in the Greek-speaking world. *Peace* was a standard greeting in the Jewish world. When Paul writes these words, he's following the custom of his day. He's extending the usual greetings to his ethnically mixed readers just as we use common salutations today.

But his words *grace* and *peace* are more than just greetings. They are statements of fact for believers. Grace is the quality of God that makes him eager to give to totally undeserving people the best he has to offer. In the word's five letters are summed up the forgiveness of sins God has prepared in his Son, the fear-free consciences he gives to those who trust his Son, and the firm hope of heaven waiting for them through his Son. When God's grace showers such gifts on me, peace is the result. Grace and peace go together. God's grace is the cause and wonderful peace is the result for me. Such grace and peace come only "from God our Father and from the Lord Jesus Christ." Because of their author, Paul's words aren't just a usual greeting; they're blessed reality for me.

Lord, through your Word bring me your grace
and peace in rich measure. Amen.

MATH AS TAUGHT BY JESUS

The man who loves his life will lose it, while the man who hates his life in this world will keep it for eternal life. John 12:25

Addition and subtraction are some of the first facts we learn in mathematics. To subtract means to take away. The more you take away the less you have. To add means to increase. The more you add the more you have. So what does Jesus mean when he says gain is loss and loss is gain?

He's warning me when he says, "The man who loves his life will lose it." All around me others are sweating, striving, and stomping on fingers on their selfish pursuit of earth's treasures. Why can't I be like them? And if I'm not, won't I lose out? Moreover, there's the road to heaven. Even when I know Jesus is the way, the devil tantalizes me with the suggestion that my efforts at Christian living, my dollars for the kingdom, my this and that surely will earn God's love. The Savior warns me, "Follow the world's math and you will end up with eternal loss."

The Savior also assures me, "The man who hates his life in this world will keep it for eternal life." To hate my life doesn't mean to see nothing good in it, but rather to get priorities straight. When I believe in Jesus and have eternal life through him, worldly living loses its glamour for me. Nothing the world offers can hold a candle to the eternal life Jesus has waiting for me. When the world gets in the way, hate is the right word for my reaction, just as gain is the right word for the life Jesus has waiting for me.

Lord, teach me your math and help me practice it in life. Amen.

⌐ OUR FAVORITE FOOD

How sweet are your words to my taste, sweeter than honey to my mouth! Psalm 119:103

What's your favorite meal? Mine is pasta and beef. When I'd return home from a trip to the mission field, my wife usually had my favorite meal waiting for me. And it was good!

God uses food to nourish my body, replenish my strength, and keep me healthy. Leafy vegetables, omega-3 fatty acids found in fish, and even broccoli are good for me. They are gifts from the hand of God. So is his Word. The psalmist describes God's Word as sweeter than honey—the sweetest thing known in his day. I don't cut the Bible up and lift it page by page to my mouth. I don't cook, bake, or fry it in order to eat it. I taste God's Word when I read it, listen to it, and hear it at church or home.

Always that Word is good for me. It may taste sour at times. The law makes my soul pucker as God's commands point out how often I've done what I shouldn't and haven't done what I should. I need the bitter taste of the law or else the sweet taste of the gospel wouldn't appeal at all. The gospel with its good news of Jesus' payment for my sins—how sweet it tastes to my hungry soul! What can delight my soul the way the gospel does when it points me to the cross of my Savior and causes me to kneel in faith beneath it?

Pasta and beef may be favorites when it comes to my body. But they're nothing like God's Word with its news of Jesus' forgiveness as sweet food for my soul.

Lord, give me a good appetite for your Word so that I be healthy in my faith in Jesus. Amen.

THE OIL OF THANKSGIVING

Always [give] thanks to God the Father for everything, in the name of our Lord Jesus Christ. Ephesians 5:20

"Always check the oil," my father drummed into me. Whether it was the tractor, the car, or the lawn mower, don't start it without checking the oil. To this day, I check my mower.

Did you ever think of thanksgiving as a lubricant? As something that makes life run better and keeps it from grinding in complaint? When I look at what my neighbor has and what I don't, envy may start its grating in my heart. When I contrast my efforts at church to that of others, self-righteousness may whistle in my ears. It's so easy to complain. But complaining can only make life bitter.

Time to check the oil. Before I can be thankful, I need to inventory what God has given me. Where should I start but at the cross of Jesus? How could he love me so much to die for my sins? How can he keep on forgiving me so often? Let my neighbor worry about his sins. I have plenty of my own. But for each of them I have God's forgiveness through Jesus' blood. My forgiving God is also my providing God. He gives me what I need for body and life. I may not always recognize the form in which his blessings come, but that doesn't stop them from being his good gifts to me. Paul told me to give thanks for everything. Do I hear you ask about the oil can? God's Word, of course. It keeps my heart lubricated so that in Jesus' name I can be thankful for everything.

Lord, fill me with the good news of the Savior so that my heart overflows with thanksgiving. Amen.

DON'T WASTE GOD'S GRACE

As God's fellow workers we urge you not to receive God's grace in vain. 2 Corinthians 6:1

My mother didn't always follow the doctor's advice. When he gave her a prescription, she'd use it for a bit and stop when she felt better. Or she'd take only one pill instead of the two it said. "Don't waste your money going to the doctor if you don't follow his advice," I finally told her one day.

Some people do the same thing with God's grace. His grace is the salvation he has prepared for sinners like me in Christ Jesus. I deserve punishment for my sins, but he forgives me in Christ. I deserve to be far removed from him and reserved for an eternal hell, but God comes to me to make me his child, an heir of heaven. That's grace. In his Word, God offers me his grace like some prescription. He wants me to use it as directed, not according to my own inclinations or whims.

How might I receive God's marvelous grace in vain? I may hear of his forgiveness for all my sins and yet let the memory of some special sin rub my conscience sore. I may hear of his great love for me and yet let the special circumstances of my life ruin my days with worry. I may hear his command to live a holy life and yet run with the idea that since he is so gracious, I can sin all I want. Or I might even throw away the prescription bottle of his grace as if I had no use for it. The opposite of receiving God's grace in vain is using it in generous doses daily for the well-being of my soul.

Help me, gracious Father, to use your Word daily. Amen.

HE LEADS ME

We live by faith, not by sight. 2 Corinthians 5:7

Waiting for the train in the Washington, DC, subway station, I watched a blind man with his seeing-eye dog. When the train stopped, the dog led his master forward, across the threshold of the car, and safely to a seat inside. That blind man must have had a lot of trust in his dog's guidance. Consider the danger he could have fallen into near those tracks.

God has promised to lead me by the hand through this life to heaven. Yet at times I feel blind. I can't see where he's taking me. Some days when sins pile up on the shoulders of my soul, it's as if I can't find Jesus' cross where he paid for me. When troubles, like dangerous gaps, come between me and the train of life, I often grope around as if fog has separated me from God's hand. And what about when the day of death draws near? So dark it can appear and so dangerous its shadows that I'm not sure I can trust God to lead the way.

God doesn't ask me for blind trust. Instead, he reminds me how worthy of my trust he is. Again and again he has shown his love in my salvation. As Paul once put it, "He who did not spare his own Son, but gave him up for us all—how will he not also, along with him, graciously give us all things?" (Romans 8:32). God loves me so much that he sent his Son to bear my punishment and die my death. Such a God I can trust to lead me to heaven even if some days I don't understand his ways.

> Lord, through your Word remind me of your love in Jesus so that I trust your leading in life. Amen.

WHY ME?

You did not choose me, but I chose you and appointed you to go and bear fruit—fruit that will last. John 15:16

"Why me?" can be a question of despair when something dreadful happens. Or it can be an exclamation of joy when something wondrously good comes into life. I don't think we need to ask what that question means when it's applied to our verse.

Why did Jesus choose me to be his own? That's right, I didn't choose him; he chose me. I didn't find him; he found me. I didn't come to faith in him; he brought me to faith. There's only one reason why I believe in him as my only Savior and way to heaven. *He chose me!* It was not because I was better than other sinners or more easily converted. My heart was just as hard in unbelief and my load of sin just as huge as all the others. He chose me out of grace and grace alone.

Doesn't that bring the joyful question: "Why me, Lord?" I just can't appreciate enough God's grace that has brought me salvation. I just can't marvel enough at God's love in making me his child and heir of heaven. The more I look at my utter unworthiness and his undeserved grace, the more I'll rejoice daily, "Thank you, Lord, for choosing me." And while I'm thanking him, I'll be telling others about him. They too need his grace. They too need to hear how he saves. I want them too to join me in asking with eternal joy in heaven, "Why me, Lord?"

Thank you, Lord, for your grace in choosing me.
Fill my heart with the joy of salvation. Amen.

WHAT GOD HAS DONE FOR ME

Come and listen, all you who fear God; let me tell you what he has done for me. Psalm 66:16

It was the day after Thanksgiving, and the grandfather of the family was being buried. Several days before his death, he had asked his pastor to use our verse as the basis for the funeral sermon. "I don't want a lot of tears," he said. "I want them to give thanks for what God has done for me."

Like that grandfather, I am a sinner. Not a day goes by when I don't sin against my holy God. But Christ died for all my sins. When the Savior carried the world's sins to Calvary's cross, part of that load came from me. When the Savior cried from the cross about sin's payment being finished, he meant mine too. Moreover, he sent his Spirit to bring me to faith in him as my Savior. What I couldn't do by my own thinking or strength, the Holy Spirit did for me, calling me to faith by the gospel. God's grace opened my eyes to see, my ears to hear, my heart to hold the Savior.

God even promises to keep me in this faith till the end. I remain a believer only because of his grace. Left to myself, my faith could only shrivel away in the ferocious winds of this world. But God's Spirit works through the gospel as I hear and read it, to continue and even increase my faith. God will do still more for me. When I take my last breath, he will carry me home to his heaven.

If like that grandfather I want people to know what God has done for me, there's no better place to start than with my eternal salvation through Christ Jesus.

Thank you, Lord, for all you have done for me. Amen.

WHAT GOD DOES WITH SIN

Blessed is he whose transgressions are forgiven, whose sins are covered. Blessed is the man whose sin the LORD does not count against him.
Psalm 32:1,2

Are you still playing the excuse game when it comes to sin? David tried it unsuccessfully, refusing to use the word *wrong* for his sins of adultery and murder. Though my sins may not be as glaring, I try it too. "Everyone else is doing it," I excuse. "I'm not as bad as so and so," I weasel. But relief comes only when, like David, I turn to God in repentance and am reminded of what he does with sin.

What does God do with sin? As a sinner I need to know. "Transgressions are forgiven," David writes. The word *forgiven* means "carried away." With eyes of faith, David saw God's Son carrying the whole stinking mess of his sins to the cross in payment for them. "Sins are covered," he also says. The word *covered* means more than using some canvas to cover them and hoping God won't catch on. With eyes of faith, David saw the precious blood of Jesus erasing his sins so that they would never again be visible to God's sight. "Whose sin the LORD does not count against him," David concludes. God cannot just write "canceled" over sin's unpaid debt. Instead, he sent his Son to settle the account by paying in full the amount due.

When the church father Augustine's life was ebbing away, he asked a friend to paint David's words on the wall opposite his bed. Upon these glorious words he gazed as the darkness closed in. What else do I need? Blessed, indeed, are those who know what God does with sin.

Lord, comfort my penitent heart with the blessed news of what you have done with my sins. Amen.

WHEN THE ROCKS FALL, CRY TO THE LORD

Out of the depths I cry to you, O Lord. . . . Let your ears be attentive to my cry for mercy. If you, O Lord, kept a record of sins, O Lord, who could stand? Psalm 130:1-3

"Danger, falling rocks," says a highway sign. On this stretch of road, rocks have tumbled down the cliff before and very likely will again. How much like the life of a Christian.

Sometimes we think that those standing on the Rock of Ages should be sheltered from all falling rocks in life. Shouldn't believers be freed from all of life's problems? How flabby faith's muscles would become if such were the case. Like some master carpenter, God uses the sandpaper of trouble to bring out the grain in our faith. Far better than the question "Why falling rocks?" is "What should I do when rocks fall?"

"Cry to the Lord," the psalmist tells me. And he even tells me where to start—with my sins. Don't misunderstand him. He's not saying that troubles come because of my sins. That would leave me comfortless as a rock-bruised believer. God has already punished his Son for all my transgressions. Rather, when the rocks fall, I need to turn to my gracious God, acknowledging that I deserve no help from him. I can make no demands on him. If he were to check my record, I wouldn't dare even knock on his door. As a darkroom is necessary to develop film, so at times God necessarily allows falling rocks to turn me to him in humble repentance and cry to him for undeserved help.

Lord, so many rocks, so often. Help me cry out of life's depths to you for undeserved help. Amen.

WHEN THE ROCKS FALL, WAIT FOR THE LORD

I wait for the LORD, my soul waits, and in his word I put my hope. My soul waits for the Lord more than watchmen wait for the morning.
Psalm 130:5,6

Waiting can be so difficult. Some of us have gone through nights when we've waited for the morning. Perhaps a night of weeping, when at the sickbed of a loved one we sat watching the clock tick away the minutes like hours. Or perhaps some night of expectant waiting, when we couldn't wait for morning to come because of the joy it would bring. Like some child waiting for gift-opening time on Christmas morning or some vacationer just waiting to leave daily drudgery behind, even more than these, the believer's soul waits for the Lord.

When the rocks fall in life, I'll never go wrong if I put my hope in God's Word. Some may laugh at my simple trust in his promises. Yet what do those people have to offer in place of this hope that has never failed my fathers and will not fail me? I prefer the gospel moorings to the scoffers' aimless driftings on seas of doubt. I prefer the chart and compass of God's Word to passing human theories. I prefer, instead of merely covering my head in fear when the rocks fall in life, to raise my head in confidence to the Lord and wait in hope for him to keep his promises. When I doubt, as I will at times, may he point me to his Son's cross where he has fulfilled his greatest promise of forgiveness for the jagged, constantly tumbling rocks of my sins. That cross is the signature of his love, guaranteeing the validity of all his promises.

> Lord, I don't ask you to keep all rocks out of my life but to raise my eyes to your promises. Amen.

WHEN THE ROCKS FALL, RECEIVE FROM THE LORD

But with you there is forgiveness. . . . With the LORD is unfailing love and with him is full redemption. He himself will redeem Israel from all their sins. Psalm 130:4,7,8

A promise is only as good as the one who makes it. Ever learn this truth from bitter experience? When a roof with a 25-year warranty goes bad and the company who laid it gives you the runaround, what can you do? They promised, even in writing, but!

God keeps his promises—always! Two short sentences in our verses remind me of this comforting truth. The first declares, "With you there is forgiveness." The second states, "With him is full redemption." Don't miss the wonder of those words. They point me to Christ the great Redeemer. They assure me that I have a God who loves me so much that he would not let me die in my sins but, instead, sent his Son to die for me. They point me to a God who loves me so much that he cannot bear the thought of having me plunged into the hell I deserved. So, instead, he, through his Son, prepared his free gift of heaven for me. Look what I receive from his loving hand—all that I need for my soul.

You know what else these words tell me? They remind me that a loving God who would do such great things for my soul will also help with my lesser needs in life. How can he, who in Christ has freely given the five million dollars my soul needs, not give the five dollars I need for my bodily life? He has said so. His Word is good. I can count on him when the rocks fall in life.

> Lord, let the rich forgiveness you give my soul assure me of your daily care for me. Amen.

COME ON! FESS UP!

When men fall down, do they not get up?
When a man turns away, does he not return?
. . . I have listened attentively, but they do
not say what is right. No one repents of his
wickedness, saying, "What have I done?"
Jeremiah 8:4,6

Spilt milk spotted the floor near the refrigerator. But little Ben, though wearing a white mustache, claimed he was innocent. "Come on, Ben," his mother said, "Fess up."

That's what God was saying to the children of Judah. His prophet Jeremiah had worked among them for 40 years, calling them to repentance. But the people of Judah weren't listening. Unlike someone who quickly jumps back to his feet when he has fallen, they just lay there stubbornly in sin's dirt. Unlike some traveler who quickly turns around after taking the wrong road, they just doggedly insisted on traveling the road away from God. Though God pictures himself as attentively bending down from heaven to hear even the slightest sigh of repentance from them, they refused.

Does God's repentance call apply to our land? Of course, but I gain more if I apply it to myself. Have I ever shrugged aside his call as if I didn't need it? ever excused my sins by comparing them to someone else's? ever blocked out the story of Christ's cross with the thought, "I know all that"? Then it's time to hear my Father say, "Come on, fess up, my child." Time to pray again: "Lord, help me see my sins. Above all, help me see the cross with its message of Jesus crucified for me."

Lord, help me see my sins and truly repent
of them. Help me see my Savior and trust
him. Amen.

TAKE THE TRUST TEST

Let not the wise man boast of his wisdom or the strong man boast of his strength or the rich man boast of his riches, but let him who boasts boast about this: that he understands and knows . . . the LORD. Jeremiah 9:23,24

Wisdom is important in this world. It has brought us computers, space capsules, heart transplants. We need to pursue wisdom with might and main. Yet if we put our trust in it, we only end up being miserable intelligently. Strength is important too. The best offense against aggression is a good defense. Yet history reveals that powers rise only to fall. And we cannot live without riches. They're the legal tender necessary to pay our bills. Someone has estimated that if you could gather the world's gold into one place, it would equal the size of a ten-room house. Yet with all that no person can buy a moment of real peace or a second of eternal happiness.

Where do I put my trust? The Lord himself answers, "Let him who boasts boast about this: that he understands and knows me." Knowing God is much more than knowing something about him. It means knowing who he is, what he has done and is doing for me, where he is taking me, and how I can get there. It means knowing that he is a Lord who doesn't deal with me as my sins deserve, but according to his love. Knowing how that love literally compelled him to send his Son to pay for my sins and satisfy his justice. Knowing that through his gift of faith, Christ's robe of righteousness dresses me for heaven. When by his grace I know and trust him, I'm safe on earth and for heaven.

Lord, you ask where my trust is. Give me faith to answer that it's in you and you only. Amen.

WHAT DOES MY EBENEZER STONE SAY?

Then Samuel took a stone and set it up between Mizpah and Shen. He named it Ebenezer, saying, "Thus far has the Lord helped us." 1 Samuel 7:12

"Historical marker ahead," says a road sign. We've learned to stop for such markers on our travels rather than speeding by. By reading them, we've learned much about past events.

If I set up such a marker on the road of my life, what would it say? Like the Ebenezer stone Samuel put up for Israel, would it detail what the Lord has done to save me? God had blessed the Israelites beyond measure, but success fogged their minds. They forgot the Lord, blasphemed his house, and lost his Word in the dust of neglect—until that day at Mizpah when the enemy army surrounded them. Finally the Israelites realized how far they had strayed. Penitently they confessed, "We have sinned against the Lord." In answer, the Lord crushed the enemy and assured the Israelites of forgiveness. Up went their Ebenezer stone for all who passed by to read, "Thus far has the Lord helped us," forgiving our sins.

So what would my Ebenezer stone say? Wouldn't it be something about victory in the greatest battle of all? How God through Christ has given me victory over sin, death, and the devil? Samuel's stone was a preview of the rocks that held Christ's cross in place on Calvary as he victoriously cried out of the battle against sin, "It is finished." Samuel's stone was also a preview of the rock rolled away from the Savior's empty tomb in witness of God's perfect forgiveness and sure heaven for me. Looking at Jesus' filled cross and emptied tomb, wouldn't I want my stone to say, "Thus far the Lord has helped me, forgiving my sins"?

Lord, thank you for this victory. Use me to tell others. Amen.

SOMETHING TO SING ABOUT—VICTORY

Then Moses and the Israelites sang this song to the LORD: "I will sing to the LORD, for he is highly exalted. The horse and its rider he has hurled into the sea. The LORD is my strength and my song; he has become my salvation." Exodus 15:1,2

"Who wants to go to heaven if all they do there is sing?" asked the teenager. The Scriptures do speak about believers singing in heaven. When we look closely, though, we note that it's not so much the singing that is stressed, but to whom and about what we will sing.

As the bodies of the Egyptian soldiers washed ashore, the Israelites sang. Let out of Egypt by the Lord, they had camped, rejoicing beside the Red Sea. But like some balloon brought too close to the fire, their joy had popped. Pharaoh's troops had been right behind them. The Israelite's situation looked hopeless till the Lord led them to safety through the dammed up waters of the sea. Then those water walls became his weapon in wiping out Egypt's strike force. It was of victory that the Israelites sang and to the One who had gained it. "I will sing to the LORD," each one said, "for he is highly exalted."

When will the world learn that fighting with God is no contest? Better still, when will we learn? All the threats against Christ's church from all those godless isms—materialism, humanism, modernism—will fail. We don't have to defend God. He's very capable of defending himself and us! The more I'm assured of his victory, the more I'll be ready to sing to him.

Lord, it's your church bought by your Son's blood. Assure us that you protect your own. Amen.

SOMETHING TO SING ABOUT—LIBERTY

Then Moses and the Israelites sang this song to the LORD: "I will sing to the LORD, for he is highly exalted. The horse and its rider he has hurled into the sea. The LORD is my strength and my song; he has become my salvation." Exodus 15:1,2

He had served 11 years of his sentence when the modern detective tool of DNA testing indicated his innocence. "You don't know what it feels like to be free," he said with a big smile on his face.

The Israelites knew. Whole generations of Israelites had never known freedom. Over four centuries of slavery in Egypt had all but erased freedom from their memories. But now as those Egyptian corpses washed ashore, the Israelites tasted liberty. And the taste was so exhilarating that they burst into song. "I will sing to the LORD," they said, "for he is highly exalted."

Much more glorious liberty is ours. And just as with the Israelites, water and God's power have something to do with it. Through the water of Baptism, connected with the power of the Word, God set me free. At my baptism he told the devil: "Hands off. This is now my child. His name is written with my Son's blood in my book of heaven." Through his powerful Word, God assures me again and again: "You're free from sin. My Son's blood still covers them." Through his blessed Communion meal he says it too: "Go in peace. Your sins are forgiven." God has set me free from sin's punishment, Satan's power, and hell's prison. Such liberty is surely something for me to sing about!

Lord, don't let me take my freedom from sin for granted. Help me rejoice in it daily. Amen.

SOMETHING TO SING ABOUT—ETERNITY

Then Moses and the Israelites sang this song to the LORD: "I will sing to the LORD, for he is highly exalted. The horse and its rider he has hurled into the sea. The LORD is my strength and my song; he has become my salvation." Exodus 15:1,2

Taking the long-range view can be difficult. Whether it's adversity or prosperity, we tend to live only for today. Today's problems tie us in knots. Today's prosperity turns our vision downward.

The Old Testament often uses Israel's victory at the Red Sea to point to the eternal victory won by the blood of God's own Son. Ahead lies the promised land to which God will lead his people of all times, that heavenly Canaan with its everlasting glory. John in Revelation 15:3 says of believers here: "[They] sang the song of Moses the servant of God and the song of the Lamb: 'Great and marvelous are your deeds, Lord God Almighty. Just and true are your ways, King of the ages.'" Looking ahead to heaven's eternal victory, the Israelites had something to sing about.

But they forgot. They let their present-day problems fog over God's long-range promise of heaven. They even let that fog cloud over the lovely face of the Savior who would lead them into eternity. The same can happen to me. Ahead of heaven's complaint window stands a long line with me as a regular in it. When I get lost in life's problems and sorrows, I lose sight of the eternal glory Jesus has prepared for me. When I take the long-range view, nobody will have to tell me to sing.

Lord, in all conditions of life, teach me to sing joyously because of the heaven waiting for me. Amen.

SOLA SCRIPTURA

Your word is truth. John 17:17

Seldom do artists show Martin Luther without the Book. From Schadow's monument in the marketplace at Wittenberg to Cranach's famous portrait, Luther is shown with the Bible in his hands.

For good reason. Remember that day at Worms, April 18, 1521? Filling the hall were the politically powerful of church and state and one humble monk from Wittenberg. Asked if he would take back anything of what he had written, the monk bravely replied, "Unless I can be instructed and convinced with evidence from holy Scriptures or with open, clear, and distinct grounds and reasoning—and my conscience is captive to the Word of God—then I cannot and will not recant." Then came that famous line: "Here I stand. I can do no other. God help me. Amen."

Luther stood on the Word—all of it, nothing more and nothing less. What the Word said, he said. What the word taught, he taught. What the Word opposed, he opposed. "Sola Scriptura" was his theme—Scripture and Scripture only.

What about me? Am I willing to abide by what Scripture says whether it always meets my fancy? Am I ready to demand that my church teach nothing but what Scripture says? Do I understand that ripping out any page of Scripture makes all the remaining pages suspect? Do I realize that to attack any part of Scripture is to attack its central teaching of salvation through Jesus? "Here I stand," Luther said, pointing to the solid foundation of God's true Word.

God, help me do the same. Amen.

THANK YOU, LORD, FOR MARTIN LUTHER

Therefore, there is now no condemnation for those who are in Christ Jesus. Romans 8:1

"I'm afraid to die," said a man in a hospital bed. A pastor, recognizing the man's need, spoke about Christ's payment for sin and the removal of death's sting. "I'm afraid of my sin," said a woman in a counseling session. A pastor, recognizing the woman's need, told her: "God has fully paid for your sin by his Son's death. Your sin is gone from you and from God's memory."

Do we realize, though, that pastors might not be telling people such wonderful news if it weren't for the work of Martin Luther? Through his servant, God restored the saving message of how "God made him who had no sin to be sin for us, so that in him we might become the righteousness of God" (2 Corinthians 5:21). Through Luther's work God placed before sinners' eyes the truth they desperately need, how "the blood of Jesus, his Son, purifies us from all sin" (1 John 1:7).

Listen to what Luther had to say once God had led him into the Scriptures and as a result to the Savior's cross. He wrote: "If the great, sublime article called the forgiveness of sins is correctly understood, it makes one a genuine Christian and gives one eternal life. This is the very reason why it must be taught in Christendom with unflagging diligence and without ceasing, so that people may learn to understand it plainly" (*What Luther Says, An Anthology,* Vol. 1, p. 514). Only because of what God gave me in his Word and enabled me to see clearly through Luther can I live in hope and die in peace. Today we mark the Reformation.

Thank you, Lord, for Martin Luther. Amen.

NEVER DONE GROWING

> But grow in the grace and knowledge of our
> Lord and Savior Jesus Christ. 2 Peter 3:18

"My, how you've grown." Remember how embarrassed you felt when some aunt at a family gathering would make that comment? "Yes," Mother would reply, "I just can't keep him in jeans."

Came a time when I reached physical maturity. Growing stopped, except around the middle where I don't want it. In one area, though, I'm never done growing. I can never learn too much about the "knowledge of our Lord and Savior Jesus Christ." "Knowledge" is my understanding of the Bible's truths. I hadn't learned them all when I finished catechism class. Nor did I understand fully what I did learn. Now as an adult I ask different questions and need fuller answers.

Also I need to keep growing in "the grace of our Lord and Savior Jesus Christ." *Grace* refers to undeserved gifts from a loving God. What could be more undeserving than his gift of salvation in Jesus? He prepared that gift for an undeserving world. That's salvation in general. He prepared that gift for me. That's salvation in particular. Until life ends, I need to grow in appreciating his grace.

How can I grow? My body does it through regular feeding. So does my soul. I need a steady diet of God's Word if I'm to keep growing in the knowledge and grace of my Lord and Savior Jesus Christ.

> Lord, make me hungry for the saving truths of
> your nourishing Word. Amen.

THE QUESTION EVERYONE MUST ANSWER

"What shall I do, then, with Jesus who is called Christ?" Pilate asked. Matthew 27:22

Some questions I can't answer. Like what the year 2020 will bring. Other questions I may refuse to answer. Like what my Social Security number is when cashing a check. To still other questions, I may just give a shrug of my shoulders because they don't interest me. But one question I have to answer, the one Pilate asked the enemies of Jesus, "What shall I do, then, with Jesus who is called Christ?"

Pilate's answer was to send Jesus to the cross. He knew Jesus was innocent. He knew what was right and what was wrong. Yet he sentenced Jesus to death and tried to wash the innocent blood off his hands. Peter's answer, at least for the moment, was to deny his Lord. The other disciples answered by running away in fear, though after Easter they all found the right answer.

What's my answer? The world advises me not to give one. To them this question is not important. Just as in Jesus' days on earth, people today choose eternal damnation instead of the eternal life he offers. They give the King of kings a cross instead of a throne in their hearts. They choose Satan's dominance instead of the freedom from sin Jesus brings. And they urge me to do the same.

God, help me through the power of your Word to answer: "He's my only Savior. There's only one thing I want to do with him. Believe him. Confess him. Follow him all the way to heaven."

> In this unbelieving world, Lord, help me answer, "You're my Lord and my God, my Savior." Amen.

MY SECRET WEAPON

I have hidden your word in my heart that I might not sin against you. Psalm 119:11

"Learn those Bible passages," the pastor insisted in my confirmation class. "You never know when you'll need them." He didn't just mean for my witnessing to others. He was also referring to defending myself against the attacks of sin.

The psalmist agreed. He spoke about hiding God's Word in his heart. Notice he didn't say in his head. Head knowledge of God's Word is like a toy rifle that can't fire. Heart knowledge is the real thing, loaded with live ammunition, ready to fire when the devil attacks. When Satan skirmishes with me, it won't do for me to tell him, "Go away." But when I raise the rifle of God's Word, he ducks for cover. Like Jesus when tempted by Satan in the wilderness, my best weapon is "It is written."

Scripture isn't exaggerating when it describes the Christian life as daily warfare. Soldiers engaged in battle want the right weapons. So do I. That pastor was right when he urged me to memorize those Bible passages. They are my secret weapons against sin's regular attacks. The best bullets are the ones with Christ's name on them. Satan, above all, attacks my faith in the Savior. I need every verse I can get about my full salvation in Jesus to fire back at him.

Lord, arm me with your Word. Help me hide its words in my heart and use them when attacked. In Jesus' name I ask this. Amen.

A WORD DIFFICULT TO UNDERSTAND

I tell you, her many sins have been forgiven—
for she loved much. Luke 7:47

Some words in the Bible are difficult to understand. For example, how would you define *eternity*? Or though the Bible doesn't actually use the word, how would you explain the concept of the Trinity? Now what about the word *forgive*?

The people of Jesus' day thought they understood what this word meant until they saw Jesus in action. Like the time when he was dining at the house of Simon the Pharisee. While they were at the table, a woman with a sinful reputation slipped into the room. She washed Jesus' feet with her tears, dried them with her hair, and anointed them with expensive oil. She was kneeling at the feet of her Savior. With her actions she was showing how much his forgiveness meant to her.

Simon objected. He thought Jesus should have sent this woman packing instead of telling her, "Your sins are forgiven." That's what he would have done. But Jesus doesn't treat people the way we do. He doesn't just show love to those he thinks deserve it. He offers his forgiveness to all. He gives it to sinners, not because they deserve it but because they need it. His love reaches for all people, even me. I don't deserve even half an ounce of his forgiveness. Yet because of his love for sinners, he tells me just as he told that woman and wanted to tell Simon, "Your sins are forgiven." Jesus' forgiveness brings me joy, even though I can't begin to understand the love behind it.

Thank you for the love that forgives me.
Help me treasure it though I cannot
understand it. Amen.

LIFE NOW

> I write these things to you who believe in the name of the Son of God so that you may know that you have eternal life. 1 John 5:13

"Life" insurance doesn't really insure life. It provides benefits when I die. And those benefits go to others, not to me. I keep paying the premiums so others I love may receive when I die.

Jesus is true life insurance for me. His policy promises not a cash benefit but life that never ends. That benefit comes not to my survivors but to me. And I do not have to die before I first collect. "You have eternal life," the apostle writes in our verse. Right now eternal life is mine. From the moment God's Spirit, through the gospel, works faith in my heart, I'm eternally alive. Membership in the heavenly Father's family, assurance of protection from him as his child, and the sure promise of a permanent home in his heaven are mine to enjoy now. I don't have to wait till I die to receive the benefits of this wonderful life insurance. I can cash it in and benefit every day. What a difference that makes in my life! As I travel its bumpy road, my heart rejoices in the eternal life I already have. I endure life's troubles, knowing that the eternal life I already enjoy will be even better in heaven.

What about the premium? God's Son paid it in full. That's why I can be sure about eternal life. Jesus, with his life and death and resurrection, paid for me the total cost for the life that never ends. Kneeling in faith beneath his cross, I can say, "I know that I have eternal life, beginning right now."

Thank you, Lord, for paying the premium. Help me enjoy eternal life already now. Amen.

A RESCUE TEAM OF ONE

He has rescued us from the dominion of
darkness and brought us into the kingdom of
the Son he loves, in whom we have redemption,
the forgiveness of sins. Colossians 1:13,14

While visiting the Coast Guard base on Kodiak Island, we were
impressed with the personnel. They braved strong winds and
high seas to launch rescue attempts for fishing boats out on
the chilly waters off the Alaskan coast. Accounts of their
heroism make for interesting reading.

Paul in our verse writes of the most amazing rescue mission
ever. Souls were lost in sin's darkness. The chilly waters of
damnation were sucking down the whole human race. Mankind
had only one way to go, not down to the bottom of some sea,
but to an eternal hell. Though sinners tried to bail out the ship
of life with their own works, it still kept sinking. Though they
pretended all was well, they floundered more and more. The
inevitable end was death on the high seas of sin.

So a loving God launched his rescue team. Only one was on
it, his Son whom he loved. That Son left the safety of heaven
for earth. He braved the worst storms that hell could devise
to pay for all the sins of all mankind. He even died on God's
rescue mission. But the third day he rose again to show that
redemption was there for all. No longer do sinners have to
drown in hell. They can live forever in a storm-free heaven.
But only through the forgiveness God's Son has won for
them. More than heroism, this rescue mission required love
as only God could give. More than reading about this mission,
I'm part of it. God's Son has rescued me. Thank God for the
faith by which I know this.

May the God of love who rescued me through
his Son keep me safe till I reach heaven. Amen.

MORE THAN ENOUGH GRACE

Where sin increased, grace increased all the more. Romans 5:20

When company comes for dinner, I can expect leftovers the rest of the week. My wife doesn't want to run out of food. So she prepares way more than we'll need.

God's grace is something like that. He always has more than enough grace to cover my needs. I pile up my mountain of sin, one dump truck load after another, in daily life till it towers like some Mount McKinley before me. But Mount Grace that my God built on Calvary always stands taller. I dig the pit of punishment for my sin so deep that, lying on its bottom, I can't even see the top. But God's hand of grace is always long enough to reach down to me. I earn death over and over again as the wage for my sins till I'd have to languish a zillion years in hell if eternity had time. But God's grace always has more than enough to cover my enormous debt. I simply cannot outsin his grace.

Such a thought dare not be encouragement for me to sin all I want. Rather, God's more-than-enough grace is my comfort when I do fall into sin. Each night when I pray on my pillow, "Forgive my sins," I don't have to add, "if they aren't too many for your grace." When I sorrow over the wreckage the tornado of sudden sin has brought, I don't have to fear, "Will this one be beyond his grace?" When my final night comes on this earth, I don't have to worry, "Are some of my sins still there, not covered by his grace?" God's grace is always more than enough to cover all my sins.

Lord, comfort me with the assurance that your plenteous grace covers all my sins. Amen.

HE'LL FINISH THE JOB

Being confident of this, that he who began a good work in you will carry it on to completion until the day of Christ Jesus. Philippians 1:6

What if my remaining in faith depended on me? What if God were to tell the believer: "There, I brought you to faith. Now you're on your own to keep faith ticking"? Some think that's the way it is. They even think faith is something they produce. And they think faith is something they can preserve. Sometimes they even go so far as to claim, "Once a believer always a believer."

Notice where Paul put his confidence. He pointed to God. "He's the one who began the good work in you," he told his readers. Just as with salvation, so with faith. It's God's good work. He makes the unwilling willing. He opens sealed hearts. He dynamites out unbelief and plants faith. Faith is God's good work in my heart.

Notice also who Paul said would carry my faith to completion. Again it's God. He won't quit with the job half done. He'll continue to assure me that Jesus is my Savior till Christ comes to take me to be with him in heaven. Though faith's creation and continuance are God's workings, he does remind me through what faith comes. It's the power of his gospel in Word and sacrament. He expects me to use these mighty means faithfully. Like the jetliner hooked up to the refueling tanker, God tells me to link to his gospel. When I do, he gives my faith the staying power it needs.

Lord, keep me close to your gospel through which you refuel my faith for heaven's flight. Amen.

HOW DO YOU MEASURE GOD'S LOVE?

I pray that you . . . may have power . . . to grasp how wide and long and high and deep is the love of Christ, and to know this love that surpasses knowledge. Ephesians 3:17-19

My wife and I take woodworking classes together. I'm the impulsive type who'll saw the board without measuring too carefully. My wife, more exacting from her years of quilting, will hand me the tape measure. "Are you sure it's as long and wide as you want?" she'll ask.

What tape measure can I use for God's love? Paul, already by adding a fourth dimension to the usual three, is telling me that such measurement is impossible. My mind simply can't stretch far enough to measure the width, length, height, and depth of God's love. How do I measure a love that sacrificed his Son for undeserving me? What numbers should I write down for a love that left heaven behind to come to earth? That took the world's sin on holy shoulders to Calvary's cross? That caused the eternal One to breathe his last on that cross? All for my salvation! My mind can't measure more than the first few inches of this love's dimensions. Such love surpasses knowledge.

God doesn't ask me to measure his love. He asks me to believe in it. And that's why Paul prays that I "may have power." Only God's Spirit, as he works through the gospel, can power my heart to believe what my mind cannot measure. I still try to measure, not to understand but to marvel even more at God's love for me.

Holy Spirit, draw me into the Word so that I may more understand and appreciate God's love. Amen.

THE SAME OLD THING

Know that a man is not justified by
observing the law, but by faith in Jesus
Christ. Galatians 2:16

"Why should I come to church," replied the straying member,
"if all I ever hear is the same old stuff?" Sometimes we might
agree. It seems like the pastor has only one sermon. Over and
over he preaches about "justification," how God has declared
sinners innocent because his Son took their guilt.

Can I ever hear too much about Jesus' blood purifying me
from all sin? When I pay my respects at the funeral home,
how does the conversation so often go? Isn't it about what a
good person the deceased was? Isn't it even sometimes the
comment that if anyone is in heaven, the one lying in the
casket should be? The erroneous thinking that salvation
depends partly on what I do is so hard to scrub out of the
heart. "Do," my heart demands aided by the devil's whispers.
Even though I hear over and over again that Jesus had done
it all, I have to struggle to push back this error.

When I deposit my weekly load of sins before the Savior's
cross on Sunday, I need to hear he has done it all. With
what comfort would I leave if the message were "Go and
help earn forgiveness"? When I lie on my deathbed, I need
to hear my salvation is a sure thing, as sure as the cross on
which Jesus prepared it. What comfort would be mine if I
had to tally up what I have done to see whether it was
enough? How can the gospel ever become the same old
thing for me? I need it too much.

Lord, open my ears to hear and my heart
to rejoice in the good news of your
forgiveness. Amen.

TWICE BORN

"How can a man be born when he is old?"
Nicodemus asked. "Surely he cannot enter a
second time into his mother's womb to be
born!" Jesus answered, "I tell you the truth,
no one can enter the kingdom of God unless
he is born of water and the Spirit." John 3:4,5

"Twice-baked potatoes?" I asked the waitress the first time I
heard of them. That didn't seem to make sense. Why would
you bake a potato twice? Now I order it whenever I can.

"Twice born?" Nicodemus asked. That didn't seem to make
sense to him either. How can a person come out of his
mother's womb two different times? Why would a grown person even want to? Obviously Jesus was talking about two different kinds of birth. The first one Nicodemus knew. He had
a mother and a birthday. The second was unknown to him till
Jesus explained.

With "born of water and the Spirit," Jesus refers to Holy Baptism. Just as I receive physical life through the whole process
of birth, so spiritual life becomes mine through Holy Baptism. In fact, the first birth is less than worthless without the
second. If all I had was my birthday to celebrate, I'd be looking forward to an eternity in hell. No faith in Jesus, no forgiveness, no kingdom of heaven for me without that second
birth. Birth is something that happens to me. I was not born
the first time because I wanted to be but because my parents
wanted me. I was born the second time, not because I wanted
to be but because God wanted me. Thank God for his grace in
making me twice born.

Thank you, Lord, for the new birth into faith in
Jesus through Holy Baptism. Amen.

HE WON'T BLOW ME OUT

A bruised reed he will not break, and
a smoldering wick he will not snuff out.
Isaiah 42:3

Reeds and wicks may not be familiar to us. Unless we are
campers, we know little about lamps with flickering wicks.
Unless we are nature hikers, we haven't seen cattails half broken off by the wind.

With these pictures the Lord speaks about faith. Not just any
kind of faith but the half-broken, flickering kind, like mine
often can be. How did he know how weak my faith can be?
how much it can smolder with doubt and misgiving? Some
days I wonder if I believe at all.

Notice that the Lord directs my attention away from me to
himself. My salvation does not depend on how strong my
faith is. If it did, how would I ever know whether my faith
were strong enough? No, my salvation depends on the Lord.
I am saved because the God of all grace sent his Son to pay
for my sins. I belong in God's family because his grace
brought me to faith. I will stand in heaven because Jesus has
prepared a room there for me. The valid question isn't "How
strong is my faith?" but "How great is God's love?" The legit-
imate concern isn't "Is my faith too weak?" but "Has Christ's
redemption lost its strength?" Even when my faith is at its
weakest, God's love and Christ's redemption are still there. His
promise assures me that even a weak faith saves. Instead of
blowing it out, the Lord wants to trim the wick and patch up
the stem by the power of his Word.

Lord, strengthen my faith. Trim and patch it by
the almighty power of your promises. Amen.

RICH THE RIGHT WAY

For in him [Christ] you have been enriched in every way . . . because our testimony about Christ was confirmed in you. Therefore you do not lack any spiritual gift as you eagerly wait for our Lord Jesus Christ to be revealed.
1 Corinthians 1:5-7

"I'd give it all away," said a prosperous farmer on his deathbed. He had spent his life chasing after more acres only to realize how poor he really was. Then a pastor told him of the treasure of salvation prepared by Jesus. "Are you sure it's mine?" the farmer asked anxiously, needing the reassurance only God's precious promises could bring.

Paul reminded the Christians at Corinth that they were rich the right way. Not only had he preached to them about the salvation prepared by Christ, the Holy Spirit had also opened their hearts to believe that saving message. When faith's hand holds Jesus, the individual is rich beyond measure. What stock or bond can compare in value to the treasure of salvation through Jesus' work? What acreage can be more valuable than the heaven where stands the believer's home? "Enriched in every way," Paul says. Rich the right way! That's what the gospel makes me when it tells me about Jesus and gives me faith to trust him.

Do I need assurance? Wrong question! Better to ask, "Where can I find assurance?" Only in one place—in God's Word, with its precious promises of all the riches God has stored up for me in Jesus.

Thank you, Lord, for making me rich the right way. Keep me rich through your promises. Amen.

HE KNOWS THEM ALL

Who can discern his errors? Forgive my hidden faults. Psalm 19:12

After years of marriage, spouses know each other quite well. They can often finish each other's sentences or predict what each other will order when eating out. But the deepest concerns are often hidden away inside. Do I know what my spouse is thinking? Does she know my inner thoughts?

The psalmist talks about "hidden faults." These are not sins I try to hide from my spouse but ones even hidden from me. I don't even know I have them. Like pet habits, they're in my daily life without my recognizing them. Is it even safe to say that there are more hidden sins than the ones I recognize? So often the ones that I confess to my God are like the few suits on display in the front window of the store, while inside the racks are bulging. Or to put it another way, if I had eyes like God, what would I see when looking at myself?

God sees all my sins. And God forgives all my sins, even the ones that I don't recognize. That's the beauty of his love. He sent his Son to pay for all my sins, known and unknown. Jesus' blood covers all my sins, the ones I confess by name and the anonymous ones I don't recognize. To his cross I carry the known ones that weigh me down. Beneath his cross I confess also the ones that are hidden from me but not from him. His eyes see them all. His eyes also see me leaving his Son's cross with them all forgiven.

Lord, assure me that all my sins are washed away by the precious blood of your Son, Jesus. Amen.

MORE THAN
A FAMILIAR FACE

The LORD your God is gracious and
compassionate. He will not turn his face from
you if you return to him. 2 Chronicles 30:9

I landed at the international airport in Yaounde, Cameroon,
alone. Finally done with immigration and customs, I ventured
into the crowd outside the terminal. Where was the missionary who was to pick me up? What would I do if he didn't
show? Suddenly, with relief, I saw his familiar face.

What would I do without God's familiar face? When sins
crowd around my soul, what if God just left me standing in
the mess, as well he might? When trouble makes it past the
immigration counter of my existence, what if God neglected
to pick me up? When death's hot breath blows upon me,
what if God didn't show up with his air-conditioned car to
transport me to heaven? These are not just "what ifs." They
are very real and happen to unbelievers who do not see
God's familiar face.

On Calvary's cross God turned his face toward me. What a face
it is—one of tender mercy and divine compassion. In his Son
God shows me how much he loves me. Not just from a distance but down in my world, under my sins, on my cross. In
his Son, God shows me what his love offers me. Forgiveness
for every sin, help for every trouble, heaven for my home.
When in true repentance I look for him on the pages of his
Word, I'll always find with joyous relief his familiar face.

Lord, thank you for turning your face toward
me on Calvary. What would I do without your
love? Help me see your face even more clearly
by fastening my eyes more firmly on your
Word. Amen.

TELL ME ABOUT JESUS

"Sir," they said, "we would like to see Jesus."
John 12:21

Someone had left a note on the pulpit for a new pastor. It was his third Sunday in a new congregation. In his first two sermons he had waxed eloquent with theological terms and high-flying language. Now this note. "We would like to see Jesus," it said simply.

The Greeks who approached one of Jesus' disciples wanted to see him too. Somehow they had heard of Jesus. Now they wanted to see him in person. Obviously they wanted more than a glimpse. A glimpse they could get from watching him in the temple or on the streets. They were eager to hear Jesus, learn more about him, benefit from him as their Savior.

A preacher who bases his message on the Bible will never run out of material. But every time he enters the pulpit, he knows what his chief theme has to be. The people before him need to see Jesus. They've come as sinners needing to hear of the Savior's cross. Yes, they need to hear how to live as God's children. They need to be reminded of God's commandments so that they feel their many sins. But above all they need to hear how through Jesus' work God has forgiven all their sins.

So do I! Perhaps I wouldn't put a note on my pastor's pulpit. But I pray that he always preaches to me about my only Savior. I need to see Jesus!

> Lord, show me my Savior on every page of your Word and in every sermon from your Word. Amen.

YOU CAN'T LOSE

Whether we live or die, we belong to the Lord.
Romans 14:8

"You can't lose," a pastor told a Christian going into serious surgery. "Either the Lord will bless the surgery so you can live for him a bit longer. Or he'll take you to live with him in heaven."

Life is at best uncertain. When I leave for work in the morning, who knows whether I'll make it back at night. When I lay my head on the pillow, who knows if I will awake in the morning. Though my health appears good at the moment, who knows when sudden illness can strike.

And yet life is most certain. As Paul put it, "We belong to the Lord." He has bought me with his Son's own blood. He has made me his own dear child with his gift of my faith. He has reserved a room for me in his heavenly mansion. He knows when it's time to take me home to that room. One thing I can be certain of as his treasured possession. I can't lose because I belong to him.

I can't lose while he still leaves me here. The days before me may have more storm clouds than sunshine. The devil with his temptations may be hitting me where I'm weakest. Sin may be swamping my boat of life faster than I can bail. But I can't lose. Jesus stands at my side to bring me safely through any storm. He reaches for me with his forgiving love. He strengthens me with his amazing power. All this he does through his Word. When I live in his Word, I'm safe.

Lord, stay close to me through your Word. Fill me with its promises in life and death. Amen.

THE CHRISTIAN'S CRUTCH

You will keep in perfect peace him whose
mind is steadfast, because he trusts in you.
Isaiah 26:3

"I don't need a crutch," scoffed an unbeliever, making fun of
his believing coworker. "I do," replied the Christian. "Without my faith I couldn't walk."

There is no peace without Christ. People may dupe themselves into thinking that they can affect peace on earth. They
build military might, labor over inventions, perfect medicine.
But when all is said and done, they still peer ahead anxiously
at tomorrow as they wipe the worried sweat from their brows
today. Peace? How elusive it can be! And perfect peace?
What's that?

Isaiah tells me. The believer has perfect peace. He "whose
mind is steadfast" knows a peace that no storm can ruffle. A
steadfast mind indicates a heart that rests solidly on God's
promises. Isaiah says so with the words "Because he trusts in
you." Notice where the prophet points me for this perfect
peace. Not to my own faith but to the Lord on whom my faith
rests. I don't keep myself in perfect peace. The Lord does. He
moors and keeps my faith anchored on his promises—above
all, on his promise of salvation. There is no peace without the
Prince of peace. In Jesus, God gives me forgiveness of sins,
deliverance from death and the devil, and eternal salvation.
That's the peace I need to walk in life. Call it a crutch if you
will. I need it. And God gives it.

Lord, keep my faith solid on Christ and his
promises so I can walk in life. Amen.

DOES HE GET IN?

Here I am! I stand at the door and knock. If anyone hears my voice and opens the door, I will come in and eat with him, and he with me. Revelation 3:20

Many of us have seen the painting "Christ at the Heart's Door." In it Jesus stands at a closed door, rapping for admittance. Looking at this scene, one little girl asked her father, "Did he get in?"

Good question. Before I answer, I need to look at the one knocking. See the nail wounds on his hands? They tell me he has done what no one else could for me. He was wounded for my transgressions. With his stripes I am healed. Look again—this time at the door. Notice how overgrown it is with branches and vines? They tell me what I couldn't do. I couldn't open my heart to the Savior's knocking. The restraining power of unbelief was something I couldn't chop away. "You did not choose me, but I chose you," the Savior reminds me (John 15:16). He not only stands knocking at the door of my heart; he opens it with the power of his gospel.

Notice why he knocks. He wants to come in and eat with me. In Jesus' day you shared your dinner table only with your closest friends. Jesus, my best friend, wants to share with me the best he offers—his pardon, peace, and promise of heaven. Eventually he wants to take me to the banquet hall in heaven where I can sit down eternally with him.

God, help me answer, "Come, Lord Jesus, be my guest and let your gifts to me be blessed." Amen.

HAPPINESS IS
A BY-PRODUCT

Blessed is the man whose sin the Lord will
never count against him. Romans 4:8

If I were to believe the commercials, I'd have to produce my
own happiness. If I buy the right vehicle, use the right cos-
metics, and consume the right medicines, the smile on my
face will stretch from ear to ear. If I were to believe the news
media, I couldn't have any happiness. Tragedy in all parts of
the world and mishaps in my own little corner of geography
make the pursuit of happiness useless.

God's Word tells me that true happiness is attainable. It
comes from something a gracious Lord has already given me.
In Christ Jesus, God has prepared for me deliverance from all
my sins. In Jesus he has shown me his saving heart, revealed
his loving face, and indicated his fervent desire to have me
live with him in heaven. The happiness that results when God
brings me to faith in Jesus is something I can't produce or
buy. It's a by-product of what God has already given me.

That's what David discovered. When God assured the king
that his sins had been charged to Jesus' account, peace
flooded David's heart. Do I want happiness? Then I need to
read and reread God's promises that he will never count my
sins against me because he has made Jesus pay for them.
Those who live in God's forgiving love have happiness in life
that no storm cloud can darken or tornado sweep away. Their
happiness will even follow them into heaven. There at Jesus'
side they will have fullness of joy and pleasures forevermore.

Lord, fill my days with the happiness of
knowing you have forgiven my sins in
Jesus. Amen.

GET THE WORD OUT

"Go to the street corners and invite to the
banquet anyone you find." So the servants
went out into the streets and gathered all the
people they could find, both good and bad,
and the wedding hall was filled with guests.
Matthew 22:9,10

What a banquet God has prepared. A wedding feast, Jesus
calls it in his parable. The tables groan under the weight of
the best food. The mood is one of happiness. And the guest
list is unlimited. The Lord wants everyone, both good and
bad, to enjoy the salvation he has prepared in Jesus. Whether
they shine in human eyes or have lives covered with grime,
all are to be invited.

And that's exactly what happened. Like a stone skipping rap-
idly across water, the invitation to God's feast of salvation
moved across countries and centuries. A walk through the
book of Acts shows how believers like Peter and Paul were
God's servants inviting sinners to the feast. A brief glance at
the early church reveals how believers carried the gospel with
them wherever they went. The chairs in God's banquet hall
were being filled.

Someone invited me too. Whether my invitation came
through a parent or spouse, pastor or teacher isn't all that
important. By God's grace I have a chair at the feast of salvation. Now it's my turn. What greater good can I offer my
family, neighbors, and people in my community or across the
world than the invitation: "Come to the feast of salvation
God has prepared. Come, and enjoy forever"?

Lord, thank you for inviting me to your feast
of salvation. Use me to invite others. Amen.

REMEMBER YOUR "THANK YOU"

Jesus asked, "Were not all ten cleansed? Where are the other nine?" Luke 17:17

"What do you say?" a mother has to prompt her child clutching Grandma's present. Thanksgiving Day, on the fourth Thursday of this month, is a reminder for me to say thank you to a gracious God.

Earlier the leper had begged with the nine, "Jesus, Master, have pity on us!" Lying in the dirt at Jesus' feet after the master had answered, the healed leper knew how much he had received. Before, he was walking death; afterward, he was restored again to his family and society. Before, he was heading for hell; afterward, he was readied for heaven. No wonder he knelt before Jesus with his humble thank you.

Why do I so often forget my thank-yous? Could it be that, unlike that leper, I forget what I deserve and how much I've received? Thanksgiving is time to remember that the only thing I deserve from God is damnation in hell. I don't deserve the Savior he has sent or a bit of the forgiveness of sins he brings. Nor do I have coming the lesser gifts in life. I have a slice of bread to butter, a stitch of clothing to wear, fresh air to inhale, a loved one to enjoy, only because he is my merciful Father. Gratitude begins with remembering my unworthiness and his abundant mercy.

Genuine gratitude colors each day. I know, as Paul put it, "Whatever you do, whether in word or deed, do it all in the name of the Lord Jesus, giving thanks to God the Father through him" (Colossians 3:17).

God, help me remember my thank-you for your grace and mercy every day. Amen.

REST IN JESUS

Brothers, we do not want you to be ignorant
about those who fall asleep, or to grieve
like the rest of men, who have no hope.
1 Thessalonians 4:13

Charged by a sultan to compile a short history of the human race, a scribe returned with "They were born. They suffered. They died." As Christians we add a fourth sentence: "They live again."

That's what Paul told the believers at Thessalonica. He comforted them by using the word *sleep* for death. *Sleep* brings rest to mind. It recalls life's earlier nights when mother tucked me into bed. Of later nights when I crawled in, exhausted by the rigors of the day. Death brings rest from my battle against sin and from the weariness caused by life's troubles.

The word *sleep* also reminds me of a continuing existence. When I fall asleep, I don't cease to be. And I don't cease to be when I die. At death my body ceases its earthly existence, while my soul goes to heaven. On the Last Day, Christ will raise my body to reunite in perfect form with my soul for unending life.

Because of this glorious rest, Paul can tell me not to grieve like unbelievers who have no hope. Of course, I sorrow when loved ones are taken from my side. But not hopelessly like some unbeliever. I have the surest hope that life is more than being born, living, and dying. Jesus lived and died to pay for my sins. Because he rose, there's a fourth chapter to my existence. I shall live again.

Lord, thank you for the comfort of knowing that
those who die in faith in you live forever. Amen.

RESURRECTION BY JESUS

According to the Lord's own word, we tell you
that . . . the Lord himself will come down from
heaven, with a loud command, with the voice
of the archangel and with the trumpet call of
God, and the dead in Christ will rise first.
1 Thessalonians 4:15,16

Paul says nothing here about unbelievers. Other portions of
Scripture reveal how their souls at death go to the torments
of hell. So will their bodies after being raised on the Last Day.
Instead, Paul speaks to believers with comfort for believers.
He says, "The dead in Christ will rise first." When the Lord of
life returns with all his holy angels, he will summon the bodies of all believers from their final resting places. Then Christians still living when that day comes will have their bodies
glorified without seeing death. Together all believers will
stand at the Savior's side in heaven's eternal joys.

Can I be sure? How do I know that death is not the end for me?
I've wondered and so have you, just as did the Christians at
Thessalonica to whom Paul was writing. "According to the
Lord's own word, we tell you," Paul asserts. He claims the highest authority for his comforting words. That authority has
already proven the validity of Paul's words. Jesus has died and
risen again. His resurrection is proof that believers will live forever. When I sorrow at a loved one's grave or think about my
own death approaching, I can do nothing better than return to
Christ's emptied Easter grave. My Jesus lives, and so shall I. He
will take my soul to heaven and on the Last Day my body also.
He says so, and his resurrection shows how true his promise is.

Risen Savior, take me through the Word to your
resurrection so that I may be sure of mine. Amen.

REUNION WITH JESUS

And so we will be with the Lord forever.
Therefore encourage each other with these
words. 1 Thessalonians 4:17,18

Two words stand out in Paul's brief description of heaven—
we and *Lord*. Heaven will be all believers forever reunited
with the Lord and one another.

Isn't that the exact opposite of what I have on earth? My
children grow up and move away, particularly in this restless
land of ours. Or else some stress arises to push loved ones
apart. Sooner or later comes death, snatching away a dear
one, leaving a hole in the family circle.

In heaven there will be no more departure or death. No more
passing away or parting from. Instead, all believers in Jesus
will gather in one large family before the throne of God to be
together with the Lord forever. Just think of it! To stand in
that heavenly family with all believers and see Jesus face-to-
face. To wear the same kind of robe made white by the Lamb's
blood as they do. To walk with them beside the Savior on the
golden streets of the new Jerusalem. To join with them in
singing the Redeemer's praises. What a reunion to look forward to!

Please, Lord, never let me forget the basis for such a blessed
hope. Jesus died in payment for my sins. He rose again to
show sin's payment was complete. Those who by God's grace
live and die in faith in him are the ones who will stand at his
side in heaven.

Lord, make and keep me one of them for your
love's sake. Amen.

I CAN HARDLY WAIT— JESUS IS COMING

When the Son of Man comes in his glory, and all the angels with him, he will sit on his throne in heavenly glory. Matthew 25:31

Ever say "I can hardly wait"? Perhaps when waiting as a child for Christmas? Or as a teenager wanting your own set of wheels? How about when waiting for the Lord Jesus to come again?

Jesus is coming. Our verse doesn't say, "*If* the Son of Man comes" or "*Perhaps* the Son of Man will come." It says concretely "*When* the Son of Man comes in his glory." Others may live as if it's never going to happen. At times I may even wonder. But Jesus says he's coming. When he does, it will not be as a judge to strike terror into my sinful heart. He'll come as the "Son of Man," a term Jesus loved to use of himself. That expression directs my eyes to a manger of straw, a cross of pain, a grave of victory. He's the one who came earlier to shoulder my sins, die my death, fill my grave. That's my Savior who's coming.

The first time Jesus came, few recognized who he was in that manger and on that cross. But just wait until he comes again. No one will fail to recognize him. All will bow down before him, the King of kings and Lord of lords. When Jesus comes in his glory, it truly will be a sight out of this world. Best of all, he's coming to take me to share in his eternal glory. That's why I can hardly wait.

> Son of Man, thank you for your first coming as Savior. Help me wait eagerly for your second coming, in glory, still as my Savior. Amen.

I CAN HARDLY WAIT—JESUS IS COMING TO CLAIM ME

All the nations will be gathered before him, and he will separate the people one from another as a shepherd separates the sheep from the goats. Matthew 25:32

Note the word *all* in our verse. We have our problems getting an accurate count in the census every ten years. But the King eternal will have no problem assembling all people before his throne. From the four corners of the earth, even from its remotest regions, his angels will gather everyone. They'll even bring all the dead, whose souls have already been in heaven or hell. Believers will come rejoicing. Unbelievers will be driven there in fear and trembling. But no one will be missing.

Note who will do the separating—the Shepherd himself. How foolish for me to say: "I'm a sheep. I belong on that right side of honor." If I am a sheep, it is his doing, not my own. The Shepherd, who once said "I lay down my life for the sheep," will divide believers from unbelievers. The Shepherd, who once said "I know my sheep and I give unto them eternal life," will on that great day show he meant every word. For those still alive when Jesus returns, that day will be judgment time. For those already dead, it will be a declaration of the earlier judgment at the moment of their deaths.

Are you curious, even concerned about who will be among the sheep and who will be among the goats? I am too. That's part of the reason why I can hardly wait. Even more so, I can hardly wait to stand on Jesus' right with all other believers, praising him forever for getting me there.

Lord, thank you for making me your sheep.
Keep me safe till you return to claim me. Amen.

STAY AWAKE—WHY?

If the owner of the house had known at what hour the thief was coming, he would not have let his house be broken into. You also must be ready, because the Son of Man will come at an hour when you do not expect him. Luke 12:39,40

Staying awake can be very difficult at times. You crank back in your recliner while watching a favorite TV program, and an hour later you wake up and it's time to go to bed. Not much is lost if I miss my program. But what if I'm sleeping when Christ returns?

Christ is coming. When's the last time I have thought about this fact? Practical people like 21st-century Americans think more about the here and now than about the then and there. When a loved one dies or an accident intrudes, I might pause a bit to think about things like Christ's coming. Otherwise it's business as usual as I muck around on this ball of mud.

Christ is coming whether I think about it or not. Cynics laugh at this truth. Scholars ignore it. Liberal theologians explain it away. But he's coming whether I'm ready or not. Nothing is more certain than the fact of his return. And yet nothing is more uncertain than the time of that return. In fact, Christ says it will be like a thief at night. He will return at a time when I least expect him. Now I know why he urges me, "Stay awake." He doesn't want to find me sleeping when he comes. He wants to find me sweeping the sky with the radar of faith, watching and waiting for him.

Lord, keep me awake and watching for my Savior's return so I can follow him to glory. Amen.

STAY AWAKE—HOW?

Be dressed ready for service and keep your
lamps burning, like men waiting for their
master to return from a wedding banquet.
Luke 12:35,36

How should I stay awake watching for Jesus' return? Should
I buy a white robe and carry helium-filled balloons with
angels on them? Should I turn on my calculator and try to
figure out when he's coming? People have made such mistakes in the past and will make them again before he comes.

Such is not the kind of readiness of which Jesus speaks. "Be
dressed ready for service," he urges. In his day servants would
tuck their ankle-length robes up into their belts so they could
move freely. "Keep your lamps burning," Jesus also says. Those
servants needed to fill the lamps with oil regularly, not just
when the master would approach the front door.

Jesus is talking about my being ready to travel with him to
heaven. He's referring to having my lamp of faith burning
when he returns. How? "Blessed . . . are those who hear the
word of God and obey it," he says (Luke 11:28). Through his
apostle he urges, "Let the word of Christ dwell in you richly"
(Colossians 3:16). Constant contact with God's Word keeps
faith's strength up, its eyes open, its attitude expectant. My
faith needs its oil regularly replenished with the message of
God's saving love in Christ Jesus. My faith needs regular
strengthening by the Spirit's work through that gospel if I'm
to be ready to travel. How to stay awake? The answer's so simple. Live in his Word.

Lord, keep me ready for Christ's return by
refilling my faith with your Word. Amen.

STAY AWAKE—
WHAT HAPPENS IF I DO?

It will be good for those servants whose master finds them watching when he comes. I tell you the truth, he will dress himself to serve, will have them recline at the table and will come and wait on them. Luke 12:37

Jesus uses a delightful picture to describe what awaits those awake when he returns. We might even call it an unlikely picture. Did you ever hear of a master taking the servants by the hand, seating them at his own table, and serving them? Among mankind such a scene is highly unlikely. But Jesus isn't talking about mankind. He's speaking of himself, my Savior for whom I wait.

What a blessed picture of the heavenly scene! I just can't find words to describe it. In heaven I, along with every believer, will be treated like a lord with the heavenly Lord serving me. By no means do I deserve such treatment. I'll be at the table entirely because of my Lord's love and working. I'll be found ready only because he gives me faith and strength to be so.

And yet in heaven he'll exalt me. On his banquet table he'll set all the holy joy he has earned for me with his saving work on the cross. The psalmist tells me that Jesus "will fill me with joy in [his] presence, with eternal pleasures at [his] right hand" (Psalm 16:11). Such delightful words are beyond me. But for now it is enough to know that such joy comes only to those awake when he returns. For now it is enough, when he says "I am coming soon," to answer "Amen. Come, Lord Jesus" (Revelation 22:20).

Please, Lord, keep me awake in faith for your return. Amen.

BAGS PACKED?

If he comes suddenly, do not let him find you sleeping. What I say to you, I say to everyone: "Watch!" Mark 13:36,37

"What am I forgetting?" my wife will ask as we leave the house. She does a good job of packing for our trips. Sometimes, though, an important item might be left out of the suitcase.

What about packing for Christ's return? When he comes, there'll be no time to jump out of bed and reach for the suitcase. When the only Savior of the sinner stands at the door of my life, it won't work to say "Just a minute while I pack." The suddenness of his coming will make the split second of an accident or the surprise of the first labor pain seem hours long in comparison. All at once he'll be at my door. I need to be ready before he comes, or I'll never be ready when he does come. Now, while my heart still beats and my world still turns, is packing time for the trip into eternity.

So what do I need in my suitcase? What should I not forget? Only one item—Christ Jesus, the all sufficient Savior. "Believe in the Lord Jesus, and you will be saved," Scripture reminds me (Acts 16:31). This requires constant packing. I need regular use of the gospel in Word and sacrament for the Holy Spirit to keep the Savior packed in my heart. Unlike the suitcase my wife packs for us, I can't pack it once and set it in the closet. This Advent season the Savior gives me a poke in the ribs. "I'm coming," he reminds me. "Is your bag packed for heaven?"

Lord, you've given me Jesus. Please keep him in my heart always through your Word. Amen.

A SURE THING

Look at the fig tree and all the trees. When
they sprout leaves, you can see for yourselves
and know that summer is near. Even so, when
you see these things happening, you know that
the kingdom of God is near. Luke 21:29-31

Do you know what a "sure thing" is? It's something that's
going to happen. Like the illustration Jesus used. When the
leaves begin forming on the trees, it's a sure sign that summer is coming. For something even more sure, Jesus points to
his coming on the Last Day.

Jesus had just finished speaking of the signs that would pre-
cede his coming. Signs in nature like floods and earthquakes.
Signs in society like wars and rumors of wars. Signs in the
church like love for the Word growing cold and false Christs
arising. All these signs, he says, will occur before his return.
All these signs, we might say, tell us that his coming is a sure
thing. It's going to happen!

I can become so wrapped up in the signs that I can forget the
reason for them. Like the markers on the street corners, signs
exist to give direction. Not the signs themselves but the
direction they point is important. So it is with the signs pre-
ceding Jesus' return. "What do they all involve? Have they all
happened?" are not the questions for me to ask. Far more
important is, To whom do they point? To the King, of course.
He wants me as a believer to be part of his kingdom of grace.
He wants his gospel to make me his very own. When he does,
I'm ready for his sure return. I even pray for it to happen.

Lord, this Advent season let the signs point my
heart heavenward to your return. Amen.

HAVE I GOT GOOD NEWS FOR YOU!

Comfort, comfort my people, says your God. Speak tenderly to Jerusalem, and proclaim to her that her hard service has been completed, that her sin has been paid for, that she has received from the LORD's hand double for all her sins. Isaiah 40:1,2

Johnny was the angel in the pageant. His mother had drilled his line into him, explaining that "good tidings" meant "good news." So on Christmas Eve it came out, "Hey, have I got good news for you!"

Isaiah had good news for Israel who was sorrowing in captivity beside the rivers of Babylon. God was going to end her separation from the homeland of Canaan. Better still, he was going to end her separation from him. Sin separates people from God. It builds a wall no sinner can crawl under, crash through, or climb over. Only the holy God, from whom sin separates us, can break down the wall. Isaiah's good news? The prophet was tenderly to soothe Israel's sinful heart. How? The only way possible—by telling her that God had paid for her sins. Indeed, Isaiah was to speak of "double" payment, so completely were her sins gone. Again we ask, "How?" Isaiah in many other verses told of the coming virgin's Son. Of the Lamb going silently to the slaughter. Of the One on whom all sins were laid and by whom all sins were paid. Better news than this Israel would never hear. Nor will I. This Advent season it's time to kneel a little closer to Jesus' crib and beneath his cross. There I'll hear the best news ever of how God sent Jesus to bring double payment for all my sins.

Lord, open my heart to rejoice anew in the good news of sins forgiven through Jesus. Amen.

ADVENT'S
ROAD CONSTRUCTION

Make straight in the wilderness a highway for our God. Every valley shall be raised up, every mountain and hill made low. Isaiah 40:3,4

"There are no mountains in my life, not even a hill. I try to do what's right. I'm a fairly good church member." Do I say these things? When I think this way, I'm mountain building. I'm piling up my works and leaving little room for the Savior. Advent is a good time for the law's bulldozer to knock down the growing mountain of my own imagined worthiness and get the road to my heart ready for Christ.

"Every valley shall be raised up," Isaiah said. When I feel that I have more sin than God has forgiveness, I need Isaiah's words. I need to hear that God's love, like some earth-moving machine, has scooped up Christ's forgiveness and dumped it into my heart's swampy spots. Away with the doubt that grows in my swamp. Let my heart be filled with the solid news of Jesus' forgiveness.

"Make straight in the wilderness a highway for our God." Let the world plot its bypasses and curves. The heart in which the Christ Child dwells seeks to follow the straight middle line on life's road. The believer wants to walk according to God's Word.

"Repent and be saved," read the notice. Underneath, some wag wrote, "If you've already repented, please disregard this notice." Not so with Advent's road construction. It's necessary year round.

Lord, knock my heart flat with your law, and then build it up with the good news of Jesus. Amen.

WE WISH YOU
A MERRY CHRISTMAS

Although you were angry with me, your anger
has turned away and you have comforted me.
Surely God is my salvation; I will trust and not
be afraid. Isaiah 12:1,2

Carolers often close with the familiar song "We Wish You a
Merry Christmas." That's the greeting Isaiah had for the
Israelites. God, in his anger over their sins, had abandoned
them for a time. Yet he sent his prophet to comfort them with
the news that salvation was coming. Christmas was still seven
hundred years away. But Isaiah saw it as if it were in his present day. With eyes of faith he knelt before the Savior's humble stall like the shepherds. He held the Redeemer in arms of
faith like Simeon. The coming Savior was the merry Christmas
Isaiah had and wished for sinners in Israel.

What about me? Do I sound like Isaiah, filled to overflowing
with what Christmas is all about? Or has my joy worn rather
thin? If I'm to have a merry Christmas, I first of all need to look
not more closely at the Christ Child but at myself. An old Welsh
poem tells how the Creator one day reviewed the heavenly bodies. As the sun, the moon, and the stars passed by, God smiled.
But when the earth came, God blushed. He saw the whole
human race corporately and individually under the dark shadow
of sin. Perhaps Christmas isn't as merry for me because I don't
blush enough. I don't look often and honestly enough at my
sins. Christmas becomes merrier for me the more I realize how
much I need its message. The good news of how God turned his
anger away and sent his Son to be my salvation is reason for joy.
Merry Christmas for me is truly Merry CHRISTmas.

Lord, make my Christmas merry with the news
of your salvation. Amen.

LET'S JOIN
THE CAROLERS

Give thanks to the LORD, call on his name;
make known among the nations what he has
done, and proclaim that his name is exalted.
Isaiah 12:4

I'm not a good singer, but there is one time when I let loose. That's when we go caroling. Somehow you can't hold back when singing Christmas hymns. Isaiah couldn't hold back either.

"Give thanks to the LORD," he wrote. Even if I sound like a bullfrog in some pond, I sing to the One who gave me the newborn King. I also use my life to thank the great Giver of Christmas. As a missionary in India preached, a man left but soon returned. After the service the missionary asked the man if he had said something to offend him. "Oh, no," the Hindu replied. "I went out to ask your driver if you were kind to him. When he said you were, I came back to listen some more, because I knew you meant what you said." Unless I live my joy, there's not much use in singing about it.

"Make known among the nations what he has done," Isaiah also urged. One sure way to increase Christmas joy is to share it. Not only do I join the carolers at Christmastime in singing "We Wish You a Merry Christmas." I use every opportunity each day to help bring to others the good news of the Savior sent by God's love. I want them to have the same merry CHRISTmas I do.

A merry Christmas? Yes, when I rejoice in Jesus my Savior and share him with others.

God help me to sing loudly all year through.
Amen.

THE LORD IS COMING

See, I will send my messenger, who will prepare the way before me. Then suddenly the Lord you are seeking will come to his temple. Malachi 3:1

"Will Uncle Jim make it?" asked the grandkids. Montana is so far away. "Will Grandma make it?" they asked too. She doesn't get around well anymore, and the weather might not cooperate. What about Jesus? Will he make it to my home this season? Or should I ask whether he's been invited?

"Jesus is coming," Malachi told the Jews of his day. It would still be four hundred years before John the Baptist at the Jordan River would prepare people for the Savior's coming. But the prophet wrote as if it were today. "He's coming suddenly to his temple," Malachi rejoiced. "Before you know it, the promised Savior will be standing in the midst of his people."

Notice what Malachi called him? "The Lord," he said. The eternal God would come down to the earth he had created to work among the creatures he had made and who in sin had turned away from him. That's the miracle in the manger. That's the real reason for my joy. Others look at the poor baby wrapped in rags and miss the meaning of Christmas. They see only a man and actually see nothing. If Jesus were only a human being, I would have no cause to celebrate. Then I could just as well forget about Christmas or change the name of the season to the "holiday whatever." Who's coming this season? The Lord himself, stooping low in love to save sinners like me.

Dear Savior, this season help me sing, "Joy to the world, the Lord has come to me." Amen.

THE SAVIOR IS COMING

"The messenger of the covenant, whom you
desire, will come," says the Lord Almighty.
Malachi 3:1

Somewhere I saw a painting of the nativity. Angels gathered round the Christ Child's manger with their songs of praise. But over in the corner one angel, holding a small cross in its hand, was wiping a tear from its eye. What a reminder! God himself came to the manger to go to the cross.

That's what Malachi tells us. When he calls Jesus the "messenger of the covenant," he refers to the beautiful one-sided agreement that God made with sinners already in the Garden of Eden. There God promised to our fallen parents that he would send his Son as the seed of the woman to crush Satan's head. Down through the centuries, God's people raised expectant eyes to the heavens waiting for the Savior to come. Now four hundred years before Bethlehem, Malachi says with obvious joy, "The messenger of the covenant [the promised Savior] will come."

This blessed season I echo the prophet's words but change the tense. "The Savior has come," I can say. By God's grace I can even add as I kneel at his manger bed, "The Savior came for me." For me he left heaven's throne. For me he took on human flesh. To save me he lived and died. If that wonderful news doesn't fill me with joy, I might as well tear the December pages off the calendar or at least cancel the month's last week. Jesus, my Savior, is coming. That's why I celebrate Christmas.

Lord, help me sing with joy, "Joy to the world,
the Lord, my Savior, has come." Amen.

THE PURIFIER IS COMING

But who can endure the day of his coming?
Who can stand when he appears? For he will
be like a refiner's fire or a launderer's soap.
Malachi 3:2

Working with a mechanic friend in his shop, I ended up with hands blackened with grease. "Here," he said, handing me a special tin of soap, "try this." And my hands came clean.

"A launderer's soap," Malachi called the coming Savior. The word means strong soap like the stuff the mechanic gave me. Like that soap, the coming Christ would scrub human hearts clean from the impossible-to-remove grease of sin. "A refiner's fire," the prophet also said. Like a super-hot smelter, the coming Christ would melt sin's impurities from precious human hearts. Hearts that the Savior has purified need not be afraid. They can stand holy when he returns in judgment. But hearts that reject the Christ will burn like the fire under the smelting furnace or like the lye eating away at the grease. Because of their unbelief, they will carry their sins into hell's everlasting pain.

Who came for me at Christmas? Thank God I can answer, "Jesus, my purifier from sin." He was defiled with my sins so that I could be cleansed by his blood. He came so that I could go all the way to his heaven. He came also to help me stay away from sin's grease. Though I still smudge my life, the stains aren't as widespread. Because of Jesus I can say: "I am not what I ought to be. I am not what I wish to be. I am not what I hope to be. But by the grace of God I am not what I was."

Savior, wash me clean from sin's grease and
power me for the fight against sin. Amen.

THE JUDGE IS COMING

So I will come near to you for judgment. . . .
I the LORD do not change. Malachi 3:5,6

"Are you a judge?" asked the girl in Children's Hospital. I had come right to my daughter's room after conducting Sunday services. Her new roommate took one look at my dark suit and shrank back in her bed. The only people she knew who wore such suits were judges.

Unbelievers will do more than shrink back when Jesus comes on the Last Day. They may have thought they could hide their sins from the One seemingly far away in the heavens. They may have thought his eyes couldn't see their hearts. But he is near. He does see. And he will punish. That threat is real. The Lord who does not change makes it. He will carry it out.

"The judge is coming," the prophet reminds me. Should I shrink back in fear? Or look for Jesus with joyous eyes? I have my answer when I remember that he who sits on the throne of judgment is the same one who lay in a manger and hung on a cross. His head, now wearing the crown of glory, once wore a crown of thorns. His hand holding the scepter is the same as the hand pierced by the nails. His tongue proclaiming the eternal judgment is the same one that said, "Go in peace, your sins are forgiven." The judge is coming. No doubt about this fact, for the Lord doesn't change his mind. Nor will he change the forgiveness with which he covers me. The One who judges me is the One who has already saved me.

Lord, remind me of my salvation when I think of you as my judge. Amen.

WHAT WOULD HE PREACH?

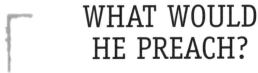

John came . . . preaching a baptism of
repentance for the forgiveness of sins. . . .
After me will come one more powerful than
I. . . . He will baptize you with the Holy Spirit.
Mark 1:4,7,8

You open the bulletin in your church bench. "Guest preacher today," it says. "Hmm," you muse, "I wonder what he'll say?" What if that guest speaker were John the Baptist? What would he preach?

First he'd have something to say about repentance. That means he'd talk about my sins. Some would rather ignore sin, putting a blindfold over the eyes of their conscience. They'd rather alibi for sin, pointing to others who are worse. They'd rather sugarcoat sin, dusting it with sweet phrases like "cultural change." But John would preach sin to me in plain terms. And I had better listen. If the Savior in the manger is going to mean anything to me, I need to know how much I need him.

With even more gusto John would preach about that Savior. In his day he pointed hearers all the way ahead to Christ's finished work. John saw Jesus, with his work of salvation finished, ascending back to heaven. He saw the ascended Savior sending his Holy Spirit to bring people to faith. He saw the Savior returning to judge the world. What would he preach to me if he filled the pulpit in my church? Above all, he'd say: "Remember the Savior who went to the cross and then back to heaven. Remember how his salvation is complete. Remember how he's coming again to take you to his heaven." I surely hope my pastor will preach John's sermon to me this Advent.

Lord, remind me of my sins so that I rejoice
that Jesus came for me. Amen.

CHRISTMAS ANXIETY

Mary was greatly troubled at his words . . . but the angel said to her, "Do not be afraid, Mary, you have found favor with God." Luke 1:29,30

Mary was afraid. Put yourself in her shoes and you can see why. In her day people looked down on unwed pregnant women. Also, what about her fiancé Joseph? How would she ever explain to him? And that holy angel! Sinful people just simply cannot stand in the presence of the holy God. They can't even stand with heads erect before one of God's angels.

"Do not be afraid, Mary," the angel had to tell her, "you have found favor with God." God's favor flows from his grace. God had chosen sinful Mary to bear the promised Savior. That was his undeserved gift to her. Through the One who would come from her womb, she could stand fearless not just before holy angels but the holy Lord himself. "God, *my* Savior," she called her child some verses later in Luke's gospel (1:47). Jesus was the answer for Mary's Christmas anxiety.

Any anxiety in my heart this Advent? The Savior in the manger won't mean much to me if I don't reexamine the reason for his coming. I need to look past the veneer I paste over life and into my heart. The sight isn't pretty, but pretty horrible. I can no more kneel before Jesus' manger than Mary could stand before that angel. But God has favored me too. He sent his Son to remove my sins with his payment. He sent Jesus so I could stand without anxiety before him this blessed Christmas season.

Lord, remove the fear from my sinful heart. Fill it with joy because of my Savior's birth. Amen.

CHRISTMAS AMAZEMENT

"How will this be," Mary asked the angel, "since I am a virgin?" The angel answered, "The Holy Spirit will come upon you, and the power of the Most High will overshadow you. So the holy one to be born will be called the Son of God." Luke 1:34,35

Mary knew biology. She knew it took two people to conceive a baby. She also knew that she was still a virgin. In amazement she had to ask, "How will this be?" The angel's answer must have taken her breath away. The Holy Spirit would miraculously begin Jesus' human life in her womb.

The virgin birth of Jesus, though disputed by some, is a very important teaching. It reminds us that Jesus was "the holy one" as the angel told Mary. Add a human father to Jesus' conception and you have eliminated him as the Savior. From a human father and mother, Jesus would have inherited the same sinful heart that I did. Also, the virgin birth reminds me that the Savior's birth is totally God's work. Man had no part in it. How could man bring about the incredible miracle of God's infinite love taking the finite shape of true man? Such a love-packed miracle is God's great doing.

"How can this be?" Mary asked in amazement. So must I. How could God become human? How could his love be so great for someone as undeserving as me? How could he work the miracle of planting the Savior by faith into my heart as he once put his Son in conception beneath Mary's heart? Christmas means amazement—joy beyond measure because of God's love-powered miracles for me.

Lord, help me sing loudly of your amazing love and what it has done for me in Jesus. Amen.

CHRISTMAS ACCEPTANCE

"I am the Lord's servant," Mary answered.
"May it be to me as you have said." Luke 1:38

In 11 more days, Christmas will be here. In 12, Christmas will be past. Is that how it'll go this year? Or will my Christmas last all year? From Mary I can gain the answer.

The angel's holy presence had at first filled sinful Mary with fear. The angel's awesome message had at first filled her with questions. With both fear and questions erased, Mary had only one reaction. In simple faith she said, "I am the Lord's servant. May it be to me as you have said." As God's humble servant she was willing to follow his commands. She found joy in doing what her Savior-God asked of her. Don't you sense her joy when she cradles her newborn Son, when she follows his ministry, and even when she is sorrowing beneath his cross? Did her joy ever cease? Or was it, "I am the Lord's servant. My Son is the loving Savior, sent by God to serve me in the highest way"?

When will Christmas end for me? The answer is obvious. Jesus wants to be my Savior throughout my life. He wants to serve me with his forgiveness all my days. He wants to take me to heaven on my final day. And I want to serve him all my days. Like Mary, life's joy is found in being the Lord's servant. Life's meaning is found in asking, "What can I do for you, Lord Jesus, who has done so much for me?" Willing obedience is the best gift I can give God during my lifelong Christmas.

Lord, wrap my hand around Jesus and my life around your will all my days. Amen.

THE HEAVENLY GUEST IS AT THE DOOR—WHO IS HE?

Praise be to the Lord, the God of Israel, because he has come and has redeemed his people . . . (as he said through his holy prophets of long ago). Luke 1:68,70

Isaac Newton, Clara Barton, Robert Ripley, and Jesus Christ have one thing in common. December 25 is listed as the birthday of all four. Some may remember Newton for the theory of gravity; Barton as the angel of mercy on the Civil War battlefields; Ripley as the creator of "Believe It or Not." But more might reply, "Who cares?" How about the birthday of Jesus Christ?

Zechariah, holding the baby John on his lap, didn't say, "Who cares?" He saw in the heavenly guest the One promised by God through his prophets. Centuries of waiting were almost over. In six months the Savior would come. No wonder Zechariah under the Spirit's guidance sang for joy.

He saw even more. The Christ Child would be God himself come to redeem his people. He who would stand at the door is the eternal God come in our flesh. Just think of it! God the Almighty—a little baby! God the eternal—a few hours old! God the all-ruling—rocked in a mother's arms! How do we describe this miracle of the ages except to point to the overwhelming love behind it? Remember the first line of that song? It goes, "The happy Christmas comes once more, the heavenly guest is at the door." God himself has come from heaven to be my Savior. That's reason to rejoice.

Lord, fill my Christmas with happiness by reminding me how you came to save me. Amen.

THE HEAVENLY GUEST IS AT THE DOOR— WHAT DOES HE BRING?

He has raised up a horn of salvation for us . . . salvation from our enemies . . . to shine on those living in darkness and in the shadow of death. Luke 1:69,71,79

How much of Christmas would be left if there were no gifts? No gifts for many would mean no importance attached to Christmas. Turn it around. Can you imagine the joy if, when Christmas comes, people everywhere would reevaluate what gifts the heavenly guest brings in his arms?

Zechariah sang of those gifts. "He has raised up a horn of salvation," he said. Like some mighty animal that butts away its foe with its horns, so Jesus tossed aside sin, death, and the devil forever. Victory over all three are the gifts the Savior brings. Like the rising sun, Zechariah said, "Jesus came to shine on those living in darkness and in the shadow of death." More than a child afraid of night's darkness, I had to be terrified of sin's blackness. More than a surgery patient slipping in anesthesia's darkness, I had to be scared of death's dark dread. No light, no hope, no joy, no heaven, no nothing without the Savior at the door this blessed season.

Does salvation's light seem as bright as ever? If not, it's time to go back to square one, to ask myself: "Am I a sinner? How much, not how little, have I sinned? Where do I deserve to go because of my sins? What would death be like without Jesus?" Then perhaps I'll be ready to sing with joy, "The happy Christmas comes once more, the heavenly guest with his precious gifts is at the door."

Jesus, blessed Savior, let your salvation light
up my Christmas and my heart with joy. Amen.

THE HEAVENLY GUEST IS AT THE DOOR— HOW SHALL I SERVE HIM?

To enable us to serve him without fear in holiness and righteousness before him all our days. Luke 1:74,75

Have you ever noticed that there are very few purple Christmas bulbs? Green, red, yellow, and blue ones we have in abundance. But not many purple lights. Someone explained that purple glass cuts off light waves and as a result dims the brightness. And, of course, we want the lights of Christmas to shine.

Isn't that what Zechariah tells us in our verse? He reminds us that the Savior comes to "enable us to serve him without fear in holiness and righteousness before him all our days." Christians are to be Christmas bulbs shining brightly long after another Christmas passes. As a believer in Christ, I'm to shine, not because I'm forced to but because I have to. It's the very nature of those who are plugged into the Light of the world, to shine with his light. And there is no switch that turns me off so that I shine only once in a while. "All our days," Zechariah said. His son, John the Baptist, did just that. He used his days to shine in a special way by preparing people for Christ's coming.

In just a handful of days, the happy Christmas will have come once more. Then what? Will the extra fervor to my faith and the extra zeal for my Savior start blinking? Will it be back to life as usual? Back to shining just once in a while with the light Christ has brought me? Or will I glow in the dark night of this world so that others might see the light who came down at Christmas?

Heavenly Guest, thank you for the light of salvation. Help me shine with it to others. Amen.

REJOICE IN THE LORD!

Rejoice in the Lord always. I will say it again: Rejoice! Philippians 4:4

Rejoice? Don't I know how? Isn't that what the Christmas season is all about? There are the gifts and the gatherings. The fun when I see a loved one open the present she hadn't even dreamed about. The joy I feel when I tear the ribbons off the gifts with my name on them. The good feeling when the family is together and enjoying one another's company. What a shame it comes only once a year.

There's nothing wrong with such Christmas joy. But my rejoicing dare not end with this. Paul wasn't thinking about people or presents when he encouraged the believers at Philippi, "Rejoice always." How could he have been? The apostle was imprisoned at Rome, jailed unjustly for the crime of talking about his Savior. He also knew what the usual exit from a Roman jail was—a head lost to the executioner's axe. Yet he urged his beloved fellow believers, "Rejoice always."

"In the Lord," he reminded them. Here's the key for joy that lasts from one Christmas to the next. As Paul put it, "You know the grace of our Lord Jesus Christ, that though he was rich, yet for your sakes he became poor, so that you through his poverty might become rich" (2 Corinthians 8:9). And then he added, "Thanks be to God for his indescribable gift!" (9:15). As a believer I have joy that never ends because I have a God whose grace is unending. In Jesus he gave me the best gift he had, the Savior from sin in whom I can rejoice every day of my life.

Lord, thank you for the gift of your Son as my Savior. Fill me with joy because of him. Amen.

⌐RELATE IN THE LORD!

Let your gentleness be evident to all. The Lord is near. Philippians 4:5

How big is my Christmas? Is it just speak a greeting, send a card, flash a smile? Have a little friendship thaw this time of the year? Is it as the poet complained in "Do Not Open Till Christmas": "Sealed unrelentingly all year long; good will and tenderness break into song. But by some curious logic, fearful men after the season seal them up again"?

What are my thoughts these days? Is it what will I get from others? What I gave them last year cost more than what they gave me? Such thinking exhibits not a spirit of gentle concern for others but selfish concern for me. Such thoughts rob me of Christmas joy. An even greater robber of joy is preoccupation with myself because of my sins. Yes, of course, I need to be concerned about my failures. But knowing the Lord is near means I bring those sins to him in repentance. I trust his Word that he has plunged them into the depths of his forgiveness. I rejoice that in his gentleness he does not deal with me as I deserve but forgives me for the sake of his Son.

People of all kinds surround me, not just at Christmas time but throughout life. Paul reminds me there's only one way of dealing with them. Just as God in his gentle love sent his Son to wash away my sins, so I'm to respond with gentleness toward my fellowman. God's gentleness in Christ is contagious. When I have it, I spread it to others.

Lord, help me to be like Jesus—meek, lowly, loving, mild. Amen.

RELAX IN THE LORD

Do not be anxious about anything, but in everything, by prayer and petition, with thanksgiving, present your requests to God. And the peace of God, which transcends all understanding, will guard your hearts and your minds in Christ Jesus. Philippians 4:6,7

"Do not be anxious about anything," Paul said. Easier said than done! Who doesn't have cares, even in this joyous season? The experts tell us that during a holiday season like this, cares seem even bigger. All around we hear "Merry Christmas," but our lives are far from merry.

Should I think that God is unconcerned about my cares? That's not the remedy Paul offers. "Present your requests to God," he urges. God knows and cares and wants to do something about my cares. So he gently invites me, his child: "Tell me all about it. There's no fear I cannot remove. No burden I cannot help you carry. No broken heart I cannot heal. No tear so bitter I cannot wipe it away. No sin, regardless how repeated, I have not forgiven."

The apostle reminds me how to bring my cares to the Lord. "With thanksgiving," he urges. Complaints are out of order. Thanksgiving is very much in order when I recall how often my gracious God has answered in the past. So I come, thankful that even as I ask for answers, I know I will receive them. Come to think of it, hasn't my God in the babe of Bethlehem given me the peace that I need? Can he who gave me the Savior withhold what I need in the changing scenes of life?

Lord, help me carry everything to you in prayer with the confidence that is mine in Jesus. Amen.

BETTER CHEER
AND COMFORT

When the time had fully come, God sent his
Son, born of a woman, born under law, to
redeem those under law, that we might receive
the full rights of sons. Galatians 4:4,5

Florida, Missouri, is today only a spot in the road. In a park
close by stands the small two-room shack in which Mark
Twain was born. By that spot on the roadside is a marker with
these words, "In this village Mark Twain was born, November
30, 1835. He cheered and comforted a tired world."

With his humorous writings, Twain brought some comfort to a
tired world. He taught people to laugh a bit in spite of their
pain. But that's as far as he could go. How much more our gracious God has done for us! When the clock of salvation struck
noon, he sent his Son to cheer and comfort a tired world. God's
love did this in a most unique way. He put his eternal Son into
human flesh through a virgin's womb. He did this so his Son
could be under the law's requirements and sin's burden. What
sinful mankind could not do, God sent his Son to accomplish.
With his perfect life, Jesus fulfilled every one of God's commands. With his innocent death, Jesus paid for every sin of
every human being. "Done," it says of God's commands. "Done,"
it says of sin's payment. I can stand in heaven cleansed of my
sin and covered with Jesus' righteousness.

"Cheer and comfort for a tired world"? Where else can I find
it but in God's Christmas gift of his own Son? What else can
bring me greater joy than knowing God sent the Redeemer
also for me?

God loves me dearly, loves even me. He sent forth
Jesus to set me free. Thank you, Lord. Amen.

THE ONLY WORD
OF ETERNAL LIFE

The life appeared; we have seen it and testify
to it, and we proclaim to you the eternal life,
which was with the Father and has appeared to
us. 1 John 1:2

An old legend tells how at midnight on Christmas Eve all the
animals pause wherever they are and kneel. In this way they
honor the Son of God, who once used their manger for his
cradle. We also pause to kneel this holy season. But do we
always remember why?

John answers. I kneel because in that manger lies the eternal God. He "was with the Father," John reminds me. In the
beginning of the world when time began, Christ already was.
At the end of the world, when time ceases, he still will be.
From eternity he is true God, face-to-face in an intimate,
inexplainable relationship with God the Father. Then at the
fullness of time, the eternal One became flesh in Mary's womb
and dwelt among people as "the eternal life." Jesus Christ is
life itself and gives eternal life to others. He is the eternal
Son of God sent by God's love to a sinful world so that people
"might live through him" (1 John 4:9).

Sometimes I wish that I could see Jesus as John did. Then I
remember that it's not the physical but the spiritual closeness
to Jesus that counts. Through the Word, the Holy Spirit gives
me eyes to see and a heart to believe in the incarnate Word
of life. With his gift of faith, I see in the manger the eternal
God who came to bring me eternal life. That's why I kneel
before him.

Lord, thank you for faith's sight. Help me kneel
in humble awe before your gift of life. Amen.

THE ONLY WAY TO THE FATHER'S FELLOWSHIP

We proclaim to you what we have seen and heard, so that you also may have fellowship with us. And our fellowship is with the Father and with his Son, Jesus Christ. 1 John 1:3

The word *fellowship* is a big one in the New Testament. It comes from a root meaning "to have things in common." Hear what John is telling us? Through the Christ Child, I can have back what Adam and Eve once had with God. They shared in all his blessings. They walked with him in all his ways. For them life was a perpetual heaven because it was a perfect relationship with God.

There's only one way back to such a blessed fellowship with the Father. Only one way for sinners like me to stand next to God. Only one way to look up at him and see him smiling at me. Only one way to stretch out my hand and have him fill it with blessing after blessing. Only one way for me to close my eyes for the last time and open them in heaven. Through the baby in the Bethlehem manger and the Christ on the Calvary cross!

In Europe I saw a nativity scene that a nobleman had commissioned Albrecht Duerer to paint. Among the holy family, the shepherds, and the wise men the artist had also painted the nobleman's family. Isn't that what the Christ Child is all about? He came to earth, took on my flesh, became my brother, to make me his brother in God's family. He came to seek and save a lost family. He came to pay for my sins and plunge himself into my hell so that I could again be one with my Father.

Thank you, Lord Jesus, for restoring the fellowship I now enjoy with my Father. Amen.

WHAT IF JESUS HAD NEVER BEEN BORN?

Today in the town of David a Savior has been born to you; he is Christ the Lord. Luke 2:11

What if Christopher Columbus or Thomas Edison had never been born? I suppose someone else would have discovered the new land or invented the electric light bulb. But what if Jesus had never been born? What if there had been no angel's announcement that night over Bethlehem's field?

If Jesus had never been born, there'd be no salvation. Then Adam and Eve would still be crying, not only at Eden's door but in hell. Then the thief on the cross would have no answer to his plea for just a corner in paradise. Then Paul would still be the chief of sinners. Then you and I would be along with all sinners most miserable and sure only of punishment in a never-ending hell.

If Jesus had never been born, I wouldn't be going to any services this Christmas Eve. Nor tomorrow or ever, because what would I have to sing about, to hear about, to rejoice about? There would be no message of hope for my eager ears to hear. It's bad enough to celebrate Christmas separated from loved ones. But just think if there were no Jesus and no promise of eternal life. There's a thought to make even the angels weep.

No Jesus—how horrible! A Savior who is Christ the Lord—how wonderful!

> Lord, help me sing tonight, "I am so glad when Christmas comes, the night of Jesus' birth." Amen. (CW 51:1)

THE PERFECT GIFT

Thanks be to God for his indescribable gift!
2 Corinthians 9:15

At times we hear about the perfect gift for someone who has everything. But what about the perfect gift for someone who has nothing and needs everything? That's what God gave me at Christmas.

When God put his Son into the manger, he gave me everything. I needed forgiveness. He gave me his Son from heaven to wash away my sins with his precious blood. I needed peace with God. He gave me the Prince of Peace, who brought back a blessed relationship with the Father. I needed power against sin. He gave me the mighty Lord, who defeated Satan in the wilderness and even more so on the cross. How can the devil keep sin's handcuffs on me when Christ is the key that unlocks them? I needed comfort in life's sorrows. He gave me the living Savior, who wipes away my tears. I needed assurance at the time of death. He gave me the risen Jesus, who has already conquered death, not just for himself but for me. I had nothing, but with the gift of the Savior, God gave me everything I needed. Thanks be to God for his indescribable gift!

Why does he lavish such a gift on me? Again the word *indescribable* fits. How do I explain the love that moved God to send his Son into the manger? What language shall I borrow to praise him for such a gift to me, his enemy? In his great love, God gave everything he had so that I might have everything I need. Thanks be to God for his indescribable love!

Thank you for giving me just what I needed in the Savior. Help me praise your love forever. Amen.

CELEBRATE *CHRISTMAS* EVERY DAY

So they hurried off and found Mary and Joseph, and the baby, who was lying in the manger. Luke 2:16

Thrilled with their first successful flight in December 1903, the Wright brothers sent a telegram to their sister. "We have actually flown 120 feet. Will be home for Christmas," it read. Their sister took it to the local newspaper. "That's nice," said the editor after glancing at the message. "The boys will be home for Christmas." Hopefully my Christmas celebration isn't missing the real news.

Shepherds came to kneel at Jesus' manger bed. People who held one of the more menial jobs in life hurried to worship the newborn Savior. That's comfort for me. By bringing the shepherds, God's reminding me that whatever my station in life, I have a Savior. From the moment of his birth, Jesus was ready to receive all sinners. That baby was born to save me.

Mary and Joseph were there at Jesus' manger bed. From the little Scripture records about these two, I learn something important about faith. They didn't hesitate but took God at his word, even when his words seemed impossible. God help me to do the same, especially with his promise of salvation.

Jesus was there in the manger bed. Never before or again will the world see a baby like him. Only he was from all eternity. Only his birth was foretold centuries before. Only he was virgin born. Only at his birth did angels sing. Only he was born to die for his fellowman. Only he deserves my worship.

God, help me celebrate *Christ*mas every day. Amen.

NAMES OF WONDROUS LOVE—WONDERFUL COUNSELOR

And he will be called Wonderful Counselor.
Isaiah 9:6

"What shall we name the baby?" expectant parents ask weeks ahead of time. Finally they choose a name. Whether it fits is another question. Seven hundred years before the Christ Child's birth in Bethlehem, Isaiah gave him some names. And all of them fit beautifully.

In Isaiah's day a counselor was one who stood at your side to offer good advice in all matters. Isn't that a good name for the babe of Bethlehem? Wouldn't we even say that the Christ of Christmas is a Counselor more wonderful than any other? He needs no teachers but is Truth himself. He needs no counselors but is the Counselor above every counselor. His advice is never lacking and is always correct. To wayward ones he says, "Your sins are forgiven." To weary ones he says, "Cast all your care on me because I care for you." To worried ones he says, "Will not my heavenly Father much more care for you?" To weeping ones he says, "Let not your heart be troubled, believe also in me."

This Jesus has experienced my wrestling against sin and Satan—my pains and my death. Even something I shall never know, the agonies of the damned in hell. That's why the name Wonderful Counselor fits him so well. He not only advises; he does. He did his work on the cross and now stands ready to help in every step of life as my Wonderful Counselor.

Savior, be with me as my Wonderful Counselor,
to guide me in life and death. Amen.

NAMES OF WONDROUS LOVE—
MIGHTY GOD

And he will be called . . . Mighty God.
Isaiah 9:6

When I look at that baby in the manger, I may fail to see in him the mighty God. That's God who is my Rock and my Fortress? Why, a rock could so easily crush him in his helplessness. That's God who is my Shield and my Defender? Why, he himself must be defended from harm and shielded from cold by a mother's arms. That's the Horn of my salvation, the mighty God who with his power would toss my enemies of sin and death into the air? Why, he's only a baby who seems to have no power of his own for anything.

Yes, indeed! That baby is the mighty God who calms storms and heals men. Even more do I see his might when with his powerful Word he sends the devil packing in the wilderness. Even more do I see his might when he shouts of sin's payment on the cross, "It is finished." Even more do I see his might when he leaves his grave empty and assures me, "Because I live, you also will live." Even more do I see his might when he arms me for my daily battle against Satan by giving me the "sword of the Spirit which is the Word of God."

My arms are so weak. My muscles so flabby. With my own might I can do nothing. But when Jesus, my Savior, stands at my side as the Mighty God, victory is always within reach. With him I can face any foe.

Savior, be with me as my Mighty God so that I have power against all my enemies. Amen.

NAMES OF WONDROUS LOVE— EVERLASTING FATHER

And he will be called . . . Everlasting Father.
Isaiah 9:6

"I'd like a father," answered a little boy. A Santa in the mall had asked what he wanted for Christmas. Back came that request from a six-year-old whose father had left.

I have a father for Christmas. Everlasting Father is another name Isaiah gives the Christ Child. What tenderness, love, and comfort are in his name. To his followers the babe of Bethlehem is like a father because of what he does. He doesn't stand aloof from his people, leaving them to shift for themselves. Instead, he does perfectly for them what an earthly father can only try to do for his children. An earthly father tries to provide what he thinks is best for his children. The Savior always provides what he knows is best. An earthly father tries to listen to his children and feel their problems. The Savior does listen, does understand, does solve my problems, if I but let him. An earthly father tries to defend his children, even putting his life at risk to do so. The Savior gave up his life to rescue me from eternal death in hell. An earthly father must at last leave his children. My Christ will never leave my side.

He's my Everlasting Father. Always he walks with me. Always his love forgives me. Always his power protects me. He'll be there to lead me even through the valley of the shadow to his heaven. My earthly father meant much to me. Jesus, my Everlasting Father, means so much more.

> Savior, take my hand and lead me as
> my Everlasting Father to your heavenly
> home. Amen.

NAMES OF WONDROUS LOVE— PRINCE OF PEACE

And he will be called . . . Prince of Peace.
Isaiah 9:6

"Make peace, not war," protestors shouted some years ago. Such protestors are always with us. They can simply spruce up their chants because wars are always with us too. Wouldn't it be something if some morning the newspaper headlines could read, "No War Anywhere in the World"?

When Isaiah calls the Christ Child the "Prince of Peace," he has more in mind than world peace. He means more than the peace that would result if no nation anywhere had any nuclear weapons or chemical bombs. If everyone of us choked off his selfishness and loved his neighbor as himself. If everyone practiced the Golden Rule, doing unto others as he wanted them to do unto him.

Such earthly peace would come about more if more people in this world were filled with Jesus' real peace. The heavenly Prince of Peace came to bring the peace that results when the war between God and man, caused by sin, is over. He came to prepare the peace that floods the heart when man knows God is his dear Friend, not his dread Foe. He came to make possible the peace that assures the dying that heaven is their beautiful home, that their inevitable destination is not hell. Jesus' peace surpasses all understanding. It enables me to live in my tense world. It sustains me in moments of sorrow. It equips me to face eternity unafraid. I need outward peace on this earth, but even more so the kind the Christ Child prepared with his manger and cross.

Savior, fill my heart with the peace that comes only through your payment for my sins. Amen.

NOT ONE OF HIS GOOD PROMISES HAS FAILED

You know with all your heart and soul that not one of all the good promises the LORD your God gave you has failed. Every promise has been fulfilled. Joshua 23:14

Some years ago the Peanuts comic strip for New Year's Eve pictured the following dialogue. "Well, here it is again," Charlie Brown says to his friend Linus. "It's the last day of the year and I did it again." "Did what?" asks Linus. To which Charlie answers, "I just blew another year."

I feel like joining Charlie. What do I see when I look back at the highway of this past year? So many of my thoughts, words, and deeds like so much litter lie in the ditch. How can I pick back up the trash of my words with which I've hurt people, not to mention my Savior? How can I pay the fine for littering the road of life with my sinful words and deeds? I've blown another year.

From the look back, I turn to the look up. What do I see when I raise faith's eyes to Jesus, who is the same yesterday, today, and forever? Wasn't he there each time I came with the penitent plea, "God be merciful to me, a sinner"? Wasn't he there in his Word and Holy Supper to assure me: "Your sins are forgiven. Go in peace"? Isn't he here tonight too one last time to repeat his sweet promises to me? Hasn't he kept his promises also for the lesser needs of my body? Won't he continue to make all things work for my good? Not one of his good promises has failed. That's why I comfortably close out the old year and confidently enter the new one.

Lord, thanks for all your mercies this past year. Please walk with me into the new one. Amen.